LORNA SAGE was professor of English at the University of East Anglia. Her previous books include *Women in the House of Fiction*, *The Cambridge Guide to Women's Writing in English*, and a short monograph on Angela Carter. She died in January 2001. *Bad Blood* was a number one bestseller and winner of both the Whitbread Prize for Biography and the PEN/Ackerley Prize for Autobiography.

By the same author

Peacock: The Satirical Novels
Doris Lessing
Last Edwardians: An Illustrated History of
Violet Trefusis & Alice Keppel
Angela Carter
Women in the House of Fiction
Flesh and the Mirror: Essays on the Art of Angela Carter
The Cambridge Guide to Women's Writing in English
Moments of Truth: Twelve Twentieth Century Women Writers
Good as her Word: Selected Journalism

BAD
BLOOD

LORNA
SAGE

4th
Estate
Matchbook
Classics

4th Estate
An imprint of HarperCollins*Publishers*
1 London Bridge Street
London SE1 9GF
www.4thEstate.co.uk

This 4th Estate Matchbook Classics edition published 2019
1

First published in Great Britain by 4th Estate in 2000
Published in paperback by 4th Estate in 2001 and 2010

A catalogue record for this book
is available from the British Library

ISBN 978-0-00-832967-9

Printed by ScandBook in EU

For Sharon and Olivia

CONTENTS

INTRODUCTION

by Kathryn Hughes

When *Bad Blood* was published a decade ago it made an unlikely star of its author, the 57-year-old academic Lorna Sage. Sage was already well known to the small but important pool of readers who followed her literary criticism in both newspapers and academic publications, but this was something else entirely. Her account of growing up in a grubby Welsh vicarage after the Second World War, getting pregnant at 16, and claiming the education, career and life which no one – family, school or culture – thought should be hers became the surprise hit of late 2000. The book sold hundreds of thousands of copies around the world, won the Whitbread Award for Biography together with the PEN/Ackerley Prize for autobiography and made Sage famous to people who would otherwise never have heard of her. In fact it was all a bit of a fairy tale – ironic when you consider that one of *Bad Blood*'s chief concerns is to cast a sceptical eye over the stories handed to us in childhood to steer by, regardless of whether they fit or hobble us horribly.

And then, just as the excitement reached a crescendo in the midwinter of 2000–2001, this late-to-the-party princess was gone. She had been felled by a complicated collision of asthma, emphysema and a fierce smoking habit, which made her cruelly short of breath. It had, though, also granted her the privileges of the chronic insomniac to read through the night, a habit begun in her childhood when she had been made restless by the face-ache of severe sinusitis.

Sage had been named after the heroine of one of her clergyman grandfather's favourite books, R. D. Blackmore's *Lorna Doone*, and if her life proves anything, it is that reading can make things happen. Not just in the old clichéd way – scholarship girl grafts her way to a life her parents could never have provided – but in the sense of giving Sage a keen sense of how stories work to shape our knowledge of self and the world. And how, most crucially of all, if a particular story doesn't make sense, then you must simply make up a better.

The irony of the timing of her death would not have been lost on Lorna Sage. Unusually for a literary academic steeped in the critical theories of the Seventies and Eighties that declared the author dead, she was fascinated by the connections between writers' lives and their works. And as an expert reader of memoir she would have known that you seldom get the neat double ending of text and life that had so spectacularly occurred with *Bad Blood*. As a result the book remains eerily intact, because there is no author on hand to expand, provoke or riff on it. We are left, as readers, an extraordinary freedom to make of it whatever we will.

Sage had been working on a memoir about her early life for some time, but it was the discovery of her grandfather's diaries in the 1990s that suddenly gave shape to the book: it came out quickly, and in such a finished form that virtually no editing was required. These were the diaries, of course, which her grandmother had used to blackmail Revd Meredith-Morris into handing over most of his stipend. Full of details of his joyless philandering, the diaries would have been highly damaging if they'd got into the Bishop's hands, which was exactly where Sage's grandmother was threatening to put them unless 'the old devil', as she called him, paid up and paid regularly.

Described like this, *Bad Blood* sounds like a parochial book, in all senses. Yet when it appeared in the early autumn of 2000 it was a national and international hit, as if people had been waiting for it without quite knowing why. Perhaps it was to do with the fact that the world was now embarking on a new millennium. The mid-twentieth century with its watershed war and the unprecedented social changes that followed was about to be left behind for good. Very soon all the detail from that time – ration books, the eleven-plus, council houses, the nascent NHS, rural buses – would slip from living memory. Here was a last chance to see that world at first hand from someone whose intellect was briskly contemporary – mostly, indeed, ahead of the pack – yet whose life and mind had been forged in another age entirely.

Bad Blood, though, is much more than a social history of the war baby generation (Sage was born in January 1943 while her father was still away fighting). It is instead a story of absolute singularity involving one of the great tragi-comic characters of contemporary English literature, the Revd Meredith-Morris of St Chad's, Hanmer, a rural parish situated in that thick finger of Wales which crooks oddly into Shropshire. The Old Devil is there for less than a hundred pages but he manages to dominate the whole book, with his great gusts of unhappiness, his boozy self-pity and of course his random lusts, which include trysts with the district nurse and his teenage daughter's best friend. It is the Revd Meredith-Morris's Bad Blood that circulates through the narrative long after he himself is gone, tainting everything it touches including little Lorna whose growing appetite for boys and books is darkly attributed to her grandfather's sticky, vicious bequest.

Nor is it just the people in *Bad Blood* who are particular. Sage locates Hanmer precisely in time and place, giving us a muddy, midgy rebuttal to any expectation that the tale we are about to hear will be a pastoral one. This is Britain in the last gasp of the tenant farming system, before agribusiness rationalised production into huge regional food factories. The mud is Flintshire mud, rich and sucky and good for beef, though bad for stuck wellingtons. There are big dirty labouring families complete with the obligatory daft son and rusty machinery that takes an age to get going. Few of Sage's readers will have experienced any of this at first hand, yet her extraordinary achievement is to make us feel that this story is somehow ours too. So while you may not have spent your early years living on rations, you know what a sly punch in the playground feels like. You may not have worn the complicated underwear that was de rigueur for older schoolgirls in the 1950s but you know what it is to feel uncomfortable in your own skin. Hanmer may have class gradations that seem as quaint as anything from Jane Austen, but which of us does not recognise that feeling of falling foul of some social tripwire we were too slow to see coming?

Still, the last thing *Bad Blood* wants is soppy identification on the part of its readers. Indeed, one of the most bracing things about the book is Lorna Sage's indifference to making us like her. This blonde princess locked up in the gothic vicarage has bugs in her hair not because of some extraordinary drama of neglect or cruelty but because no one can be bothered to do anything about it. Her gaze, she tells us, is shifty and her default state sly. Had you known her as a child she almost certainly would not have wanted to be your friend, nor you hers. There is nothing remotely cosy here. And any idea that Sage is writing a misery memoir or asking for our pity is simply obscene.

The great joy of the book – and it is a joy – remains the way that this comic nightmare is delivered in the cleanest and clearest of language. As Professor of Literature at the University of East Anglia, Sage was sometimes required to be dense in her academic prose but you can really feel her exultation when she writes, as she did in her much-admired reviews in the *Observer* newspaper, for the Common Reader. She had a huge admiration for those authors such as Anthony Burgess who hacked to pay the bills, and a corresponding determination to reach the widest readership possible. And her talent is gloriously on show here, with that miraculous ability to conjure the Hanmer landscape, tricky turns in Britain's post-war social development, and the inside of a priapic vicar's brain, all without boring or baffling the reader for a moment.

Despite her scepticism about the coerciveness of certain kinds of stories, Sage does give us a happy ending of sorts in *Bad Blood*. She tells us how her life played out in ways that are clearly a matter of quiet pride. The Bad Blood, it seems, had finally been faced down. There was, though, one bit of the story which her sudden death in January 2001 left unfinished. She had been thinking about her memoir for so long. Now here it was, an enormous hit, making her famous around the world. What would she have done next? Another volume of autobiography? A novel even? Or more of that brilliant literary criticism which seemed to crack open the world of contemporary fiction with such deceptive ease? We will never know now and that, perhaps, provides the most tantalising ending of all.

PHOTOGRAPHS

PART ONE

PART ONE

I

The Old Devil and His Wife

Grandfather's skirts would flap in the wind along the church-yard path and I would hang on. He often found things to do in the vestry, excuses for getting out of the vicarage (kicking the swollen door, cursing) and so long as he took me he couldn't get up to much. I was a sort of hobble; he was my minder and I was his. He'd have liked to get further away, but petrol was rationed. The church was at least safe. My grandmother never went near it – except feet first in her coffin, but that was years later, when she was buried in the same grave with him. Rotting together for eternity, one flesh at the last after a lifetime's mutual loathing. In life, though, she never invaded his patch; once inside the churchyard gate he was on his own ground, in his element. He was good at funerals, being gaunt and lined, marked with mortality. He had a scar down his hollow cheek too, which Grandma had done with the carving knife one of the many times when he came home pissed and incapable.

That, though, was when they were still 'speaking', before my time. Now they mostly monologued and swore at each other's backs, and he (and I) would slam out of the house and go off between the graves, past the yew tree with a hollow where the cat had her litters and the various vaults that were supposed to account for the smell in the vicarage cellars in wet weather. On our right was the church; off to our left the graves stretched away, bisected by a grander gravel path leading down from the church porch to a bit of green with a war memorial, then – across the road – the mere. The church was popular for weddings because of this impressive approach, but he wasn't at all keen on the marriage ceremony, naturally enough. Burials he relished, perhaps because he saw himself as buried alive.

One day we stopped to watch the gravedigger, who unearthed a skull – it was an old churchyard, on its second or third time around – and grandfather dusted off the soil and declaimed: 'Alas poor Yorick, I knew him well . . .' I thought he was making it up as he went along. When I grew up a bit and saw *Hamlet* and found him out, I wondered what had been going through his mind. I suppose the scene struck him as an image of his condition – exiled to a remote, illiterate rural parish, his talents wasted and so on. On the other hand his position afforded him a lot of opportunities for indulging secret, bitter jokes, hamming up the act and cherishing his ironies, so in a way he was enjoying himself. Back then, I thought that was what a vicar was, simply: someone bony and eloquent and smelly (tobacco, candle grease, sour claret), who talked into space. His disappointments were just part of the act for me, along with his dog-collar and cassock. I was like a baby goose imprinted by the first mother-figure it sees – he was my black marker.

It was certainly easy to spot him at a distance too. But this was a village where it seemed everybody was their vocation. They didn't just 'know their place', it was as though the place occupied them, so that they all knew what they were going to be from the beginning. People's names conspired to colour in this picture. The gravedigger was actually called Mr Downward. The blacksmith who lived by the mere was called Bywater. Even more decisively, the family who owned the village were called Hanmer, and so was the village. The Hanmers had come over with the Conqueror, got as far as the Welsh border and stayed ever since in this little rounded isthmus of North Wales sticking out into England, the detached portion of Flintshire (Flintshire Maelor) as it was called then, surrounded by Shropshire, Cheshire and – on the Welsh side – Denbighshire. There was no town in the Maelor district, only villages and hamlets; Flintshire proper was some way off; and (then) industrial, which made it in practice a world away from these pastoral parishes, which had become resigned to being handed a Labour MP at every election. People in Hanmer well understood, in almost a prideful way, that we weren't part of all that. The kind of choice represented by voting didn't figure large on the local map and you only really counted places you could get to on foot or by bike.

The war had changed this to some extent, but not as much as it might have because farming was a reserved occupation and sons hadn't been called up unless there were a lot of them, or their families were smallholders with little land. So Hanmer in the 1940s in many ways resembled Hanmer in the 1920s, or even the late 1800s except that it was more depressed, less populous and more out of step – more and more islanded in time as the years had gone by. We didn't speak Welsh either, so that there was little national feeling, rather a sense of stubbornly being *where you were* and that was that. Also very un-Welsh was the fact that Hanmer had no chapel to rival Grandfather's church: the Hanmers would never lease land to Nonconformists and there was no tradition of Dissent, except in the form of not going to church at all. Many people did attend, though, partly because he was locally famous for his sermons, and because he was High Church and went in for dressing up and altar boys and frequent communions. Not

5

frequent enough to explain the amount of wine he got through, however. Eventually the Church stopped his supply and after that communicants got watered-down Sanatogen from Boots the chemist in Whitchurch, over the Shropshire border.

The delinquencies that had denied him preferment seemed to do him little harm with his parishioners. Perhaps the vicar was expected to be an expert in sin. At all events he was 'a character'. To my childish eyes people in Hanmer were divided between characters and the rest, the ones and the many. Higher up the social scale there was only one of you: one vicar, one solicitor, each farmer identified by the name of his farm and so *sui generis*. True, there were two doctors, but they were brothers and shared the practice. Then there was one policeman, one publican, one district nurse, one butcher, one baker . . . Smallholders and farm labourers were the many and often had large families too. They were irretrievably plural and supposed to be interchangeable (feckless all), nameable only as tribes. The virtues and vices of the singular people turned into characteristics. They were picturesque. They had no common denominator and you never judged them in relation to a norm. Coming to consciousness in Hanmer was oddly blissful at the beginning: the grown-ups all played their parts to the manner born. You knew where you were.

Which was a hole, according to Grandma. A dead-alive dump. A muck heap. She'd shake a trembling fist at the people going past the vicarage to church each Sunday, although they probably couldn't see her from behind the bars and dirty glass. She didn't upset my version of pastoral. She lived in a different dimension, she said as much herself. In her world there were streets with pavements, shop windows, trams, trains, teashops and cinemas. She never went out except to visit this paradise lost, by taxi to the station in Whitchurch, then by train to

Shrewsbury or Chester. This was *life*. Scented soap and chocolates would stand in for it the rest of the time – most of the time, in fact, since there was never any money. She'd evolved a way of living that resolutely defied her lot. He might play the vicar, she wouldn't be the vicar's wife. Their rooms were at opposite ends of the house and she spent much of the day in bed. She had asthma, and even the smell of him and his tobacco made her sick. She'd stay up late in the evening, alone, reading about scandals and murders in the *News of the World* by lamplight among the mice and silverfish in the kitchen (she'd hoard coal for the fire up in her room and sticks to relight it if necessary). She never answered the door, never saw anyone, did no housework. She cared only for her sister and her girlhood friends back in South Wales and – perhaps – for me, since I had blue eyes and blonde hair and was a girl, so just possibly belonged to *her* family line. She thought men and women belonged to different races and any getting together was worse than folly. The 'old devil', my grandfather, had talked her into marriage and the agony of bearing two children, and he should never be forgiven for it. She would quiver with rage whenever she remembered her fall. She was short (about four foot ten) and as fat and soft-fleshed as he was thin and leathery, so her theory of separate races looked quite plausible. The rhyme about Jack Sprat ('Jack Sprat would eat no fat, / His wife would eat no lean, / And so between the two of them / They licked the platter clean') struck me, when I learned it, as somehow about them. Looking back, I can see that she must have been a factor – along with the booze (and the womanising) – in keeping him back in the Church. She got her revenge, but at the cost of living in the muck heap herself.

Between the two of them my grandparents created an atmosphere in the vicarage so pungent and all-pervading that they accounted for everything. In fact, it wasn't so. My mother, their daughter, was there; I only remember her, though, at the beginning, as a shy, slender wraith kneeling on the stairs with a brush and dustpan, or washing things in the scullery. They'd made her into a domestic drudge after her marriage – my father was away in the army and she had no separate life. It was she who answered the door and tried to keep up appearances, a battle long lost. She wore her fair hair in a victory roll and she was pretty but didn't like to smile. Her front teeth were false – crowned, a bit clumsily – because in her teens, running to intervene in one of their murderous rows, she'd fallen down the stairs and snapped off her own. During these years she probably didn't feel much like smiling anyway. She doesn't come into the picture properly yet, nor does my father. My only early memory of him is being picked up by a man in uniform and being sick down his back. He wasn't popular in the vicarage, although it must have been his army pay that eked out Grandfather's exiguous stipend.

The grandparents weren't grateful. They both felt so cheated by life, they had their histories of grievance so well worked out, that they were *owed* service, handouts, anything that was going. My mother and her brother they'd used as hostages in their wars and otherwise neglected, being too absorbed in each other, in their way, to spare much feeling. With me it was different: since they no longer really fought they had time on their hands and I got the best of them. Did they love me? The question is beside the point, somehow. Certainly they each spoiled me, mainly by giving me the false impression that I was entitled to attention nearly all the time. They played. *They* were like children, if you consider that one of the things about being a child is that you are a parasite of sorts and have to brazen it out self-righteously. I want. They were good at wanting and

I shared much more common ground with them than with my mother when I was three or four years old. Also, they measured up to the magical monsters in the story books. Grandma's idea of expressing affection to small children was to smack her lips and say, 'You're so sweet, I'm going to eat you all up!' It was not difficult to believe her, either, given her passion for sugar. Or at least I believed her enough to experience a pleasant thrill of fear. She liked to pinch, too, and she sometimes spat with hatred when she ran out of words.

Domestic life in the vicarage had a Gothic flavour at odds with the house, which was a modest eighteenth-century building of mellowed brick, with low ceilings, and attics and back stairs for help we didn't have. At the front it looked on to a small square traversed only by visitors and churchgoers. The barred

THE VICARAGE HANMER

kitchen window faced this way, but in no friendly fashion, and the parlour on the other side of the front door was empty and unused, so that the house was turned in on itself, against its nature. A knock at the door produced a flurry of hiding-and-tidying (my grandmother must be given time to retreat, if she was up, and I'd have my face scrubbed with a washcloth) in case the visitor was someone who'd have to be invited in and shown to the sitting-room at the back which – although a bit damp and neglected – was always 'kept nice in case'.

If the caller was on strictly Church business, he'd be shown upstairs to Grandfather's study, lined with bookcases in which the books all had the authors' names and titles on their spines blacked out as a precaution against would-be borrowers who'd suddenly take a fancy to Dickens or Marie Corelli. His bedroom led off his study and was dark, under the yew tree's shadow, and smelled like him. Across the landing was my mother's room, where I slept too when I was small, and round a turn to the right my grandmother's, with coal and sticks piled under the bed, redolent of Pond's face cream, powder, scent, smelling salts and her town clothes in mothballs, along with a litter of underwear and stockings.

On this floor, too, was a stately lavatory, wallpapered in a perching peacock design, all intertwined feathers and branches you could contemplate for hours – which I did, legs dangling from the high wooden seat. When the chain was pulled the water tanks on the attic floor gurgled and sang. In the other attics there were apples laid out on newspaper on the floors, gently mummifying. It just wasn't a spooky house, despite the suggestive cellars, and the fact that we relied on lamps and candles. All of Hanmer did that, in any case, except for farmers who had their own generators. In the kitchen the teapot sat on the hob all day and everyone ate at different times.

There was a word that belonged to the house: 'dilapidations'. It was one of the first long words I knew, for it was repeated like a mantra. The Church charged incumbents a kind of levy for propping up its crumbling real estate and those five syllables were the key. If only Grandfather could cut down on the dilapidations there'd be a new dawn of amenity and comfort, and possibly some change left over. Leaks, dry rot, broken panes and crazy hinges (of which we had plenty) were, looked at rightly, a potential source of income. Whether he ever succeeded I don't know. Since the word went on and on, he can't have got more than a small rebate and no one ever plugged the leaks. What's certain is that we were frequently penniless and there were always embarrassments about credit. Food rationing and clothes coupons must have been a godsend since they provided a cover for our indigence. As long as austerity lasted, the vicarage could maintain its shaky claims to gentility. There was virtue in shabbiness. Grandfather had his rusty cassock, Grandmother her mothballed wardrobe and my mother had one or two pre-war outfits that just about served. Under-wear was yellowed and full of holes, minus elastic. Indoors, our top layers were ragged too: matted jumpers, socks and stockings laddered and in wrinkles round the ankles, safety pins galore. Outside we could pass muster, even if my overcoat was at first too big (I would grow into it), then all at once too small, without ever for a moment being the right size.

In those years almost the whole country wore this ill-fitting uniform designed for non-combatants – serviceable colours, grating textures, tell-tale unfaded hems that had been let down, bulky tucks. Our true household craziness and indifference didn't express itself in clothes, but in more intimate kinds of squalor: for instance, nearly never washing the bits no one could see. This was almost a point of vicarage principle, a measure of our hostility to the world outside and separateness from it. Inside our clothes civilisation had lapsed. And this wasn't to do with money.

Grandma had the scented soap, but she didn't use it – she bought it for its smell, and kept it wrapped in tissue paper in drawers and trunks. Her line was that her skin was too sensitive for soap and water. We even had a bathroom, but somehow the only way to wash was to boil the kettle and fill a bowl, and do bits – very little bits and usually the same bits – at a time. The resulting tidemarks, in my case round my neck, wrists and legs, would be desperately scrubbed at from time to time. Hair was another problem, a tangle of troubles: brushing was usually felt to be enough of a trauma, without the business of tangling it up all over again with washing, so that my pigtails stayed plaited for days on end. Our secret grubbiness was yet another thing that set us apart. If other children were dirty, that meant they were common, their parents were foully neg-lectful and slummy, you could catch things from them. One of

Grandma's favourite terms of abuse, in fact, was 'dirty' – villagers were dirty, callers were dirty, I mustn't play with dirty children. So there were two different kinds of dirt, theirs and ours. It was a most metaphysical distinction, as befitted the vicarage.

As if to demonstrate the point, next door to us, also fronting on to the square, was a sixteenth-century tumbledown timber and brick cottage crammed with children I wasn't supposed to mix with – the Duckets, one of Hanmer's most shameless tribes. The wall that divided us from them provided me with a perch from which I could look down into their back garden. Our side had a lawn with borders and apple trees, and was neglected and overgrown and peaceful. Theirs was like a bomb-site, a muddy, cratered expanse with twisted pieces of old prams and

bike frames, and shards of crockery embedded among straggly weeds and currant bushes. The Duckets epitomised what my grandmother meant by 'dirty': they were openly poor (the father was a farm labourer), they bred like rabbits and they spilled out of their house wearing their ragged hand-me-downs for all to see.

The vicarage was a secret slum, but the Duckets' doors were always open, so you could see Mrs Ducket with her hair in curlers running about bare-legged in slippers, or – even more scandalously – sitting down with a cup of tea and a fag. They had no secrets. Their kitchen drain (on the opposite side to us) disgorged a slow stream of soapy slime and tea-leaves into the open gutter that ran along the main village street. The Duckets kept yappy dogs and skinny cats, and had kittens and ferrets in their pockets; they didn't go to church, although sometimes one or two of the children would be spruced up and sent to Sunday School. While I was forbidden the square, they were positively driven out of their house, back and front, in all weathers, clutching wedges of bread and damson jam. They reached over our wall and picked the apples, according to Grandma. And (the crowning horror) they had bugs in their hair.

The Duckets made me feel lonely. Even the bugs were more fascinating than frightening. Once or twice I managed to 'play' with Edna, the girl nearest to my own age, through the crack in our side gate. She squatted in the square, I squatted in the vicarage kitchen yard; I squeezed my dolls through the gap one by one for her to look at and she squeezed them back. But otherwise I'd climb the wall and sit astride, watching Duckets in the plural, whenever I was left to my own devices. Which wasn't often. Grandpa and I must have pottered about in church almost every day, and the echoing spaces, the stained glass and the smell of Brasso, chrysanthemums, damp pew-oak and iron mould from the choir's surplices were heady compensations for isolation. He'd tell me stories and read me to sleep at night, when he'd often drop off first, stretched out on the couch, mouth open, snoring, his beaky profile lit up by the candle. In fact, he got so impatient with my favourite books (which both he and I knew by heart) that one momentous day, before I was four, he taught me to read in self-defence. This confirmed me as his creature.

I knew my name came out of one of the blacked-out books – Lorna from *Lorna Doone* – and that he'd chosen it. Now he'd given me a special key to his world. We were even closer allies afterwards, so that when he took me with him in the rattling Singer to Whitchurch, and into the bar of the Fox and Goose down Green End, it never occurred to me to tell on him. There were several expeditions like that. He was well known in drinking circles and was looked on as something of a speciality act, a cynical and colourful talker, always with his dog-collar to set him apart. I was the perfect alibi, since neither my mother nor my grandmother had any idea that there were pubs so low and lawless that they would turn a blind eye to children. Few were willing to, however; and there were other times when I found myself sitting outside on the steps of one of his favourite haunts, an unfriendly place with a revolving door called the Lord Hill, in the company of streetwise kids a lot more scary than the Duckets. Perhaps I did tell about that, or perhaps someone spotted me: at any rate, the pub outings came to an end.

Not the collusion, though. I'd kneel on the threadbare rug in his study while he worked on his sermon, or talked to the odd visitor, pulling out the books and puzzling over big words. Sometimes he'd show off my reading to strangers, but for the most part I was meant (this was the point of it, after all) to be quiet. When he was in very good moods he would draw pictures for me, starting mysteriously from the vanishing point and drawing out the rest into perspective. I learned that trick too, never very well, but well enough to disconcert people. Our mutual 'minding' turned by untidy stages into a sort of education. Since he was a man of many wasted talents, not only with words and images but also music, I might have had a full set of pre-school 'accomplishments', except that I was tone-deaf. Despite that, I was made a member of the choir as soon as I could sit still long enough – under strict instructions to open and shut my mouth in silence, along with the words. I was quite useful, in fact: I could be shifted across from the girls' bench to the boys' (my pigtails bundled up into my cap) depending on where there were the most gaps. Watching Grandpa dress up in the vestry, processing behind him, listening to him intone the liturgy and preach, I basked in his reflected glory.

I took to lining up my toys in a corner of the garden I called 'the secondary school', where I lectured them and told them stories. More than once they got left out overnight and were brought in sodden in the morning, to be dried out in the oven of the kitchen range. My teddy, a utility bear with a flabby square stomach made out of flowered cotton, was scorched ever after. An omen there.

I was going to have to go to school soon and that meant the village school, which would make nonsense of the dirt distinction, and – as it turned out – leave scorch-marks on my spoiled soul too. There was some reluctance to send me there sooner than need be, but the temptation must have become irresistible. When Grandpa was out, or hung-over, or not in the mood, I would wander the house in an ecstasy of self-pity, wailing 'What can I do-o-o?' over and over again, tears dripping down. This was my own precocious contribution to the economy of frustration and want, and nobody could stand it. If the day was fine, Grandma might take me out into the garden, where we'd exorcise my misery by attacking the brambles and nettles with sharp scissors, pretending they were Grandpa, or Duckets, or other people on her hit list ('Ugh! Nasty old thing! Wicked old devil!'). She got even more fun out of this than I did, but she often didn't feel energetic enough for such games. So at four and a bit I went to school, and the whole village gave a shake and rearranged itself. I got bugs in my hair and started to lead a double life: one of the many – Hanmer school had a hundred-odd pupils, aged four to fourteen, in 1947 – and yet the sole vicarage child. I put about the story that you could play in the churchyard if you played with me.

II

School

Perhaps I really did grow up, as I sometimes suspect, in a time warp, an enclave of the nineteenth century? Because here are the memories jostling their way in, scenes from an overpopulated rural slum.

First there was dinner money, then the register. Then Miss Myra would hang up a cracked oilcloth scroll with the Lord's Prayer printed on it in large curly letters. She prompted, we mumbled our way through, getting out of sync during the trespasses and catching up with each other to arrive in unison at 'For ever and ever. Amen.' Next we'd be set to copy it out with chalk on jagged slices of slate. If you got to the end you simply started from the beginning again and went on until it was time to stop. You spat on your slate and rubbed it with your finger when you made mistakes, so sooner or later the letters all got lost in a grey blur. Not many in the babies' class learned to read or write by this method. That didn't matter too much, though. Hanmer Church of England School was less concerned with teaching its pupils reading, writing or arithmetic than with obedience and knowing things by heart. Soon you'd be able to recite 'Our Father' and the multiplication tables with sing-song confidence, hitting the ritual emphasis right: 'And *twelve* twelves are a *hund*red and forty-*four*. *Amen.*'

After a couple of years in Miss Myra's room you moved to

her sister Miss Daisy's, and after that to the biggest class, belonging to the headmaster, Mr Palmer. He was a figure of fear, an absentee deity. Offenders from the lower classes were sent to him for the stick and were known to wet themselves on the way. His own class, too, regarded him with dread. He liked to preside over them invisibly from his house next door, emerging when the noise reached a level deafening enough to disturb him, to hand out summary punishment.

The further up the school you went, the less you were formally taught or expected to learn. There was knitting, sewing and weaving for older girls, who would sit out winter playtimes gossiping round the stove, their legs marbled with parboiled red veins from the heat. The big boys did woodwork and were also kept busy taking out the ashes, filling coke buckets and digging the garden. None of the more substantial farmers sent their children to Hanmer school. It had been designed to produce domestic servants and farm labourers, and functional illiteracy was still part of the expectation, almost part of the curriculum.

Not long after I started there, this time-honoured parochial system was shaken up when some of the older children were removed to a secondary modern school over the nearest border, in Shropshire. This thinned out the population and damped down the racket in Mr Palmer's room, although quite a few restive overgrown kids still stayed on until they were fourteen and the law allowed them to leave. Passing the eleven-plus ('the scholarship') was unheard of; and anyway harder than it might have been, since grammar schools in neighbouring counties had quotas for children from the real sticks, i.e. the Maelor district. When my time came, Mr Palmer graciously cheated me through. Strolling past my desk on his invigilation rounds, he trailed a plump finger down my page of sums, pointed significantly at several, then crossed two fingers behind his back as he walked away. So I did those again.

Perhaps the record of failure was starting to look fishy. The world was changing, education was changing, and the notion that school should reflect your ready-made place in the scheme of things and put you firmly back where you came from was going out of fashion even in Hanmer. It was against the grain to acknowledge this, though. The cause of hierarchy and immobility was served by singling out the few children whose families didn't fit and setting them homework. Mr Palmer drew the line at marking it, however. The three of us were given sums to do, then told to compare the results in a corner next morning. If all three, or two of us, arrived at the same answer then that was the correct one. If — as often happened — all three of us produced different answers then that particular long division or fraction retreated into the realm of undecidability. Most of our answers were at best odds-on favourites. I developed a dauntingly Platonic conception of arithmetical truths. The *real* answer must exist, but in some far-removed misty empyrean. Praying ('. . . and forty-*four*. Amen') seemed often as good a route as any to getting it right.

Sums were my cross. Numeracy was not one of Grandfather's gifts; we never played with numbers, which were a subdivision of dilapidations and no fun at all. I went to school armed against the spit-and-chalk routine – words went on working – but with sums I struggled like the rest, since it was never part of Mr Palmer's plan (the school's plan) to reveal that the necessary skills were *learnable*. If you passed the scholarship, that was because you were somebody who should never have been at Hanmer school in the first place, was his theory.

One day he lined up his class and went down the line saying with gloomy satisfaction 'You'll be a muck-shoveller, you'll be a muck-shoveller . . .' and so on and on, only missing out the homework trio. As things turned out he was mistaken – by the time my Hanmer generation grew up there were very few jobs on the land, the old mixed labour-intensive farming had finally collapsed, farmers had gone over to machinery, and the children he'd consigned to near-illiteracy and innumeracy had to re-educate themselves and move on. Which they did, despite all the school had done to inculcate ignorance. Back there and then in our childhoods, though, in the late Forties, Mr Palmer seemed omniscient. He ruled over a little world where conformity, bafflement, fear and furtive defiance were the orders of the day. Every child's ambition at Hanmer school was to avoid attracting his attention, or that of Miss Myra or Miss Daisy. We all played dumb, the one lesson everyone learned.

We'd have seemed a lumpen lot: sullen, unresponsive, cowed, shy or giggly in the presence of grown-ups. A bunch of nose-pickers and nail-biters, with scabbed knees, warts, chapped skin and unbrushed teeth. We shared a certain family resemblance, in other words. Some of it was absolutely, organically, real: seven or eight huge families accounted between them for nearly half the population of the school. There were brothers, sisters and cousins who slapped, shoved and bossed each other unmercifully, but always stood up for their own flesh and blood (thickened, it was rumoured, by incest) in the end. 'You leave our Doreen alone.' Or else.

Having big brothers or (much better) big sisters – since the big boys had their own separate playground and didn't usually deign to intervene – seemed the first condition for survival in the infants' class. In fact, though, these rough, protective clans were already on the way out. There were quite a few parents who'd worked out that one way of escaping poverty was having fewer children, and a subtle eye could have detected among the mass of rowdy, runny-nosed urchins a small sub-class of better-dressed, prissier and slightly more respectable children. The girls wore hairslides and newly knitted cardigans, the boys were 'nesh' (the Hanmer word for anything from clean to feeling-the-cold to cowardly) and were endlessly tormented. Being an only child – as I was, for the time being – was a mixed blessing at best when it came down to the gritty realities of the playground. The 'nesh' ones I despised and it was entirely mutual, since I was dirty, precocious and had never been treated like a child. And the tribes despised me for being sole, pseudo-clean and 'stuck up'.

So the playground was hell: Chinese burns, pinches, slaps and kicks, and horrible games. I can still hear the noise of a thick wet skipping rope slapping the ground. There'd be a big girl each end and you had to leap through without tripping. Joining in was only marginally less awful than being left out. It's said (truly) that most women forget the pain of childbirth; I think that we all forget the pain of being a child at school for the first time, the sheer ineptitude, as though you'll never learn to mark out your own space. It's doubly shaming –

22

shaming to *remember* as well, to feel so sorry for your scabby little self back there in small people's purgatory.

My first days at school were punctuated by fierce contests in the yard, duels almost, complete with spectators, with the one girl who might have been expected to be my friend. In fact, she did become my very best friend, years later, when we went round holding hands painfully fast and giggling together hysterically, but for now she was my sworn enemy. Gail (she even had a funny name, like me) had hair in ringlets, green-hazel eyes and pale, clear, slightly olive skin stretched tight and shiny over her muscles, and she was nearly a year older than I was. She'd have won our war in any case, though, since she was so physically confident, in charge of her body even when she was five. Was she already going to dancing lessons? I don't remember. In adult life she became a teacher of physical education and modern dance herself, and even in the days of our adolescent intimacy she would sometimes win an argument by twisting my wrist. I was convinced at the start, anyway, that she was simply better at inhabiting her body than I was – not only better at face-pulling, hair-pulling, pinching, scratching and every sort of violence, but wiry and graceful, so that she made me feel like an unstrung puppet.

Once she'd thoroughly trounced me in public, Gail ignored me and held court in her own corner every playtime. She remained something of a loner, however. Other little girls might admire the ringlets and the dresses with smocking on the yokes, and the white socks that stayed up, but she was not allowed out to play in the square after school and everyone knew that she had to sit for hours every night while her grandmother twisted her hair in rags. What really set her apart, though – even more effectively than the vicarage set me apart – was the fact that her mother was divorced.

Given that quite a few kids in Hanmer didn't know who their father was – or at least knew that he wasn't the one he was supposed to be – it may seem odd that divorce stood out as a social sin. But its novelty was against it. It was untraditional, new-fangled and (worst of all) above Gail's mother's station. Someone like Lady Kenyon (the Kenyons were the other local grandees, a lot richer and more dashing than the Hanmers) might be divorced and that was fittingly aristocratic; for the local garage owner's daughter to do it was very different. Who did she think she was? People saw her as some new brand of fallen woman.

She was disapproved of in the vicarage, too, but mostly for reasons of envy. There was a history behind this: Gail's mother and my mother had been friends before the war. They had starred together in the pantomimes my grandfather had put on in the village hall in the days before he had been overtaken by booze and bitterness. My mother, whose name was Valma – another of Grandfather's romantic choices, although I've never known where he got it – and Gail's mother, whose name was Ivy, had played Prince Charming and Cinderella respectively. They stood there in a surviving photograph, two slim young women with their arms clasped around each other's waists in the middle of the assembled cast, their big, hopeful, lipsticked smiles looking black and glamorous. Gail's mother, being divorced, looked pretty much like this still, except that she was even skinnier. She also had a job driving the local taxi. Whereas my mother, thanks to a combination of marriage, poverty and her parents' crazy demands, lived in (comparative) purdah. This was what made Grandma furious. She said that Ivy looked like Olive Oyl in the Popeye cartoons, or like a stick of liquorice. And that she was common. But it was all sour grapes. Secretly Grandma must have thought divorce a good idea –

her notion of marriage, after all, was that a man signed you up to have his wicked way with you and should spend the rest of his life *paying through the nose*. But her expressed opinion coincided with village wisdom.

Even playground games, in the intervals of thumps and pushes, were all about the changeless order of things. 'The farmer wants a wife,' we'd chant, joining hands in a ring – 'Heigh ho, heigh ho, the farmer wants a wife.' And when the snotty little boy in the middle had chosen his bride, 'The wife wants a child . . . The child wants a dog. Heigh ho, heigh ho' – which sounded like 'ee-oh!', this farmer was related to Old Macdonald – 'The child wants a dog.' This doggy extension of the nuclear family seemed to join human arrangements on to the whole wealth of species, top to bottom, patriarch to pup. And then the climax – 'The dog wants a bone.' The bone, by tradition a tiny, would be vigorously bounced, thrown into the air and caught on the way down, by the farmer, wife, child and dog, while we all shouted triumphantly, 'The bone – won't – stand! Eee oh! Eee oh! The bone – won't – STAND!' Being chosen as the bone was a mixed delight, scary and painful as well as thrilling, so I wasn't sorry that my turn seldom came round. This game, all the games, were a bit like those horrible group therapy exercises where you're meant to let yourself fall in order to learn to trust the rest, who catch you. Mutual dependence – farmer, wife, child, dog, bone, representing the great chain of being. And you couldn't be outside of it. Gail and I and the other milder misfits curried favour with the pack in our separate ways.

My great advantage was the churchyard. Mr Downward, the sexton, would turn a blind eye to all but the most boisterous grave-hopping games if I was involved in them. He seemed to regard the churchyard as an extension of the vicarage garden

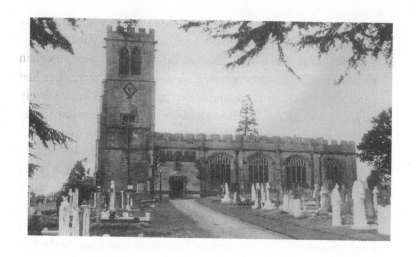

and indeed the wall between them was so tumbledown in one place that the boundary was only a pile of long-fallen bricks in a nettle patch. As the vicarage child I was a licensed trespasser and I shared out my immunity among the 'dirty' children I could persuade to play with me after school, or on Saturdays. I was especially popular when there had been a Saturday morning wedding: we all collected confetti, but its dolly-mixture colours didn't last long in that rainy region, you had to pick up the little pink bells and white bows and silver horseshoes quickly or they dissolved away. We especially treasured the silvered sort and scorned the cheap variety stamped out of waste paper, often mere dots with cryptic fragments of print on them. Once there were drifts of silky paper rose petals on the path, each shaded from cream to crimson, and these we saved up reverently.

Funeral wreaths were even better, although only for looking at until they were thrown on to the rubbish heap in the corner, when if you were lucky you could salvage a carnation or lily or chrysanthemum still blooming – luxury flowers a cut above the sweet williams, wall-flowers and Michaelmas daisies of village borders. We marvelled, too, at the glass and porcelain immortelles under their glass globes, and the graves that had shrubs growing on them and shorn grass looked impressively tidy, but it was the bunches of flowers people brought to lay on the graves that gave us our chance really to join in the grown-ups' mourning games. There's nothing small children enjoy more than parcelling things out according to some system of just deserts and it was obvious that many of the dead were being short-changed. This a gang of us – mostly girls – set about putting right, redistributing the flowers in jam jars and empty vases filled at the sexton's pump so that everybody had some. We weren't strictly egalitarian, however. Certain graves, particularly one with a soulful baby angel in white marble belonging to a child who'd died in the 1930s, always ended up with the best bunches.

It's tempting, now, looking back, to see in our pious and partial efforts a dim reflection of post-war social policies. Certainly Hanmer churchyard was a pretty good microcosm of inequality. None of those children who puddled around so busily at the pump, and solemnly divided up the daffs and the pinks, had any graves of their own, as it were. Their families must have been buried there, but the graves were unmarked, they had no more property in the churchyard than anywhere else. My family had none there either, of course, but that was because they had recently moved to Hanmer. Nowadays my mother lies there under her stone, alongside my grandparents' grave. I wonder if any of my generation of upwardly mobile Duckets or Williamses or Briggses have invested in graveyard real estate? Back in the late 1940s their families inhabited anonymous, untended tussocks after they died. I think we kids took it for granted that life after death was a class matter. I know we spent many fruitless hours searching for the entrances to the Hanmer and Kenyon vaults, in the expectation of meeting real ghosts: it was clear to us that the only reason they needed those underground apartments was because they were somehow undead. Or perhaps this was a theory I suggested. Away from the playground, on church territory, I set up as an expert on such spooky topics and managed – on some blissful days – to feel accepted, a member of the child world of Hanmer.

Well, the bugs thought so, I had the school doctor's word for that. I was sent home with a note, like most people (but not everyone: that line about lice preferring clean hair is just a propaganda ploy to get the middle classes to own up) and predictably Grandma said: one, that I'd caught them from those dirty children; and two, that there was no point in applying the magic bug-killing mixture recommended because it would mean boiling too many kettles and anyway I'd only get re-infected. And *anyway* we couldn't be seen buying that stuff in local towns, we'd have to do it in a strange place where no one knew us. So I spent the rest of my time at junior school blithely passing on head lice. The first year at grammar school, too, to my utter chagrin – but that comes later. For the moment, I sort of belonged.

The high point of my career as a dirty child was also, coincidentally, inspired by the school doctor. Medical examinations were a complete novelty to most Hanmer families, and for us kids the beginnings of the National Health Service licensed elaborate games of doctors and nurses, which took place in the bushes at the bottom of the vicarage garden. Nowhere else was private enough (no one else's family was so oblivious) and so I became, while the craze lasted, everybody's friend.

We queued up behind a hazel tree, knickers round our knees,

clutching leaves for 'papers', and shuffled along to have our bottoms examined by Kenny or Bill or Derek, who, after having a good look and making dubious predictions, always prescribed the same thing: another leaf, which might, excitingly, be a nettle, but never was. This one was stuck on with spit if you were a girl, and threaded over your willie if you were a boy, and you were supposed to keep it on like a poultice as long as you could. For most of one summer this illicit clinic was convened once or twice a week, until we got bored, or the weather turned. Never again was there quite such a good occasion for kidnapping other kids on to my territory.

When I think back to that time, it's not such heady, forbidden games that really represent its feel, but other much more routine memories – like lining up with the others outside on raw winter days, all wearing damp, knitted pixie hats and rubbing our chilblains while we waited to be marched over to the parish hall for our regulation school dinner of whale-meat stew. Thinking of that produces a mingled brew of fear and longing that seems the very essence of school.

Bit by bit the fear came to predominate. I became a timid, clumsy, speechless child – agonisingly shy. In my last year at school Mr Palmer would promise me sixpence for every time he spoke to me and I didn't cry. I think I earned a shilling. More and more I lived in books, they were my comfort, refuge, addiction, compensation for the humiliations that attended contact with the world outside. But books were nothing really to do with school, not this school. I was a real dunce at the things I was supposed to learn – how to be neat, tidy, dexterous, obedient, punctual. My sewing turned to a grubby rag, it had been unpicked so many times. My knitting was laddered with dropped stitches. I couldn't write a line without making a blot. So I was mystified when I passed the 'scholarship' at ten, and felt sure it was a mistake and someone was going to find me out.

They didn't and still haven't, I suppose. Hanmer school left its mark on my mental life, though. For instance, one day in a grammar school maths lesson I got into a crying jag over the notion of minus numbers. Minus one threw out my universe, it couldn't exist, I couldn't understand it. This, I realised tearfully, under coaxing from an amused (and mildly amazed) teacher, was because I thought numbers were *things*. In fact, cabbages. We'd been taught in Miss Myra's class to do additon and subtraction by imagining more cabbages and fewer cabbages. Every time I did mental arithmetic I was juggling ghostly vegetables in my head. And when I tried to think of minus one I was trying to imagine an anti-cabbage, an anti-matter cabbage, which was as hard as conceiving of an alternative universe.

III

Grandma at Home

Hanmer's pretty mere, the sloping fields that surrounded us, and the hedges overgrown with hawthorn, honeysuckle and dog roses that fringed the lanes, might as well have been a cunning mirage as far as Grandma was concerned. They did nothing to alleviate the lousy desert that made up her picture of village life. She lived like a prisoner, an urban refugee self-immured behind the vicarage's bars and shutters. None of my new school friends were allowed in the house. You could get into the vicarage garden via the side yard, or by climbing over the walls, and that was the way we did it. The whole thing was clandestine, the other children weren't supposed to be really *there* at all, any more than that picturesque backdrop of lake and trees and cows. Meanwhile, insulated and apart, vicarage life went on. In the church, in bars, in books (Grandpa) or in a scented bedroom fug of dreams of home in South Wales (Grandma). That is of Tonypandy in the Rhondda, which rhymed with yonder, but with its Welsh 'd's softened into 'th', so that it seemed the essence of elsewhere.

Her Welsh accent was foreign – sing-song, insidious, unctuous, converting easily to menace. Asthma lent a breathy vehemence to her curses and when she laughed she'd fall into wheezing fits that required a sniff of smelling-salts. She had a repertoire of mysterious private catchphrases that always sent her off. If anyone asked what was the time, she'd retort 'just struck an elephant!' and cackle triumphantly. Then, 'Dew, Dew,' she'd mutter as she got her breath back – or that's what it sounded like – meaning 'Deary me' or 'Well, well', shaking her head. That 'ew' sound was ubiquitous with her. She pronounced 'you' as 'ew', puckering up her small mouth as if to savour the nice or nasty taste you represented.

She had lost her teeth and could make a most ghoulish face by arranging the false set, gums and all, outside her lips, in a voracious grin. This clownish act didn't conceal her real hunger, however. She projected want. During the days of rationing she craved sugar. Its shortage must have postponed some of the worst ravages of the diabetes that martyred her later, for once the stuff was available again she couldn't resist it at all. She was soft and slightly powdery to the touch, as though she'd been dusted all over with icing sugar like a sponge cake. She shared her Edwardian generation's genteel contempt for sunburn and freckles, and thanks to her nocturnal habits her skin was eerily pale. And just as she maintained that soap and water were too harsh for this delicate skin of hers, so she insisted that she couldn't chew or digest gristly, fibrous meals with meat and vegetables, but must live on thin bread and butter with the crusts cut off if she couldn't have tarts and buns. This, she'd repeat to me, was what little girls were made of, sugar and spice and all things nice – and I knew she was thinking of the sticky blondness of butter icing. Her ill-health had aged her into a child again in a way: a fat doll tottering on tiny swollen feet. But in her head she'd never been anything else, she still lived in the Rhondda in her mother's house, with her sister Katie. So powerful was the aura of longing surrounding the place that it *ought*, by rights, to have been entirely fantastical, or at best only a memory. But no. True,

32

her mother was long dead, but home actually still existed.

In the summer holidays we went there to visit, Grandma, my mother and me, leaving Grandpa behind. (This was called 'letting him stew in his own juice'.) South Wales was an entirely female country in our family mythology, despite the mines and miners. A female place, an urban place and a place all indoors. Going there was like sinking into fantasy for all these reasons – and for one special reason above all, which was that home was a shop and we lived over it, and when we were there all the money horrors were magically suspended. Life was unfallen, prelapsarian, as though paying for things hadn't yet been invented. When you wanted a chop or a teacake you just went and helped yourself without even having to cross the street. It was a self-sufficient kingdom, or almost: a general stores that stocked everything from tin trays to oranges to sausages to sides of beef and cigarettes, with a special line in Lyons cakes, and when I was small I could entirely sympathise with Grandma in her resentment at having been persuaded to swap this blissful set-up for the vicarage and the dilapidations. Life at 'Hereford Stores' – named for her mother's native town – was her ideal of luxury and gentility, the source of her unshakeable conviction of social superiority to everyone in Hanmer.

Her sense of what class amounted to was remarkably pure and precise, in its South Wales way. Owning a business in a community where virtually everyone else went down the pit for wages *would* have seemed, in her youth, thoroughly posh. And the simple fact of *not working* when all around you were either slaving away or – worse – out of work would have been sufficient to mark you out as a 'lady'. What could be grander than lounging around upstairs, nibbling at the stock when the fancy took you, brushing out your curls? She and Katie would still spend hour upon hour getting ready to go out – to Cardiff,

or to Pontypridd, to some teashop, or to the pictures – recapturing the world of their girlhood, before men and money had turned real.

Katie was in her forties and had never married. She too was very plump and a bit breathless, but her hair was still red, her teeth were her own and her laugh had a tuneful trill to it, so that she tended on the face of things to bear out Grandma's belief that you were better off without men. There *was* a shadowy man on the premises – their elder brother Stan – but he didn't really count, because (after, so they said, a dashing, brilliant youth) he'd had a colossal breakdown and was never quite right again. Now, in his fifties, he was seedy and skinny, with a faraway gleam in his eye, due to stubbornly wearing his mother's spectacles instead of getting some of his own. Stan hardly dented the atmosphere of scent and vanishing cream and talc I thought of as Hereford Stores. He slipped through it sideways like a ghost. There were two other brothers, but they'd long ago left home and were thought about as outcasts:

elderly Tom, who looked after the butchery part of the business, was a pariah because he lived with a housekeeper, who was not very secretly his mistress, and thus belonged to the same vicious male sect as Grandpa; and Danny was talked about in the past tense as though he was dead, because he had actually had the gall to set up a shop of his own in another valley. So the magic circle of sweet, stale dreams stayed intact, up the crooked stairs over the old double-fronted store, with their family name, 'Thomas', fading over the door.

The house was overheated with high-quality, jet-black, sparkling coal, swapped for groceries with the miners who got it for perks. There was a big old range in the kitchen, which was behind the shop on the ground floor in point of truthful topography, although imaginatively speaking it was upstairs. Here a serial tea party like the Mad Hatter's was in full swing all day and every day except Sunday, when Katie would ceremoniously roast a joint of meat (picked out by Tom) and get very red in the face. Otherwise we lived on Grandma's favourite diet of bread and butter, toasted teacakes, scones, sponges and so on, eked out with tinned fruit and condensed milk. It was understood that cooking, cleaning and washing-up were properly the duties of a 'skivvy', which is glossed by the *OED* as a maid-of-all-work (usually *derogatory*) – first example 1902, so very exactly a Grandma word, she'd have been ten in 1902 – but if you didn't happen to have one then you tried to get through as little crockery as possible, for instance, by hanging on to your cup all day, just giving it a cursory rinse once in a while. South Wales habits accounted for a good proportion of vicarage dirt I suppose: certainly it would have been very difficult to wash clothes, dishes or oneself with any regularity or thoroughness there, since the taps mostly seemed to be rusted up in disused outhouses in the yard and the skivvies who'd once upon a time carried water upstairs for bedroom washbasins were no more. Still, somehow, in the Rhondda we never seemed so shamingly grubby as when we were in Hanmer. And the housework that spelled such unending, ineffectual drudgery for my mother in the vicarage simply wasn't done, for the most part, and nobody much cared.

Hanmer hemmed us in and threatened to expose our secret squalor, whereas neighbours in Tonypandy's steep, jerry-built streets seemed to have lost interest in the ways of Hereford Stores. Katie and Stan gossiped with customers and this functioned as a kind of insulation – a protective barrier of chat within which their eccentricities were contained, unquestioned. They no longer had a social life otherwise and, having quarrelled with their relations, they lived as they liked. There was something pleasurable and even thrilling about this, at a time when advertising and women's magazines were so venomously clean-cut and conformist in their versions of how to be. You were supposed to cringe inwardly when you saw those Persil ads: a little boy's head swivelling on his neck as another boy, the one with the Persil-bright shirt, strides proudly by. 'Persil washes whiter – *and it shows*!' Competitive cleanliness. Hereford Stores sold soap powder all right, and the miners' wives scrubbed away on their washboards and competed with each other in the whiteness of their lace curtains and doilies and antimacassars (an endless battle, in that atmosphere) but Grandma and Katie scorned it all. They were heretics, they wouldn't play by the rules. If society wouldn't supply them with skivvies they were damned if they were going to slave away.

My mother, however, got the worst of both worlds. She inherited the contempt for housework and she was also imbued with the notion that it was a sacred womanly duty. So she dusted and scrubbed and mopped and ironed, but with self-scorn, and – what made it infinitely worse – no idea at all how to set about it. All housework is futile in the sense that it has always to be done again. Hers was more blatantly so, since the vicarage didn't even look briefly clean when she'd 'finished'. When my poor mother mopped a floor she merely redistributed the grime – *and it showed!* That this wretched syndrome was magically suspended in South Wales added to the feeling of playing hookey from reality. *Everyone* was a girl again – not just Grandma, who perhaps always was, but my mother too.

In the drawers upstairs were scented hankies, fake pearls, ends of embroidered ribbon, painted buttons, scraps of lace, lavender sachets, dyed feathers. They hoarded. Grandma especially loved anything made of mother-of-pearl. For her its rainbow sheen was the epitome of prettiness and its very name was shadowed with extra glamour in that house. Their father had left nearly no impression, but their mother was invoked daily as the standard of grace, sweetness, refinement. When Grandma and Katie looked in the mirror, and titivated and sighed, it was their mother's face they were looking for. And when they unhooked their creaking corsets after an outing, eased off their tight shoes and made yet another pot of tea, they were mothering themselves as she would have done. She must have spoiled them hugely, for they reposed in the mere idea of her, although nothing they said about her – nor her rather blank-looking photographs – gave her much character. Except for the hair. Her hair they rhapsodised about: naturally wavy and not yellow, not red, not copper-coloured, but *golden*. 'The colour of a sovereign,' they'd sigh, for all the world as though she'd been a fairy-tale princess, able to spin riches out of her hair. When they remembered her, one or the other of them would sooner or later repeat the phrase 'like a sovereign'

– it became her motto, the sign of her mysterious charm.

Hereford Stores was silted up with mementoes of her era. There were hundreds of picture postcards filed away in chocolate boxes: glazed, embossed and glowing with unnaturally beautiful colours. One I particularly pored over from the time of the First World War (Katie's first bloom) showed a handsome officer reclining in the arms of a pretty nurse, with a small, scarlet stain on his bandaged temple and discreet puffs of smoke to indicate a battle in the distance. But all the pictures were sanctified by association. They belonged to the world of mothballed hopes, that eerie wonderland of kitsch innocence where, in some unimaginable corner of time, a juvenile Grandpa and an even younger Grandma had met and married, and inaugurated hell.

How had it come about? How had he managed to fall for a girl with nearly no brains at all, and nearly no conversation except for curses and coos? With absolutely no interest in books or music or painting or anything much except peppermint creams and frilly blouses? And why did she accept a lean and hungry curate with his way to make? A clever, passionate, talented man if you believed in him, but a bookish boaster, lecher, snob, ham actor and so forth if you didn't. They must have been mutually blinded by their dreams and needs: presumably he fell for her icing-sugar-and-spice flesh, not yet run to flab; and she for the pleasure of being courted, the prestige of being married. It seems safe to assume, from the outrage with which she referred to the whole messy business, that she married in entire ignorance of the mechanics of intercourse and childbirth, and found them hideous.

His discovery that she was barely literate and thoroughly philistine was (one imagines) less traumatic. After all, marrying a pretty, empty-headed girl was considered par for the course and still is, even in a world where couples get to know each other first. Hilda Thomas and Thomas James Meredith-Morris, back then in decorous 1916, wouldn't have been very well acquainted. In that they were simply figures of their generation. What made their marriage more than a run-of-the-mill case of domestic estrangement was her refusal to accept her lot. She stayed furious all the days of her life – so sure of her ground, so successfully spoiled, that she was impervious to the social pressures and propaganda that made most women settle down to play the part of wife. Sex, genteel poverty, the responsibilities of motherhood, let alone the duties of the vicar's helpmeet, she refused any part of. They were in her view stinking offences, devilish male plots to degrade her. When he took to booze and other women (which he might well have done anyway, although she provided him with a kind of excuse by making the vicarage hearth so hostile) her loathing for him was perfected. He was the one who had conned her into leaving her *real* home, her girlhood, the shop where you never had to pay for anything, the endless tea party. It was as though he'd invented sex and pain and want and exposure. She turned patriarchal attitudes inside out: he *was* God to her. That is, he was making it up as he went along, to spite her *and with no higher Authority to back him up*. There was no Almighty in charge, to excuse him, in Grandma's world picture. She was an unreconstructed pagan herself, her sacraments a toasted teacake and a cup of tea, her rosary woven out of her mother's hair. And she treated this life he offered, his shabby malicious invention, with contempt and cocooned herself in memories. The visits to Hereford Stores were her lifeline back to the world before.

Life at the shop was running down, though. Bit by bit they'd gone off their mother's gold standard. Tom's butchery department still seemed fairly solid, meat-rationing had buoyed it up somehow, or at least disguised the falling-off in business. But once you turned your back on his suet-and-sawdust-smelling counter and faced into Katie and Stan's domain (which smelled acridly of tobacco, cheese, yellow soap) you could see that trade was anything but brisk. Customers came out of habit, the older ones, and because they couldn't carry shopping bags up the hill. They bought tiny quantities in any case, rationed by poverty as much as by coupons. As I grew and 1950 loomed, the world in general began cautiously to cast off austerity, leaving Hereford Stores behind, stranded and getting gradually dustier and emptier. When I could count money well enough to be allowed to play shop, I sold untipped Woodbines in ones and twos out of an opened packet we kept by the till. My customers were stooped men with permanent bronchitis and big boys of thirteen or fourteen mysteriously off school. Men in work and their wives shopped elsewhere, except sometimes after hours, when Katie and Stan could be relied on to serve latecomers. It was the sort of shop that had almost as many customers when it was closed as when it was open. Feckless, improvident types rattled at the door at all hours wanting a few fags or half a loaf. And, of course, in search of that increasingly rare commodity that was turning out to be Katie and Stan's special stock-in-trade: tick.

Katie doled out credit with a mixture of scandal, resignation and sympathy, clicking her tongue and sighing as she settled back into the kitchen's fireside warmth to gossip about the after-hours callers ('There's cheek for you, sent that Jimmy round again, poor little tyke'). But Stan had his own infinitely more elaborate and clandestine methods, which he'd evolved during the Depression. This was all meant to be a secret – part of his furtive lunacy – but he was proud of his system, and took me on a tour of the stockrooms and the lofts above to show me how it worked. This whole building was separate from the house, a ramshackle barn-like wooden place with missing floorboards and shaky stairs. There were soap boxes, candles, piles of tin trays and jute mats, cigarettes in cartons on top away from the damp, nothing very exciting at first glance. It was only when you edged your way past this sensible stuff that you entered Stan's Aladdin's cave.

Piled up high, glinting and dusty, were curly metal antlers and wiry spines and whiskers that on closer inspection resolved themselves into dismembered bicycles – handlebars, wheels, plus the occasional fork or seat. There were smaller sets of wheels, too, that came in fours, from prams, and even some whole prams, parked dangerously on top of one another like an accident. He was proudest, though, of the contents of the sacks he kept, for fear of thieves, on the upper storey where the holes in the floor acted as booby traps. Here he had sacks full of ivories: confiscated piano keys, which for Stan, you could tell, represented (together with his other trophies) a cunningly accumulated fortune, the wealth of the world, pretty nearly, infinite riches in a little room.

His plan had been to confiscate people's most vital pos-sessions – their mobility and their music – as pledges against bad debts. They were never redeemed. Yet Stan didn't mind, didn't mind at all. In fact, he was as excited and pleased as if he'd invented his own currency and was a secret millionaire in it. He cherished the ivories and the bike wheels, and looked on the storerooms as a sort of safety deposit. This was his treasure, his equivalent to the collections of scented sachets and beads his sisters kept in the bedrooms. They for their part tut-tutted over his inexplicable affection for this junk, but even at the time when I was small I think I somehow understood – since I *liked* the prams and bikes, and was mystified and

41

impressed by what I imagined to be the stolen teeth of all those pianos – that here was yet another annexe to the fantasy edifice of Hereford Stores. They had (save butcher Tom) all but forgotten that keeping a shop was about swapping goods for money; its real function was as a shrine to the past. Mother's emotional generosity, her gift for giving, had turned all three into obsessive hoarders.

Their bankrupt idyll lasted for nearly ten years after the war. And even when Katie finally married, and died of a stroke horribly soon, confirming all the myths about men, Hereford Stores went on providing the ghost of a living for my mother's disreputable brother, Uncle Bill, who joined Stan in the shadows until – some time around 1960 – he was done for receiving some hot Daz, and the CLOSED sign went up for the last time and finally meant what it said.

Grandma eked out her visits with other fantasy gratifications. She could hoard wherever she was and, although Shrewsbury and Chester were in her view not a patch on Cardiff, they would help recapture the security of streets, and their cafés and cinemas would cocoon her against the hostile whispers of the trees and the whiffs of manure. These outings were all-female, too, and involved hours of getting ready, then a lift to the train from a blaspheming Grandpa, or sometimes a taxi, all so that she'd be able to repose in the life-giving fug of a matinée at the Gaumont or the Majestic. The plush seats, the dimming of the lights and the sheen they caught on the swagged curtain as it rose, the box of chocolates, were as important as the film itself, almost. Although she loved the whole thing and entered into the spirit of the illusion so enthusiastically that she swept aside the dimension of fiction altogether. The latest Ava Gardner movie was just the most recent report on what promiscuous Ava had been up to since you saw her last: the changes of costume and setting and name were feeble disguises, and didn't fool Grandma for a minute. She was there to witness when Joan Fontaine, for all her icy blondeness, fell for Harry Belafonte and would (she said) never trust Joan again. Grace Kelly she watched like a hawk for signs of similar leanings and was semi-confirmed when Grace married an Eye-tie. (She herself wouldn't touch dark chocolate, even, and anyone who acquired a suntan was suspected of a touch of the tar brush.) Once television arrived in our lives she became an addict of soap operas and in particular *Emergency Ward 10*, which saved *her* life day after dreary rural day. The box eventually became her babysitter, the last, many times removed substitute for her mother. By then I was treating her with contempt, as a senile infant, although she scared me a lot, in truth, because she represented the prospect of never growing up.

Once upon a time in South Wales, when a friend of Katie's came to stay, I had had to spend the night in a feather bed, sandwiched between Katie and Grandma, and that ambiguous sensation of sinking back and back, down and down in a deep nest of feathers and furbelows and flesh, came to stand for the Rhondda. Infinite regress threatened down there: promised, and threatened. It was pleasurable – how could it be otherwise? – to return to the smothering, spongy womb of the Stores. And yet I was always glad to get away. As I grew, Grandma got shorter, so that she sometimes looked almost spherical. She and Katie were such an exclusive club, really, that even my mother wasn't a full member and I was even further removed from the inner sanctum because I couldn't recall my great-grandmother, so had to take her praises on trust.

There were other Welsh voices I could have listened to. Occasionally – and to my great surprise – people who dropped in to the shop would congratulate my mother on my bookishness and talk with pride about how their grandchildren were 'getting on' and going to the grammar school. People in Tonypandy, as in other mining districts, were enthusiastic about education, in sharp contrast to Hanmer's conservative scorn and inertia. The future was real and a good thing, and even if you went down the pit like your da you weren't expected to give up reading, thinking, arguing or politicking; autodidacts flourished still in those days. Nonetheless the atmosphere of Hereford Stores dominated my sense of the place, so that for me the journey south was like slipping into a pocket of the past. I didn't know who I was, there – didn't need to know. It was as though I hadn't been born yet.

Grandma saved paper bags inside paper bags inside paper bags ... Years later, when she died, and my mother and I were going through the trunks that by then held the compacted residue of her lifetime's squirrelling, we came on a cache of letters from my grandfather, tied in the inevitable banal shred of pink ribbon. His courtship compositions, they were, full of quotations from the poets, sentimental flourishes, promising plans. We looked at them with awful embarrassment and agreed (how I wish now that we hadn't) to burn them, because they seemed shaming evidence of the mutual confidence trick of that hateful marriage. There was cash in the same trunk, folded notes cunningly dispersed among the photos of Katie done up to the nines, and the bars of waxy soap and sugar lumps put by against the return of rationing. And that money was the clue to another part of her story. Where did she get it? Where, for that matter, did she acquire the substantial sum – around five hundred pounds – she'd accumulated in my name (so that my father couldn't inherit it, she told me once) in National Savings? I didn't think very hard about it at the time and I took the theories that circulated in the family as tall tales.

However, Grandma's way of blurring the boundary between fantasy and reality, and her power to draw me back into the past have long outlived her.

About the money: I was asking my father just the other day whether some of the wilder things I recalled about the grandparents had any basis in truth. For instance, what about the story that Grandma had blackmailed Grandpa for years, by threatening to show his private diary to the Bishop unless he handed over part of his stipend every quarter? Well, yes, said my father, that was certainly true. But how do you *know*? I asked. Simple, he said, I've got the diaries, two of them. (Because she'd kept them as well in one of the trunks, although my mother had never let on.) Anyway, with a bit of persuasion, reluctantly, my father handed them over: two small, cheap, reddish diaries, for 1933 and 1934, both published by John Walker & Co., Farringdon House, Warwick Lane, EC4, filled with very small writing and decorated at weekly intervals with coloured stamps he stuck in to mark the church calendar. These left him even less space to write down the compromising details of his daily life, but he managed enough.

IV

The Original Sin

There is no doubt that Grandma preserved Grandpa's diaries for 1933 and 1934 as evidence against him. Indeed, the 1933 diary has a couple of scathing marginal comments in her hand – *Here the fun begins* (Friday, 25 August) and *Love begins (fool)* exactly a week later. If he refused to produce the cash that lined her luggage, paid for her outings to the cinema and her teatime meringues at the Kardomah, and fed the National Savings account she eventually put in my name in case some man got hold of it when she died, then she would take the damning documents to the Bishop, threaten scandal and divorce, and lose him even the rotten living he had.

Reading these diaries turned out to be a bit like eavesdropping on the beginnings of my world. 1933 was the year the grandparents arrived in Hanmer from South Wales. This was how the Hanmer I grew up in had been created – how life in the vicarage got its Gothic savour, how we became so isolated from respectability, how the money started not to make sense and (above all) how my grandfather took on the character of theatrical martyrdom that set him apart. 1933, he did not fail to note, was the nineteen-hundredth anniversary of Christ's Passion: 'This is the Crucifixion Year AD 0–33, 1900–1933. A Holy Year.' He wasn't thiry-three himself, but forty-one and fearful, before he was offered this new, sprawling country parish in the north, that his career in the Church of Wales had ground to a shaming standstill. He'd been twelve years in the same place. 'Here we are at the end of winter time,' he writes on 8 April, on Saturday night, doing some spiritual stock-taking and already assuming his Sunday style, 'and I am still at St Cynon's. O God give me a little chance now at last. Thy will be done.' But the South Wales parish he was after at the time, Pencoed, went to someone else the very next Thursday and the day after that, Good Friday, he is making the most of his misery, preaching on the theme, 'Who will roll away the stone . . . ?'

It isn't until later in Easter Week that he learns – or at least confides to his diary – the full extent of his humiliation: 'They have really cast me aside in favour of a young fellow who has only been ordained since 1924. Well this is the limit. What on earth am I to do now? No hope and no chance.'

But he has learned to live with hopelessness, that's the worst of it. He fritters away his time and turns his back on the drama of rejection. The great shock of opening this compromising little book, for me, was that for the first half – with the exception of the few desperate and frustrated *cris de coeur* I've culled – it was the record of a pottering, Pooterish, almost farcically domesticated life. The sinner I was expecting was guilty of pride, lust and spiritual despair, not merely of sloth and ineptitude. This was the diary of a nobody. So I nearly censored January to June 1933 in the interests of Grandpa's glamour as a Gothic personage. But in truth this is what we should be exposed to – the awful knowledge that when they're not breaking the commandments, the anti-heroes are mending their tobacco pipes and listening to the wireless.

He had been 'jolly miserable' (that middle-class oxymoron!) during those last stagnant months in South Wales. You could do nearly nothing in the Church of Wales and get away with it, no one took official notice, a vicar was a gentleman after all. Chapel would have been different, much more a matter of openly devout busybody closeness with the congregation, but he managed to nurture his depression in private. He'd surface late from sleep or sulks, affronted by the weather: 'It is a terrible trial to get up in these very cold mornings' – and light the fire in the study. Or that was his plan. Often things went wrong, as he expected: 'Lit a fire in the study but heaps of soot fell down and put it out,' he reports, as late on as 6 May. 'Could not get on with my sermon at all today. An aeroplane overhead at teatime . . .' It's uncharacteristic of him to notice what's going on outside, he is so fed up with his surroundings (his parish, his prison). But perhaps the plane flew past his defences because it belonged to the skyey regions of the weather, which he regularly records as a mirror or a foil to his moods. He's good at the rhetoric of the barometer: with freezing rain comes the pathetic fallacy, sunshine equals irony, with the snow everything grinds gratifyingly to a halt.

Also, the aeroplane was *new* and a machine, like his addiction, the wireless. With his ear to the speaker he takes to the airwaves himself and communes with the wide world so intimately it seems inside his head. 'Toothache,' says one entry, 'Earthquake in Japan.' Hitler comes to power in Germany (31 January), Roosevelt's oath-taking is relayed (4 March). Grandpa registers the facts, but doesn't comment, he's more interested in the quality of reception he's getting on short wave, the placing of the aerial and whether to buy a Pye or a Murphy. He tries each out on approval, squeezes in little drawings of the rival sets on the page and after some enjoyable dithering – 'Spent the whole of the day trying to decide between the Pye and the Murphy' – splashes out £17.17s.0d on the Pye, 'bought . . . outright'.

This is hugely extravagant, the better part of a month's pay (his stipend was £73.4s.4d per quarter), but he owes it to himself, since listening in and twiddling the knobs is what makes his idleness and boredom feel busy. He sees few people, even on the Almighty's business. He boycotts the meetings of the Rural Dean and Chapter ('lost any desire to meet the clergy of the Rhondda – they are all such a lot of place-seekers') and records punctually and with a kind of glum relish the lousy church attendances in harsh weather: 'Got up for H[oly] C[ommunion]. No one at HC.' The wireless, by contrast, is a friendly presence. 'Spent the whole of the afternoon tinkering with my old wireless set in the study,' reads an almost happy entry long after he has acquired the superior Pye. The hums and crackles and cosmic whistles of interference probably served nearly as well as the programmes to provide him with a private cocoon of distraction. He does read of course as well, and in the same impatient spirit, science fiction stories about other worlds for preference. On 17 January, for instance, 'the Radio programme is very monotonous and dull. Took up Conan Doyle's *Lost World* and read it right through.' He is an accomplished mental traveller. In March he actually spends a day or two pretending to have been called away, in order to escape parish business – 'Am supposed to be away from home today. Stayed in and did some reading . . . Lit a fire in the study and sat there all day reading Jules Verne's *Journey into the Centre of the Earth* . . .' Sometimes he sat in the kitchen instead, sometimes he complains of a headache rather than a toothache. On his official evening off he would sit in the study and watch people going to church.

He had his smokescreen too. He smoked a pipe. Or that was the theory. In practice he evolved his own extra rituals to make his habit more complicated and satisfying-because-unsatisfying. Fiddling with pipe-cleaners and bowl scrapers didn't suffice, partly because he hankered after cigarettes – although they woke up an 'old pain' in his chest – and partly because it hurt to grip a pipe-stem with those aching teeth. Anyway, he doesn't just mess with pipe accessories, he goes further. In a sort of parody of a handyman, he *whittles*: 'Shortened my pipe – the Peterson – and spoiled it,' reads a terse entry in January. Was he chagrined? Probably not, although one can't tell whether he has yet worked out his pipe plot. Does he know that what he really wants is (by accident of course) to spoil his pipe and thus make 'work', plus an opportunity to get back to cigarettes? In February he buys another Peterson ('no. II') and on Saturday, 22 April he experiments again and supplies a full rationalisation: 'After I had dinner I turned my Peterson pipe into a cigarette holder as this is the more satisfactory way of smoking to me. The full weight of the pipe is too much for my teeth.' In May: 'am still on with the cigarettes but must go back to the pipe I think'. In fact, he buys a new nameless pipe the very next day, but immediately rejects it in disgust – 'too rotten to smoke. A cheap pipe is useless.' Whereas a dear one provides hours of pleasure and distraction for a bad-tempered bricoleur. On 15 May he buys another Peterson, 'a Tulip-shaped Peterson No. 3' this time, and manages to destroy it fairly fast: 'Saturday May 27th. Broke my Peterson pipe. It seems I must keep to the cigarette holder.' By Monday he records proudly in the diary that he has 'finished turning the Peterson pipe into a cigarette holder'; and so gratifying is this that the week after he goes out and buys another 'light' pipe (3 June) and two days later turns *that* into a cigarette holder too. On 9 June he buys a Peterson No. 33 . . .

As his frustrations mount, the pattern of destructive tinkering speeds up to match, turning smoking into another pseudo-occupation to fill his seething sedentary hours and days. His sensibility is in perpetual motion – he's self-absorbed and self-repelled at once, and the pottering alternates with bleak vistas of pointlessness. 'Spent an unprofitable day feeling liverish and miserable' (March). 'Spent a useless sort of day in the study' (April). Although he is always at home, wearing out the chairs with his bony behind, his family barely exist for him – *except for my mother*. And this was the second surprise of the South Wales part of the 1933 diary, that his teenage daughter Valma (she turned fifteen on 14 March) lives on the inside of his loneliness. She is his one human task, he has been tutoring her at home for a year (he records in May) and she figures in the same sorts of sentences as the wireless, the books and the pipes, where her presence suddenly populates the house – 'Spent the morning and the afternoon taking Valma's lessons. Came on to Latin at tea-time'; 'sat in house all this afternoon giving Valma her lessons'. He plans out schedules of study and sets her exams. She's his go-between with the outside world, in more senses than one, for she also runs errands and posts letters.

It's my mother who posts the letter asking for the Pencoed living, after he's hesitated for days over committing himself, fearing to be snubbed (as he was). She is his hostage to fortune. She stands for a possible future. And the reason this was such a surprise to me was that she always led me to believe that she had never been close to him, and that he had never shared with her the bookish complicity I had with him when I was little. In my mother's account of her growing up the Latin lessons and piano lessons (she was musical, like him and unlike me) had been erased without trace. Why? Why had she taken my grandmother's side and when? The story that was about to unfold in Hanmer does explain, I fear, exactly why. But for the meantime she is his creature, as I became. He is distant and callous-sounding about his son Billy, who only attracts his notice when he plays truant from school and is duly beaten for it. And already there is (to put it mildly) no love lost between him and my grandmother. She must have been very ill that freezing winter of 1932–3, because he notes in his diary for Wednesday, 5 April: 'Hilda went out for the first time since Christmas.' But that's not all. He only names her to record her absences. She goes out a lot as soon as she's able, often back to her real home at Hereford Stores, leaving him to stew in his own juice. The diary simmers on: 'Well here is injustice if you like. I believe we have got a lot of madmen in authority in this diocese . . . I pray that this may be my last Easter at St Cynon's.'

And out of the blue his prayers were answered, when he least expected it. The resurrection of his ambitions and energies was only weeks away. It's on 13 June that the long winter of discontent finally melts into spring – 'At last the day of hope has dawned. The Bishop has written to ask me to come and see him about the living of HANMER with TALLARN GREEN.' And he breaks out the green ink to celebrate. After this things move very fast. He travels north by train to visit Hanmer on 25 June, inspects the vicarage two days later ('a nice old place and I can't imagine myself in it') and accepts the living on 3 July, so that on Friday, 28 July he's able to read the announcement of his appointment in the *Church Times*, which makes it real – 'O father at last I see the fruition of my desires . . .' – and within weeks the fun began, as we know.

Everything is suddenly on the move, unfixed, the old land-marks of his depression left behind in the Rhondda – along with his wife and son and Valma too, for the moment, since the vicarage in Hanmer is to be cleaned and refurbished a bit, and in any case they need time to pack up. All at once he's alone in this new place ('a lovely spot') where people don't know him from Adam. Mobility. Freedom of a kind. He must take up his duties immediately, now that the old Canon, long ailing, has finally admitted defeat and been persuaded to go. His two churches are three miles apart down shaggy, meandering country roads blistered with cow pats and hemmed in by weedy ditches. He acquires a bicycle, and finds himself walking it up gentle hills (no mountains here) and freewheeling down again on the other side. The diary shows him threading his way along a necklace of new place-names – Bangor-on-Dee, Wrexham, Ellesmere, Horseman's Green, Eglwys Cross, Bronington, Bettisfield, Whitchurch – marking out a map on which, more and more often, his path crosses that of the district nurse, Nurse Burgess, who of course has a bicycle too . . .

Just days before, ironically enough, he is all prepared to be lonely and bored. 'Hanmer is very quiet,' he notes ominously, 'very . . . Time hangs somewhat on my hands in this place.' Then the new bike arrives. There's an August heatwave, the kids are swimming in the mere just as we would twenty years on (except that in 1933 it's only the boys) and on the very day he admits to taking his first ride *with* the nurse ('*Here the fun begins*') they are both summoned to the mereside in their professional capacities, because one of the young men has drowned. It's the beginning of a tragic sub-plot that keeps up a kind of background thrumming for months to come: drowned Jack is Molly's young man, bereaved Molly comes to work in the vicarage as a maid, loses her mind, Nurse Burgess tries to get her put away and so forth. For now, though, Jack's death is the main, telling event, a focus for feeling. It permeates the humid atmosphere and puts paid to any illusion of serenity. His body doesn't surface for three days and the whole of Hanmer keeps a vigil, people standing in hot huddles talking under their breath, gazing at the innocent flat water only dimpled with fish taking flies. He was a strong swimmer, too, so there's a niggling element of mystery about his death: cramp, or weed, or cold currents must have got him and it's true – was still true twenty years later – that sometimes when the water near the edge was soupy warm you'd suddenly find your legs entwined with chill streams snaking in under the lily pads, just before the bottom shelved right away.

Grandpa was swiftly out of his depth as well, but he was having a marvellous time and only noticed how far he'd gone when his family actually turned up. Out of his depth, and *in his element*. He and Nurse Burgess, now MB for short in the diary, pedal to paradise every day of the week, including Sunday. Trailing a cloud of midges, they'd hump their bikes off the road, through some muddy gateway and, behind the hedge, hug and knead each other among the mallows and Queen Anne's lace and nettles dusty with pollen. Perhaps they spread his tobacco-scented black cassock on the ground to protect them from ants and the crawling wasps drunk on crab apples. Or more likely they'd keep their uniforms on and each get to

know the other's body in bits. He is lean and wiry, MB in her starched blue linen is substantial but not yet stout, well muscled because of all the exercise she gets, her arms mottled pink and white from soap and sun. She has a midwife's hands. His fingers are inky and curve to caress an imaginary pipe bowl, or a preacher's palmful of air, and – now – the generous breast where her watch ticks away. It's nearly always afternoon, they are supposed to be out to tea, strawberry jam and fruit cake, and so they are, so they are. Cattle watch incuriously, sidling towards the gate, ready to herd along the lane for milking. And they wrestle each other into submission, and relax a long moment, listening with half an ear to the trickling ditch the other side of the hedge, where duty calls. Although it's hard to hear the summons for the rooks and wood pigeons.

So I imagine them celebrating in advance their private Harvest Festival, the event in the church calendar that strikes the richest chord in this pagan place, as he'll discover. 'We plough the fields and sca-a-a-tter / The good seed on the land.' Was that how they managed contraception – *coitus interruptus*, aggravating the sin of adultery? Deliberate infertility, the luxurious, forbidden pleasure of *taking pleasure by itself*, must have spiced their lovemaking. Theirs was a feast of blissful barrenness. MB may well have used a sponge and a spermicidal douche. A nurse, being a professional spinster, was assumed to know about these things; and in any case all nurses had lost their conventional aura of feminine innocence – their collective *moral* virginity – because of their intimacy with other people's bodies. They administered enemas and sponged the sick, and washed the dead and laid them out and plugged their orifices. They helped other women's babies into the world. At the same time, since a nurse couldn't keep her job and marry, she was a bit like a nun – a nun in a salacious story.

Nurses were suggestive. And so, for slightly different reasons, were priests of the Church of England, who could and did marry. Grandpa had the shamanistic glamour associated with the magical ability to transform the bread and wine, of course, and he combined it with licensed access to other people's private *spiritual* parts. He officiated at a distance in church, but also close to, at home. He talked with women, and with the aged and the sick, during the day when other (real) men were out at work. An Anglican vicar was, in terms of cultural fiction, a eunuch of sorts. Yet everyone knew that actually he wasn't vowed to celibacy, hence the comic naughtiness associated with his situation, too. Perhaps that is why it's inviting to picture this love affair – the Vicar and the Nurse – in the style of a Hogarth etching of carnival appetite on the rampage. Flesh triumphs over Spirit. An allegory of hypocrisy. The holier (or in MB's case, certainly cleaner) than thou rutting away in the ripe season, no purer than the peasants to whom they preached hygiene and holiness.

Peering down the years, a voyeur through that dense bramble hedge, it's hard to see them except in outline, etched in archetypal postures. But why not remake them out of Arcimboldo fruit and veg, since it's a less moralising transformation? O father, at last I see the fruition of my desires, in apple cheeks, cabbage curls and a damson mouth.

On 31 August he pauses for a second to count his blessings: 'The end of a wonderful month for me. Thanks be to God.' A couple of days later he foresees possible 'complications' with MB, but for now he's so happy he steps right out of character and simply refuses to brood. He has to admit to having a good time: 'Well I must take life as I find it and make the best of every circumstance,' he writes, for all the world like a saintly stoic accepting the delights the Lord has seen fit to pelt him with.

He makes a brief return trip to South Wales, where Hilda and the children are staying at Hereford Stores, packed up to leave. While he's there he sneaks some vertiginous glimpses of his hated old parish – 'went for a walk over the Coronation Hill within sight of the parish of Ynyscynon' – before travelling back north on his own, to be met in Wrexham by MB. Then, on 13 September, the family ARRIVE IN HANMER in capital letters. Hilda has brought her beloved sister Katie along to help and to soften the blow of leaving the Rhondda, but this doesn't prevent her from being 'very down in the mouth' at her first sniff of country air. 'She is utterly miserable this evening,' he tells the diary. The next day she is no better ('terribly miserable') and the day after that he sends them off to go shopping in Whitchurch, the nearest town, six miles away, with the same result – 'Hilda again miserable.' On Saturday, taking stock, he finds his own secret sense of well-being wearing a bit thin: 'Am not feeling very well again. This is due to the pressure of moving and Hilda's lack of spirit.' He seems to feel, rather unreasonably, that she should be sharing in his elation, sympathising with the revolution in his feelings. 'I have to bear everyone's burdens and my own,' the entry ends, with a surge of self-pity.

Of course, Grandma didn't yet know about MB. Once on the bicycle, on the byways of the parish, he was off her mental map. And in any case from Hilda's point of view MB was only one of a set of local ladies who had taken doting possession of their new vicar during his first lone weeks. Chief among them was widowed Lady Kenyon, who was (it turns out) the real head of the Hanmer community, and outshone the eponymous Hanmers in both rank and wealth. The diary records that he was frequently chauffeured around in her car, and that he was regularly invited up to Gredington, the comfortable

Kenyon pile, for tea and for dinner tête-à-tête. Then there's Miss Crewe – the headmistress of the parish school – and her friend Miss Kitchin, who ran the bakery and doubled as the church organist. Miss Crewe, too, owned a car, which Miss Kitchin drove, and they gave him lifts to Chester, Shrewsbury, Oswestry and so on, and more invitations to tea. He was, it seems, God's gift to all the grander single women of the parish. It must quickly have become apparent to these new female friends that he and Hilda were a most ill-matched and disaffected couple. She hadn't the health, inclination or the social background to play the role of the vicar's wife. And this unhappy fact must have added to his air of availability for them all, and particularly for MB.

She called shortly after the family's arrival and walked Hilda to the church 'for the first time' (as the diary records, possibly with irony). Instead of cooling down, their affair intensifies: 'Went to Tallarn Green . . . met MB. A lovely day altogether' (19 September). He is hardly ever in his new vicarage and often eats supper or goes to play cards with the people at the lodgings he stayed in when he first arrived in the village, where MB often drops by, too. And very soon this family – the Watsons, who keep the shop – are in on the secret. As the autumn closes in, and the weather gets wet and foggy, his double life keeps him idyllically busy. Official parish duties even promise fun, too: 'Went to the meeting at the Parish Hall for entertainments . . . there will be quite a lot to do at Hanmer as time goes on.' Although the pace occasionally gets hard to sustain, it seems, for on Saturday, 7 October he reverts to the old ploy of hiding in his study and pretending he's elsewhere: 'Decided to be away all day so as to have a quiet day.'

It's the day the clocks go back. He finds himself pausing for reflection and – for the first time – misgivings. Has he been led down the garden path? 'Thank thee O God for hearing my prayer to get a removal from Llwynypia. But I wish I could have removed to some other parish in S. Wales instead of coming up to the north.' Or perhaps he isn't as smitten as he first thought, for the entry ends enigmatically, 'My heart is in the south.' But the very next day he goes to the Watsons after evensong, where he meets MB and 'stays late'. There's a gratifyingly 'huge crowd' at church for Harvest Festival a week later and he's able to rest on his laurels, since MB is going away for a short holiday. And then, suddenly, just as he relaxes, there comes a stroke of fate that whisks away the very means of his freedom.

In other words, he had an accident on the bike. He was speeding alone down the dark lanes between services when he came a cropper – 'tore the cartilage of my leg. Laid up at Pritchards' farm. Dr McColl set my leg and brought me home,' he writes, staccato style with clenched teeth: immobilised, grounded, trapped in the vicarage. That dawns on him gradually. By Wednesday the leg 'is far from getting right', on Thursday the doctor calls and tells him he won't be fit for his duties on Sunday and things start to look serious. Lady Kenyon sends a pair of crutches. And MB, who is after all the district nurse, returns from her holiday to find him in the new position of patient – flat on his back.

She knows just what to do. She bustles into the vicarage armed with her professional innocence. Now their assignations take place *in his bedroom*. On 1 November she calls and stays till midnight. 'Am feeling very tired,' he tells the diary before falling asleep. MB is tenderly solicitous. She gives him a 'dental pipe' as a present, plus tobacco, and a walking stick 'for me to get about'. Except that she doesn't seem to be leaving him much time or energy for hobbling out of the house. The diary is dominated by her home visits. After about ten days, when the level of intensive care must have been starting to look a bit excessive, a new and magical word turns up: massage. The leg is on the mend, but needs daily massage. Bliss, you might think, to be in her capable hands. The accident has turned out to be a blessing in disguise, now that the weather is foul and the nights are drawing in.

But reading between the lines – which are getting pretty repetitious, there's massage and more massage – he's not altogether enjoying this domesticated transgression. For instance, there is an interesting double-take in the entry for 16 November: 'The nurse (MB) came in the morning and gave me another massage.' On the eighteenth he's 'rather depressed . . . shall be glad when my leg is well enough to get about'. On the twenty-third the massage leads to 'a long serious talk with MB all the morning'. On the twenty-fifth he strikes a querulous note: '*Have* to be massaged in the afternoon' (my italics, but his resentment, surely?). It's not just the nights that are closing in. Perhaps in some perverse way it's almost a relief when at last on 27 November Grandma, who has been distracted (presumably) by homesick dreams of the Rhondda, wakes up to what's going on.

There's a huge row. 'Hilda in tantrums.' No more massage sessions with MB. He goes to see the bone-setter at Church Stretton and the leg is soon cured. Not so the ache of passion. There are more long, serious talks ('It is a very miserable position for MB') and more rows with Hilda – 'Heart-breaking in this country silence,' he says, suddenly, dazedly, missing the background hum of traffic, the life of noise in South Wales. Still, he's out and about again, and there has been a gratifying flurry of invitations, including one to the Hanmers' house, Bettisfield Park, for late supper (leading to a 'thumping' hangover the next morning). He keeps away from the vicarage as much as possible and sees MB at the Watsons', as he did before the accident. Things have changed, of course, the complications he dreaded have materialised. On 9 December he swears her a sinner's oath on the Bible – promising to stay faithfully unfaithful. Thick fog blankets Hanmer and some days he is stuck at home. 'Had to sit in the kitchen through perpetual bothering and misery,' he writes on 19 December. 'Don't know what is going to come of this.' Even when he contrives to stay out all hours, Grandma – already an insomniac – is quite capable of raging till dawn: 'Spent a most awful night with Hilda again. Up the whole of this night and in deep misery about everything.' He notes grimly that the Watsons have called the vet to put their dog out of *its* misery. He was no animal lover, obviously he envied the brute.

This misery was of an altogether different order from the old dull depression, however. This was live, vivid, *mythic* misery that marked the festive season with its own secret significance: 'So the most notable Christmas of all has commenced.' He was full of energy, absorbed and fascinated by the spectacle of his life. 'How will all this end?' he asked himself, clutching the edge of his seat. His feelings were volatile and contradictory. Certainly there were moments when he wanted to be free of MB. She had become a liability, another burden. And yet she still represented the lure of adventure. On 27 December he sent her a 'letter of renunciation' – 'This is now the end.' But the very next evening, when he went to church to collect his robes, 'MB followed with a scene . . . a pathetic pleading night. I do not know what to make of all this. What a situation is now developing. Hilda begins her tantrums again about MB. So it goes on endlessly. Did not go to bed but remained in study all night long . . .' As the year ends, and the diary too, he's very attracted by the pull of an ending, but also by the opposite desire, for more intrigue, the plot to come. Rounding off 1933 he's keeping his options open: 'So ends a most memorable year for me. I have had the move I wished for to a lovely country church. Here I have met many most kind people. But I fear that the work will be too much for me. I have met MB too and therein hangs all the tale of the future. What will that be I wonder?? God knows since it is His doing that all this has come about. So then I commit the future to God.' So MB was God's idea.

She was not the whole story, for he had other projects. In the new year private drama had to share space in the new diary with the public kind. The parish entertainments committee that started meeting back in the autumn had generated a real show, his first Hanmer pantomime – and suddenly all the world's a stage. He limbers up on New Year's Day by doing a 'turn' himself in the parish hall, as part of a very amateur concert, a monologue as 'Fagin in the Condemned Cell'. But for the panto he's the prime mover – mostly from behind the scenes – recruiting the band, rehearsing the cast, and painting the scenery. The diary entries take on a surreal savour, when you remember the real-life drama he's escaping from. Armed with bolts of cloth and cans of paint, he is levitating out of the rows and scenes to create in their midst scenes from another world, the innocent, archetypal land of *Cinderella*: 'Got up this morning to start painting the scenery. Commenced with the woodland glade and got on well with it until 4.30 . . . sat in study thinking out a scene for the kitchen . . . finished scene 1 this morning. Put it out to dry this afternoon.'

He's wonderfully well insulated from the raw real. Everything takes on an extra dimension of *theatre*, or to put it another way, *bad faith*. Thus he resolves to simplify his life and make a moral choice – 'I must make up my mind what to do' – but actually he is revelling in all the complications of indecision, the beauty of both/and: 'So this is the end or is it the beginning of a new era for me.' The personal plot thickens – Mrs Watson talks to him about MB, MB and Hilda row face to face . . . The village is a carnival of gossip. He is defiant and grandly outrageous. These days he and MB are meeting in the church, God's safe house. It's not the emotional logic of adultery that shapes events, though, but pantomime preparations. The show must go on – 'a long and serious talk' with MB gives way to 'a good rehearsal'. He has finished the final ballroom backdrop (1 February) and is now hanging the whole sequence of scenes and painting the wings *in situ* in the parish hall. 'Had a row with Hilda in the house during the day,' he notes on 3 February. 'After that went to the Hall and continued painting. MB brought me a cup of tea.' He's cutting it fine, for the first matinée is only four days away, but it's a real labour of love. He is exercising his vocation to the full at last – the hard-working wizard making magic for the crowd.

He has started to turn into the Grandpa I remember – except that he has yet to taste the bitterness of being *really* found out. The pantomime was a triumph. He put on evening dress to conduct the orchestra, Sir Edward Hanmer publicly praised him from the stage and so – on the final night – did Lady Kenyon. So far, no one held his sin against him, MB was apparently a mere peccadillo compared with the major magic of *Cinderella*. Indeed, it looks as though people somehow felt it was all part of the show. He was having a love affair with the parish. No wonder he was suddenly forlorn and lonely when the curtain fell. His life was as much of a tangle as ever, but it struck him as banal. He remarked that time hung heavy on his hands – which is exactly the phrase he used just before he met MB. He

was restless, impatient to affront the next phase of his fate. This time the cast would involve my mother (she hadn't starred in the first panto, nor had he been paying her much attention) and this time things would go badly wrong, and he would fix the future.

V

Original Sin, Again

The quiet of Hanmer gave Grandpa the willies whenever he slowed down sufficiently for it to invade his consciousness. He heard time passing, then. Depression lay in wait and he would see the prospect of a more vivid life, *the life his talents deserved*, dissolving away like a mirage. I think this is why scenery-painting for the pantomime absorbed him so blissfully. He could create the illusion of perspective without having anywhere to stand to check he'd got it right (mostly he painted with the canvas spread out on the floor of an attic) and this trick was a version of the moral trick he needed to play on himself constantly. The moral trick – or more truly the *morale* trick – was harder, however. The show he put on that first Hanmer winter gave him a taste of carnival freedom and yet its very success left him in post-coital gloom: 'The village is very quiet tonight after all the excitement of this week. What a week!'

The affair with MB had developed along similarly perverse and disappointing lines, since she had not only become the theme of endless Hilda rants, but also a kind of wife number two, part of the furniture of his frustration. So it was horribly convenient that the village – or at least the influential people, like Lady Kenyon – seemed disposed to blame MB for the scandal. If he cast her off he'd be allowed to get away with it. And he was ready (for the wrong reasons) to do the right thing. In short, he behaved like a complete cad towards MB.

He heard a whisper that she had another lover and longed to believe it – 'This may be a way out, let it come quickly.' It didn't and after another 'terrible week' of rows, he was feeling very sorry for himself as he took stock on a cold Saturday night in mid-February: 'I hope to my God that it will all end now. Hanmer has brought me much misery. Got my thoughts in order for tomorrow but H— keeps on and on . . . I do think that MB is very greatly wronged and after all her only fault is that she has said that she thinks a lot of me. Well I only hope that everybody will shut up now and that the whole business will end.' He is the injured party, besieged by Hilda and Hanmer gossip. At the same time, however, he is magnanimous enough to spare a thought for poor MB, a fellow victim and all because she cares for *him*. . . He is afraid of scandal, but even more on his guard against self-contempt. He is quite ruthless when it comes to preserving his own good opinion – not above implying, for instance, that MB (now that he has rejected her) is to blame for making him feel 'lonely', by which he means sexually starved, after all that autumn plenty. Then again, he wouldn't be feeling lonely if she hadn't existed in the first place, which was probably the Almighty's fault. Anyway, that it had all turned out such a mess was the cross Grandpa had to bear.

And with a kind of poetic justice, God's cause in Hanmer was being sold short as a result, for doing without MB was affecting his performance in the pulpit. 'This loneliness is reacting upon my spirit. I cannot preach as I used to do.' That particular Sunday (25 February) there was a good congregation, but his sermon was 'rotten'. 'I must buck up if I want to keep the crowd,' he adds crudely, fearing the loss of his magic. MB (like Hilda) demoralises him, she's an incubus puncturing his self-love, draining away his confidence and *spoiling the show*. 'The loneliness of Hanmer is awful and MB is the cause.' Unlike Hilda, however, she can be got rid of.

It's a painfully drawn-out process and more than once his 'loneliness' gets the better of his resolve. But he perseveres until bit by bit he comes to hate MB and – given the way he's behaving – maybe it's mutual. One sad sub-plot to the end of their affair involves poor Molly, whose young man was drowned in the mere in the August heatwave that first brought vicar and nurse together. Molly had been working on and off for Hilda in the house, but on 26 April she broke down and drank 'paraffin oil', and MB took charge of her. The next day, he records in the diary, 'MB is now driving the case against Molly. Molly is taken to the Wrexham workhouse and looks like being charged with attempted suicide.' The day after that Hilda talks to the inspector and as a result 'Molly is to return to us from custody. But she must leave Hanmer as soon as possible . . .' It looks very much as though Molly had become a pawn in the game. The vicarage can hardly have been much of a sanctuary for a girl mourning her lover, and now Hilda and MB were using her plight to score points against each other. For once Hilda came out on the side of humanity in Grandpa's account, so pleased was he to have evidence that MB was overbearing, callous, sadistic even. Summing up the whole wretched episode, he concluded (Molly already forgotten): 'I have come to detest MB, really and properly.' All the same, it wasn't until June that they made the final break. That gave him an opportunity to put the boot in by writing her a Dear Nurse letter on her birthday in May, only to retract it a week later, plus other refinements of torment.

Neither of them was disposed to drink paraffin oil for grief, that's certain. Only the lower orders dreamed so naively of oblivion, or got moved on. *They* both lived still in Hanmer, tied to their posts, hating each other and Hilda, who hated them both. This is another aspect of rural life that's lost now that the middle-class diaspora has populated the countryside with property-owning vagrants: the peculiar hell of having to live with such substantial ghosts from your past. It's this that gives the story of Grandpa and MB its tragicomic character – they're too resilient for tragedy, too horrid for comedy. In Shakespeare's tragicomedy *Measure for Measure* an inept moralist called Elbow, who's wiser than he knows, pronounces the most harsh and inescapable of life sentences – 'Thou seest, thou wicked varlet, now, what's come upon thee: thou art to continue, now, thou varlet; thou art to continue.' That's what happened to them. If the Almighty had been watching their goings-on, he couldn't have sentenced MB, Hilda and Grandpa to a more appropriate fate than Hanmer.

MB was a survivor, she was still doing her job in the late 1950s, in her fifties. I remember her very well. She'd be a bit out of puff sometimes after she'd pushed her bike uphill, her rosy cheeks showed broken veins if you got close, and her curls were white, but she was hale and stout and all of a piece, every firm inch the district nurse. The reason I remember so exactly is that after Grandpa's death, when Grandma had been evicted from the vicarage and was living with us, Nurse Burgess called every day to test a urine sample (Grandma couldn't be trusted not to binge on sugar) and give her her insulin injection. Grandma was unable to inject herself because by now she also had Parkinson's disease and shook too much, and my mother refused because she was squeamish. So Hilda and MB were reunited daily, when MB would sterilise a big needle (this was before throwaway syringes, but Grandma insisted she kept a specially blunt one for *her*), briskly rub Grandma's soft, flabby arm with surgical spirit and plunge in the cruel point. After she'd gone, Grandma would complain that her treatment was 'rough' as was only to be expected of a woman so *coarse* (a very strong word back then). The ritual was rendered fascinating, of course, because *everyone knew* – even *I* knew – that Nurse Burgess had been Grandpa's girlfriend once upon a time, and that was why she and Grandma loathed one another.

What I didn't know until I read the diary, for it hadn't become part of local folklore, was the story of his next amorous adventure, the one that would really count against him. Perhaps gossip as a communal art form actually censors out the unacceptable, rather than exposing it? At any rate, compared with MB, Marjorie (Marj for short) was a most suppressed and insubstantial ghost. When I asked about her people remembered

her perfectly well, though. Marj was my schoolgirl mother's brand-new best friend. Valma, my mother, had just turned sixteen that spring of 1934, and Marj was a year or at most two years older. She'd left school and was at a loose end, waiting for a hospital place to train as a nurse. She spent a lot of time at the vicarage, almost lived there, because she had in a sense no home. Her maiden aunts, the two Misses Griffiths who taught at Hanmer school, had taken her in – she was their sister's illegitimate daughter. Marjorie was socially ambiguous and morally at risk (no patriarchal protector), just the sort of young person the vicar should be taking a fatherly interest in. His affair with her wasn't just bad behaviour, it was sin squared. Or possibly cubed, for he used his own daughter as a kind of bait and as camouflage.

Or maybe he wasn't quite so calculating. It's true that after vanishing from his diary for months Valma suddenly resurfaced that spring. In January he'd arranged for her to attend the Whitchurch Girls' High School (fee-paying pre-war) and he bought a dress for her first ball, given by Lady Kenyon at Gredington. This was just at the time when he was messily disposing of MB, in post-panto gloom, and perhaps he was suddenly charmed with the young woman his daughter had become (a real-life Cinderella?) when he flirted and worse with her friend Marj. The paradox is that if you add a hint of incest, the whole thing looks more innocent, or at least more impulsive. He was now desperately in love with youth, potentiality, the fleeting sense of lightness and freedom, and the future stretching ahead unresolved. It was his own youth he was reaching out for: 'I wish I was free of all encumbrances so that I could go where I liked,' he wrote on 3 March. He got his bicycle out and oiled it for the spring, also noted that time hung heavy ... He wanted to feel that life was still before him. And there was Valma, slender, pretty, at the beginning of things. And there was Marj, right next to her, a bit older and more knowing, hungry for attention, wanting a father figure, *asking for it*. According to the diary it was Marj who made the running. On 21 April Valma and Hilda went to Chester, and Marj took advantage of their absence to tease him: 'Marj has worried the house all day . . . I don't know what to make of her.' Except that he did, for he adds melodramatically, 'Must alter my handwriting after this entry.' There's a certain lack of logic about this resolution. If he'd really wanted secrecy he'd have written backwards, or in code, or in invisible ink. But it's the gesture that counts – always the showman, Grandpa, even (or especially) when he's talking to himself. His handwriting stays just the same.

He was still disentangling himself from MB and perhaps had as yet no fresh offences to report. On the face of it he was making a *new* new life, starting again. He worked hard in the garden, cut the grass and rolled the lawn until it was once more flat enough for a game of bowls. He did the housework, too, after Molly's departure: on 11 May he 'scrubbed the passage and kitchen', and a week later he 'cleaned the study and all the rooms downstairs', while Val and Marj rode off fancy-free on their bikes to Ellesmere. (Hilda took no part in any of this skivvying; already she was concentrating on going to the pictures.) Despite his labours, there are fearful tracts of boredom – 'To bed tired out with inertia,' says one entry in early June; and 'spent a very useless sort of day' another confesses irritably. The old futile busyness seems just around the corner.

He reports on Val and Marj's comings and goings like a fretful voyeur – only occasionally does he even contrive to freewheel alongside them on their rides. Indeed, he might never have got closer if puckish providence hadn't supplied him with a go-between, in the form of the curate he'd been asking for for months. This young man, whose name was Percy Davies, turned up in June. To start with Grandpa was sour and suspicious – 'he is a blinking snob I think. I would like to have a human being with me . . .' But he changed his tune almost immediately, for Percy Davies (or PSD) was an obliging and convivial young fellow, and what's more he had a motorbike. Two days after PSD's arrival, Grandpa is riding pillion and life speeds up again. PSD has only just been ordained, nonetheless he can perform the magic that matters and redeem the time. He receives a rare and real accolade: 'The curate has now had a whole week here and the week has passed quite quickly.' Soon he is almost one of the family – like Marj, and like Grandma's plump younger sister with the musical laugh, sweet Katie, who's come for a holiday.

This family, though, is dangerously fissile, falling apart, orphaned, since nobody wants to play the part of parent. Grandma regarded the role of wife and mother with revulsion even before Grandpa justified her by carrying on with that coarse nurse. Grandpa is doing his best to keep up appearances (you might think) by scrubbing the kitchen and dusting the drawing-room, but then that in itself would have seemed shockingly bohemian in the 1930s – not at all manly or proper. No one in the vicarage that summer of 1934 admits to belonging to the older generation, it's an extended family with nothing to hold the pieties in place. No one sits still for a moment. It's as though the old house is a centrifuge – expelling its inhabitants in every direction, in ever-changing permutations, off to Wrexham, Chester, Shrewsbury, Llangollen.

It's also the season of garden fêtes and trips to the seaside – the bell-ringers, the Sunday School, the Choir, the Women's Institute all have their outings to Rhyl or New Brighton. On the last day of July the whole vicarage tribe piles on to the Tallarn Green Choir bus to Rhyl: 'We are quite a little party – *ego*, Val, Katie, Hilda, Billy, Marj and PSD' (even Hilda will join a 'party'). All the fun of the fair. He sounds as if he's still on the big dipper when the August anniversary of his arrival in Hanmer comes around: 'A year ago I came to this parish. On the whole I have been very happy and I have known misery also. PSD is a good friend. MB is a big disappointment. I trusted in her but she is a complete failure, a woman of no principle at all. I have done with her finally. This has been a happy week and I think that we have spent a decent time . . .' Naughty Marj has been gossiping about her rival's promiscuity and in any case he's free to discard the boring truth about his affair with MB because he's living all in prospect. Their relationship, as it turns out, *had no future* and that suffices to damn her by the logic of now. Meanwhile he's taking his turn to hitch lifts on the back of the curate's machine, trailing clouds of glorious exhaust fumes.

As the hot days pass a pattern emerges in the vicarage party's seemingly random excursions. There's a kind of phantom four-some (now you see it, now you don't) who never exactly go out together, but who match and mirror-reverse each other. PSD takes Valma off on his motorcycle, and *ego* and Marj find themselves alone. This time Grandpa at least has the grace not to try to claim that it's God's doing. Indeed, he sounds for almost the first time consciously wicked, daring the big police-man in the sky to punish him. On 6 August: 'Val and curate go off for a ride. Marj on my lap in the study. So ends this day. What of it!' Well, no thunderbolt strikes and so he does it again, and again. And on the surface of things there's only a jolly family party. He even survives a holiday plus Hilda and Katie and children but minus Marj and PSD back in the South.

But Katie stays behind in the Rhondda to go back to work in the shop and bit by bit the summer's party atmosphere dissipates. In September he meets MB in a cold professional capacity over a parishioner's deathbed, which strikes him poetically as an emblem of the transience of passion – 'All that is at an end.' Only as far as MB is concerned, however, for he adds slyly, 'Time does fly even in the country.' Outings to the cinema on PSD's bike (Marlene Dietrich, in October, in *The Scarlet Empress*) keep the illusion alive, as do secret assignations with Marj under cover of Valma's jaunts with the curate: 'PSD takes Val to pictures at Wrexham.' (23 November) 'So the days fly by.' Days with wings are code for cuddles with Marj.

Even his cover wasn't very respectable. 'Fast' would have been the world's kindest word for the public aspect of vicarage life. But given Hanmer and his history with MB, people suspected the worst and started to draw away. Lady Kenyon herself, although too grand to fear contagion, was giving up on Grandpa. True, she took the trouble to chivvy Marj to make ready to leave for her nursing training; but invitations to Gredington were fewer and further between. Cynically, you might say that the Marj affair was a snub to the charms of maturity and so caused extra offence to the Hanmer ladies who'd patronised him. There'd have been genuine shock, though, too – especially at the way he blithely encouraged his daughter to compromise her reputation. The sheer moral untidiness of the breaking down of boundaries between generations and classes (Marj being neither respectable nor safely an outsider) would have had a real whiff of decadence about it, sexual intrigue apart. And in a sense Hilda also colluded, refusing her wifely duties and (even worse) her maternal responsibilities too. The all-night rows – which now started up again – only spiced the witches' brew of badness. You can see how the vicarage began to be surrounded by a cordon sanitaire of scandal, spoken and unspoken, and became a moral slum.

But what went on *inside*? When did Valma realise what her father and Marj were up to? When did she understand that she too was being talked about? What would she even have known about sex, when *her* mother believed it was (all of it, always) vile? She must have 'known' about MB, from the rows, but clearly that had not alienated her from her father. This affair did, because this time of course (I realise) he was being unfaithful not so much to Hilda as to *her* – betraying her with her friend, making use of her, shaming her in public, turning her into a sexual object before she'd even properly recognised her own wants . . . She must have been burningly ashamed, especially if she felt jealous of Marj, as she may well have, given her old role in her father's Rhondda life, when he was her tutor and she his main link with the world.

And there was another bitter betrayal. He seemed to have forgotten that she was a clever girl, and lost all interest in her mind and character, in his hectic obsession with the mere fact of youth. He may or may not have damaged Marj's young life (she seems to have gone off to her hospital training on time and to have revisited Hanmer later at odd intervals when the fancy took her) but he certainly scarred his daughter's sensibility horribly. She lost all the confidence and hopefulness you can glimpse in the dashingly virginal girl of 1934. She became fiercely censorious about bodies and their wants, so much so that it always seemed a bit of a miracle that she'd managed to make an exception for my father, and marry and reproduce at all. And she was shy, fearful, mislaid most of what she'd learned from Grandpa or at school and saw herself apologetically as inept, unable to cope with life. She wouldn't talk about intimacies of almost any kind – and that's how I know that despite the gossip her 'fast' adolescence was entirely innocent, for she'd reminisce about Percy Davies and his motorbike, and light-hearted times before the war quite openly. Then the blackout curtain in her head would be drawn and she'd be closed off again.

Her alienation didn't happen all at once, though, and in any case it was never complete. There was one corner of her personality in which she remained always her father's daughter, his girl. Although in real life they became strangers, in the magical world of unreality – of theatre – they shared common ground. She starred in *Aladdin* and *Dick Whittington* and his second *Cinderella* in the years between Marj and the war. She did go on with singing lessons, too, and sang in the church choir, doing solo parts in the anthems for special feasts so long as he officiated in Hanmer. The panto songs she still hummed around the house when I was little and she was back among the cinders. One I well remember went 'I wonder who's kissing her now' (which I think rhymed with 'showing her how') / 'I wonder who's looking into her eyes / Breathing sighs / Telling lies . . .' When she acted and sang my mother was the other she might have become – radiant, accomplished, glamorous, often funny, shamelessly extrovert. As I grew up I found her metamorphoses in Women's Institute productions and the local Amateur Operatic and Dramatic Society shows achingly embarrassing. The gap between her selves was so great it made me feel queasy. I didn't somehow connect the stage persona with Grandpa, so implacable was her disapproval of him. But this *licensed* magic was what lingered of his influence.

Not much more remained to him of his dreams of freedom, either. His offences went unpunished – except that Hanmer became a life sentence. 'Thou seest, thou wicked varlet, now, what's come upon thee: thou art to continue . . .' He was

76

licensed to perform, that was his 'character' and he was trapped in his role for ever after. He contrived to live with himself by savouring the ironies of his situation, contemplating the waste of his talents and making the most of his hopelessness in dramatic sermons. He consciously took on some of the glamour of the undead. Womanising became a routine vice – he no longer believed that sex was any sort of passport to a different future and seems to have taken up with the kind of understanding spinster who had affection to spare. And he added booze to his list of bad habits. Already in the 1934 diary he's making a home from home of the Fox and Goose, and sits there doing his correspondence. He goes back to whittling cigarette holders and fixes the radio aerial to the topmost branch of the apple tree, where I remember it trailing its wires as I looked up from the rope swing that hung from a lower branch, dreaming away the days.

Later on, much later, after his death, my mother's worst insult was to say, 'You're just like your grandfather.' This was in my adolescence and what she mainly meant (but couldn't bear to spell out) was that I was promiscuous, sex-obsessed. I took it as a great compliment. This, of course, confirmed her in her opinion, for Grandpa's pride in his own awfulness was his distinguishing trait. Otherwise, when you think about it, why write these diaries? Who is he writing *for*? The answer seems to be: himself. He is justifying himself. This involves not only making excuses (although he does plenty of that, blaming Hanmer, Hilda, MB, the Author of the universe and so on), but also simply *making it all real*. If you write things down, however compromising ('Marj on my lap in the study'), then life is redeemed from the squalor of insignificance – which is (I'm sure he believed) worse than wickedness.

His secrets are like the secrets of a character delivering a stage soliloquy who 'doesn't know' he has an audience. Grandpa was always writing for Grandma in a certain sense, inconvenient though the consequences of her getting her hands on the written 'evidence' may have been. By the same token, he was writing for me too, reaching out a scrawny hand across the years. For instance, on 27 October 1934, out of the blue: 'Today I had the old inspiration back again to write. I wonder shall I try! I lose it so when I have to work at other things and then too I don't get much encouragement.' And on 8 December, 'I make another resolution to spend my time in journalism and writing. I think I can make good now. Marjorie's taunt [his underlining] determines me in this matter.' Marjorie must have jeered at him for his line about getting away and making a new life. That freelance existence never materialised for him. Here are his words, though, in print at last.

He keeps some secrets still. As I made my way through the cramped scrawl towards the end of 1934, and he began to fiddle with his pipe once more and listen to the wireless, I was troubled by a vague intuition and an even vaguer memory. This sounded like where we came in – ostracism and boredom, plus (it's true) pantos and rows, which didn't figure in his last months in South Wales. But still . . . I went back and reread 1933 and there – in September, right at the beginning of the affair with the nurse – was the source of my troubling memory. The entry was indistinct, so I hadn't transcribed it, but on closer inspection it surely said: 'MB and self set out at 2 p.m. We stop at Bangor . . . I am in this eternal triangle again.' *Again?* Puzzling over the word, I don't want to believe it. But there it almost certainly is. Had he done it all before? Was that why he'd been stuck at St Cynon's? Very possibly, thought my father, when I asked. My mother had said that there was a rumour in South Wales of another woman, even possibly a child, but was never willing to say more, in any case didn't want to know ... Well, it would figure. The sin I'd thought the start of the story perhaps wasn't so original after all. The old devil was never to be trusted.

VI

Death

He would rub dry leaves between his palms and mix them with shreds of tobacco, and when he lit his pipe it smelled like an autumn bonfire. This was after his first stroke, when I was seven or eight years old, and he was supposed to cut down on smoking but instead extended his meagre ration and fed his habit with more or less anything combustible. He could walk with a stick, but his whole left side was stiff and the old cynical expression on his face had got an extra involuntary twist to it. His words were a bit slurred. He hadn't long and knew it, and perhaps cared as little as he claimed – not because he was saintly and resigned but because he was exasperated. 'Damn it all!' he'd say defiantly. Although he hadn't yet reached sixty he was at least threescore and ten at heart, and had long affected a familiarity with death. Before his illness he even looked like pictures of the grim reaper, robed in his cassock, with his scythe, cutting the long grasses growing to seed on the lumpy lawn. Some of the lumps were bowls buried in the grass, waterlogged and cracked and mysterious, toys from before the war.

All around us things rotted gently and it looked peaceful but wasn't. So married were Grandpa and Grandma that they offended each other by existing and he must have hated the prospect of gratifying her by going first. On the other hand she truly feared death, thus he could score points by hailing it as a deliverance and embracing his fate. It was, in any case, a line he'd rehearsed for years. Sometimes the parish dead would lie coffined in the church the night before their funerals, and he would go and watch beside them. He found their company, he'd announce to no one in particular, more amusing than his wife's and then he'd set off through the churchyard with his lamp for a private wake. There were horrid hints – his own, or perhaps Uncle Bill's – about the creaks and gurgles corpses produced. Uncle Bill, my mother's younger brother, had converted to Communism in rebellion against Grandpa and was a militant materialist, but he often indulged in such ghoulish thoughts under cover of his socialist realism. Anyway the point about bodily decay mimicking the signs of life merely served to strengthen Grandpa's unflattering comparison between live Hilda and a dead villager.

When they first arrived in Hanmer it must have looked unlikely that she would outlive him. I'm not at all sure, looking back at some of those diary entries, that he wasn't actively expecting God to take her off. Indeed, dropping Him a hint – 'I have met MB . . . and thereby hangs all the tale of the future. What will that be I wonder?? God knows since it is His doing that all this has come about. So then I commit the future to God.' If you think about it and about that oath he swore to MB on the Bible, it looks as though he may have been entertaining a contingency plan for remarriage in the sad event of Grandma's demise. True, he would soon become disenchanted with MB, but that may have been in itself partly a consequence of the Almighty failing to oblige and so refusing him the respectable widower's escape route to an alternative life. MB no longer, as it were, had the endorsement of providence and was in every sense too heavyweight for mere dalliance.

It was probably the move to Hanmer – although she hated it – that saved Hilda from death by bronchitis and asthma. She sounds from the diary much fitter than she was in smoky, damp, industrial South Wales. And as a result the balance of domestic power shifted in her favour. Once she had possession of the diaries she granted herself a secret DIY divorce, complete with alimony. He was to pay the housekeeping, all family expenses and also a separate sum each quarter which she would squirrel away. Given his own financial priorities (tobacco, drink, women and simply getting out of the house) it's no wonder that the grocery bills weren't paid and our underwear was in rags. The crises of credit fuelled more rows and so it went on. Bit by bit their war turned cold, and the anger bubbled away volcanically under the surface.

'God moves in a mysterious way' indeed (hymn number 373 in the book, recommended for use 'In Times of Trouble'). Grandpa must have come to the conclusion that the Lord was a bit of a practical joker. He didn't lose his faith, but it took on a jaundiced complexion, nicotine-yellowed and steeped in bitterness. Hymn 373 says we're not to worry, since God's frowns often hide smiles, and draws the moral that it's rash to think you can read His purposes. Grandpa's trials had been more subtle and mocking, and worked the other way round – smiles hiding frowns – but they spelled out the same message. He had been led up the garden path, disappointment was his vocation now and he could testify to the hollowness of the world's promises with real conviction. One of his sermon notes reflects on the value of human imperfection. Under the heading 'Man is Heaven's Ambassador to Man' he writes: 'An angel can only speak in the second person – "For unto you a child is born" – but man can speak in the first person – "For unto us a child is born" – and you all know that a preacher is never

so effective as when he speaks in the first person . . . *An angel may be a fine teacher, but the world needs a witness.*'

He was no angel, as everyone knew. He preached theatrically (what else?), his style was deliberate and yet devil-may-care, as though he had nothing to lose. His past followed him like a long, glamorous, sinister shadow. Worldly unsuccess was an asset in the pulpit. There his disillusionment with life gave him spiritual distinction. I wasn't seeing it from the point of view of the congregation back then, of course: I sat in the choir stalls and had a bit part in the show. His part was the one he played all the time, so I stayed spellbound when other members of the cast returned home to reality. It wasn't as though being allowed behind the scenes spoiled the illusion, much the reverse. The musty-smelling vestry where we robed and disrobed, where he kept the wine in a special cupboard, where the organ's bellows wheezed, was a marvellous place to me. That was where we came into our own. We had the key to the side door of the church, and came and went casually at odd hours. I'd slot the white cards with black numbers into the wooden frame, to spell out the hymns for the next service, he'd tut over the choir's messy accumulation of service sheets and half-sucked mints and Victory-Vs hidden under their desks, and have a quiet swig, communing with himself.

All of this lent extra charm to the public service, his sermon the climax, when he'd nerve himself to solemnity, grip the pulpit edge with one hand and raise the other in the orator's timeless pose. His gestures were vigorous, I remember, and the diary offers confirmation of a sort, for after one of his *other* acts, the 'Fagin in the Condemned Cell' monologue, he notes the next morning that his arm is aching 'from the acting'. The diaries don't have sermon notes, though, only teasing lists of his themes (in autumn 1934 'The Picture of Dorian Gray', 'Priggishness', 'The Ethics of Job'). For fuller versions he kept separate little red books, of which one has survived. This relic was definitely not preserved by Grandma, but handed on along with the books and pipes and walking sticks. It's a motley collection of outlines, ideas and scripts, some of them dating from years before he came to Hanmer. Nonetheless it helps to give some flavour of his preaching style.

He was best on other worlds. This didn't only mean heaven and hell, for his favourite writers were Shakespeare and the metaphysical poets, Scott, Dickens, Wilde, Wells, Conan Doyle and Jules Verne. However, he was also surprisingly well supplied with earthy anecdotes. For instance, under the heading 'The Mountain and the Valley' (ecstasy vs. prudence), there's a note that goes:

> Illus: Martha and Mary
> Countryman asked which he would prefer
> Martha before dinner
> Mary after dinner

And there's a pungent political fable – undated but surely designed for Bolshie South Wales sensibilities.

> Illus: Tom Paine's *Rights of Man* was a book so obnoxious that the government of the day strictly interdicted its sale. An old bookseller in Glamorganshire strongly suspected of Radical proclivities discovered that he was being watched by government spies, and one day he wrapped up a book in brown paper and wrote on the back of it these words, 'The Rights of Man', and placed it in his little shop window for sale. The government spies eagerly purchased the book for much more than its market value, hurriedly opened it, and found to their bitter disappointment that it was a copy of the Holy Bible. That old Welshman was a clever trickster; but he was something more – he was a true seer . . .

He rose to different occasions with relish, and like a jackdaw picked up eye-catching phrases and stowed them away. There's a list of famous last words, which – he notes – are often revealingly characteristic; and rather unfairly he juxtaposes Lord Palmerston ('Where are those Belgian dispatches?') and Chesterton ('Give the gentleman a chair') with Jesus – 'Father forgive them, for they know not what they do.' Even his humour tended to black.

The sermon for which the most layers of notes survive is a 'Special Sermon for Holy Week' about the infamy and agony of Judas. You can see him working it up from fairly tame beginnings: 'Ambitious . . . But his ambition was wholly secular . . . not repentance but remorse . . . A lump of ice.' Gradually Judas's character acquires new depths and his fate starts to look more dubious. The thirty pieces of silver for which he betrayed Christ are only about £4 in current money, so that the profit motive won't work; and there is something 'horribly suggestive' about the fact that there were no tears, for even Judas might have been saved if he'd truly repented. And then, in the final version, Judas becomes a fully tragic and paradoxical figure:

One heretical sect invented the story that Judas, knowing it to be the will of both Father and Son that Jesus should be brought to suffer death by an act of betrayal in order that the world might be free, had sorrowfully taken the eternal infamy upon himself. If this were so he would in a sense deserve as much merit as Jesus.

These enterprising interpreters were wrong, of course: Judas's real motives were to force Jesus to declare himself King and to take credit for his foresight by becoming a power in the new regime. When he found out how wrong he'd been he committed suicide in self-pity and disappointment. No tears, but 'possibly there mingled with his agony . . . some confused thought that in the world of the dead, behind the veil, he might meet his Lord and confess his guilt'. Did Judas kill himself to rejoin Jesus? Well, perhaps not . . . Having sown the seeds of his own near-heresy, Grandpa returns to the fold with the metaphor of the frozen heart that cannot relent – 'You might pound a lump of ice with a pestle into a thousand fragments but it would still continue to be ice . . . A man may try to make himself contrite . . . But come to Jesus. Let him bask in the beams of His Sun of righteousness.'

The real mystery lies in Divine Grace. But that leaves plenty of room for our own vertiginous speculations. He was very taken with the baroque devices of seventeenth-century poets, who also enjoyed punning on sun/Son and whose work was only then becoming fashionable again. His favourite seems to have been saintly but insidious George Herbert, whose poem 'The Altar', which is altar-shaped on the page, he copies out

86

in full. 'A broken Altar Lord Thy servant rears, / Made of a heart, and cemented with tears . . .' Herbert's habit of posing as a plain man, the mere vicar of a country parish, while actually cultivating deep, dizzying ironies, must have appealed to him a lot. It certainly intrigued me. Herbert figured large in the thesis on 'Poems about Poetry in the Seventeenth Century' I wrote in the 1960s. I only realised later, with a small shudder, that I was dissecting Grandpa's quotations, recognising the lines he'd picked out. I must have filed them for future reference unawares. Now, not even a conscious effort of memory will put the words into his mouth and bring back his speaking voice, although I can see him readily enough in my mind's eye, gaunt and tense with the effort of persuasion.

That's how he was standing when the first stroke got him – in the pulpit, in mid-flow. A couple of basses from the back row of the choir scooped him up and he was carried cradled in their arms not, for some reason, across to the vestry, but straight down the main aisle and through the doors in the wooden screen into the belfry. The rest of the choir processed behind and then we all stood around waiting for the doctor for what seemed a long time, although one of the Drs McColl would surely have been among the congregation.

Grandpa lay on the floor with his head cushioned on some threadbare hassocks in the dazzling sunshine that poured through the high windows. The vestry was dark and stuffy; here it was bright, the bare wooden ceiling with the holes through which the bell ropes dangled was more than twenty feet up and there was a great expanse of empty air. On the walls hung a few brittle pieces of armour from the Civil War which Mr Downward's predecessors had unearthed in the churchyard. The Hanmer family were Royalists and Cromwell's soldiers had stabled their horses in the church, and left behind gauntlets with missing fingers, bits and spurs to prove it. These flaking relics apart, the belfry was bare and clean and open, and Grandpa looked dreadfully out of place there, exposed in that flat light. For a long moment everything was still. Then the doctor bent over him with a stethoscope, we were shepherded away and when I saw him next he was in a chair in his study, back from the brink and in a very bad temper.

Finding him himself again I was even more sure that he was immortal. The permanence of grown-up people is something children tend to take for granted and my generation was doubly smug, for the war had given death by violence, bombs and bullets such imaginative currency that ordinary mortality faded out of the picture. Grandpa's closeness to death was part of his character and his job, so that his having got closer didn't alert me to the truth. He just became more bony and bloody-minded. He'd sit by the kitchen fire with a toasting-fork watching the bread blacken. Or he'd plan a feast and bury potatoes in the embers to bake, and then dismantle the fire an hour later looking for them, beating lumps of coal to smithereens with the poker. He'd dun visitors for extra, forbidden tobacco. One way or another he contrived to surround himself with a cloud of smoke, which kept Hilda at bay and added to the general grime. He even claimed he cleaned his teeth with soot, since it was gritty, which was all that mattered. But he had so few teeth of his own (and those so stained) that it was hard to tell if it made any difference. Housebound, for me he simply converged with his myth.

I needed him to stay the same so that I could go on playing the vicarage child. Even being locked down the horrible cellar by Grandma for being naughty, although terrifying, was not so threatening as the return of my father from the army and the birth of my brother when I was six. My real family didn't seem congenial to me at all but – a bit like school – interested in tidiness and obedience, and things I was no good at. My claims to specialness were books, the church and my fund of creepy stories – Grandpa's gifts, all associated with the dark spaces of the vicarage and the vestry, and with the familiar feeling of discontent and want, in which Grandma shared too. So I clung to the idea of him in the face of his decline and I sided with him in secret, listening from the stairs when my father joined in the shouting matches about the bills and dilapidations, and deplored the muddle and irresponsibility of vicarage ways.

And it wasn't just a question of accounts that didn't add up. The grandparents stood for anarchy of all sorts. She was like a travesty of the new feminine housewifely virtues (too feminine to wash or clean) and he wasn't at all a manly man, despite his philandering. It was probably the way he colluded with women, at least the aspiring ones and the ones at a loose end, that made him attractive. His not having an outdoor job, even one that took him to an office, and his habit of living irritably in his imagination, charmed his spinster fans as well as me. What authority he had was actorish and equivocal. So post-war moral rearmament, with everyone conscripted to normality and standing to attention, didn't get far in the vicarage. My parents, though, were moving out into a new council house up the lane from Hanmer, a house designed for the model family of the 1950s ads: man at work, wife home-making, children (two, one of each) sporty and clean and extrovert. I was going, too, but the upheaval happened in slow motion. We moved piecemeal. I called at the vicarage every day after school and we still went into church at all hours. The new open-plan living-room wasn't where I lived, yet.

Thanks to the vicarage I'd been programmed with a love of

dark corners and ingrained with disrespect. I knew how to hide in books. If need be I could build a kind of nest out of any old scraps of print I found around. The taste for words Grandpa had given me was thoroughly promiscuous. I read everything, in no particular order – Rupert Bear, Captain Blood, Tarzan, Alice, Valma's and Billy's adolescent annuals featuring biplanes tied together with string and schoolgirl intrigues made more mysterious by bobbed hair and gymslips, and games like lacrosse. Edgar Rice Burroughs has Tarzan learn to read all by himself in the jungle: he comes across his dead parents' camp and discovers mouldering books alongside their nice clean bones. At first he thinks the black letters are insects, and tries to pick them off the page and eat them, then he understands. But although he can read and even write, he can't speak at all. This was more or less my condition too, I got more and more clumsy in speech as I grew, and I felt for Tarzan. True, I hadn't figured out literacy alone and unaided, but once Grandpa had taught me to read, he simply set me loose to pore and skip as I pleased. There was nothing reverent about reading, nor was reading the only thing you could do in this paper forest. He licensed me to misbehave. Once, when I was five and bored, he'd shown me how to use the big scissors and I cut out – or cut up – the ladies from the Oxendales catalogue in their New Look long skirts and picture hats. This caused a memorable fuss when my mother and Grandma came home. Playing with sharp things was utterly forbidden, of course; and also – maliciously – he'd encouraged me to mutilate the very stuff of their dreams.

If he had lived longer we'd doubtless have grown apart. He'd have got fed up and I'd have lost faith in him. But he didn't betray me as he had all the others. Instead, he died and cunningly vanished into the dark with his mystique intact. The second stroke, in 1952, a couple of years after the first, poleaxed him. He lay in bed in a coma in the small back sitting-room downstairs, the doctor came and drank whisky and left, callers were turned away and the house was full of hopeless whispers.

Grandma, unrelenting to the last, insisted on having him shifted, moribund as he was, so that she could change the bed under him – otherwise, she said, he'd only spoil the good mattress with the incontinence of his end. Nothing had changed for her, he was as offensive as ever, possibly even doing it on purpose. Death could not part them any more than life already had – but that meant that his dying didn't release her from her outrage and resentment. She was the only person at the time who made me feel better in my disbelieving and desolate state, because she made him seem still alive in a way. Sensing this, Uncle Billy – ever the zealous realist – was determined that I should see for myself that physical death was final and that was that. Despite my mother's protests he hauled me in, squirming, to kiss the corpse goodbye. Grandpa lay on the bed in his black skirts, not coffined yet, hands crossed on his hollow chest and his jaw tied up with a big white handkerchief knotted on the top of his head like Marley's ghost in *A Christmas Carol*. He was the first dead person I'd seen and would be the last for a long time, and if Billy had really wanted to dispel my sense of Grandpa's unique mystery he didn't succeed. This last scene, so dramatically in keeping with his character, completed Grandpa's apotheosis.

I blurted out at school the story of our last macabre meeting, with shaming results. On the day of his funeral, which I wasn't allowed to attend, the whole class was supposed to be sitting in respectful silence. Actually, we were whispering and smothering giggles. The church bell was tolling, almost directly over our heads it seemed (the school was next door to the church), and we had worked ourselves up into a state of creepy euphoria. Maybe he wasn't quite dead after all. Nerys Jones, the pale girl I sat next to, sent a shudder round by suggesting that the noise of the bell would be bound to wake him up. He'd sit bolt upright in his coffin, his jaw bound up as though he'd got toothache – so we pictured him – and give the grand congregation a real fright. We convulsed with laughter at this tasteless vision and roused the headmaster from his reverie. He'd been about to slip into church at the last minute. Now he took extra time out to give Nerys a tremendous telling-off that reduced her to tears. Decorum dictated that I couldn't be held responsible and she became the scapegoat, poor Nerys, who died young herself of a heart weakened by childhood rheumatic fever. Although Mr Palmer didn't punish me, I cried bitterly too. My bad behaviour was, I suppose, part of the private ritual by which I buried Grandpa in my mind, where of course he lived on, my malcontent mentor. He was the source of my sense of having an inner topography, a sort of vicarage soul; also the author of my bookishness, who looked over the shoulder of the actual author of every book I read for years afterwards.

The land of the living certainly presented a chilly prospect without him. We lost caste immediately. Our lack of substantial claims to respectability was obvious – he left no money and no property – and the moral claims had, of course, been forfeited long before. The Church chivvied Grandma to leave the vicarage to make room for the next incumbent, and the dusty accumulations of twenty years were brought out into the light: pieces of the good dinner service that had survived the plate-throwing days, chairs with tattered upholstery and tobacco burns, brittle curtains, moth-eaten rugs and mountains of old newspapers. Most of the furniture went into store, the piano and the books were squeezed into my parents' council house, where they looked alien and apologetic, and made the shortage of space even more acute.

And after acrimonious discussions, Grandma was squeezed in too. She had been plotting to return to sister Katie and South Wales, and the paradise lost of the shop, but to everyone's surprise their brother Stan found the desperate courage to say no. The worm turned. He wouldn't be smothered with sisters and anyway the shop couldn't afford her (this was perfectly true, but then it couldn't afford Katie and Stan either). So with a very bad grace Grandma moved in with my parents. It must have seemed like a bad dream – no sooner had they escaped the poisonous atmosphere of the vicarage than it followed them in the form of this short, fat, ill-tempered incubus smelling of cold cream, stale talc and mothballs. Grandma, of course, blamed fate, and my parents, for her disappointment, and never stopped complaining about the discomfort of her surroundings, even further (if that were possible) from shops and cinemas. The raw council estate, where cows wandered over the unfenced garden plots on their way to the fields and *the neighbours could see in*, was for her Hanmer squared, essence of Hanmer, and she scorned it with a passion.

She was horrible to live with, but at the same time she was a link with the lost past. One day, when she was still sorting through the stuff in the vicarage, where everything seemed to me to be wearing thin and getting see-through, as though a spell were dissolving, she told me a tale that epitomised her witchiness. I'd called by after school, and found her muttering and wheezing with laughter, so I could tell she had some malicious story she wanted to impart. After a whiff of smelling-salts she got it out. Going up to bed that morning, as was her habit, she'd passed an apparition on the stairs – Grandpa getting up, as always. I was suitably thrilled and impressed, not so

Grandma. With her characteristic lack of imagination (which had at moments like this its own surreal genius) she assumed that it was just the sort of cheap theatrical trick he *would* pull. 'If the old bugger thinks he can frighten me that way,' she wheezed triumphantly, 'he's got another think coming.' And she went back to packing paper bags inside paper bags, sliding the odd ill-gotten pound note in between, doubtless. And I went away with food for thought – 'another think coming' – hoarding the stories that would keep me going in the open-plan future.

PART TWO

VII

Council House

The cement strip of front path was hardly dry when we moved into our brand-new council house and it was months before the electricity was connected, although the wiring was all there and the waiting switches. Bright lights and straight lines were signs of the times. Hanmer was catching up. The very existence of houses not owned by the Hanmers or the Kenyons (or the Church) was itself a new departure. Those council semis, built in the early 1950s on a flattened field at the top of a windy rise half a mile out of the village, made a square hole in the old social map. The address had a mysterious sound – 'The Arowry' (we were number 4) taken from 'Yr Orwedd', the Welsh name for a medieval Hanmer family manor. In prosaic fact, however, the present-day Sir Edward had simply sold the Rural District Council a scrubby site, with one empty, tumbledown black-and-white shack on it which was duly demolished – to make way for a dozen families who couldn't be accommodated in the old pattern of farms and smallholdings and tied cottages.

In Hanmer, up until then, your house came with your liveli-hood, more or less, and most roles had been passed on through generations. My grandfather's tenure at the vicarage had been a matter of less than twenty years and now we were among the new people. Council-house people were socially mobile – upwardly in most cases, although not in ours. We all shared a sense of being out of place, on the move. Some of the men were self-employed builders, carpenters, or joiners. Some worked for firms outside the village. One ex-serviceman was a security guard on the new Wrexham Trading Estate. They were local people but they didn't work on the land, they were in Hanmer's version of limbo. And so were we.

For me the loss of the vicarage and my small share in Grandpa's shadowy prestige was awful. I made up for it by becoming for the first time truly a country child, a native of Hanmer, wandering the fields and footpaths in squelching well-ies. Most of the Arowry families had brand-new children much younger than me, so in the mornings I'd join the straggling band of true Hanmerites who walked to school along a bumpy little road called Striggy Lane. They made the journey as lengthy and devious as possible by dawdling, wading along the muddy ditches, or crawling like commandos through the prickly undergrowth on the steep hedge banks. These kids progressed in a sort of noisy silence, with yells and whistles and hoots, breathing hard. In cold weather you watched your breath on the air.

No one talked much. There were two wild and weedy girls, twins, who had invented a private language of their own and otherwise didn't talk at all. They were Briggses, who lived up at the Mere Head, the 'back of beyond' according to Grandma and my mother. Briggses were many and skinny and big-boned, and out-at-elbow and sometimes sockless. Grandma had a story about them. She said she'd once given a very nice pullover to one of the boys in the family, only to see the scrawny patriarch himself, Mr Briggs, shamelessly sporting it the very next day. There were (I always felt) things wrong with this story. For a start, why would she have given away a good pullover when we wore matted, moth-eaten woollies? I was being literal-minded. Looking back, I can see that she was enjoying a fat woman's joke against a thin little man (as on the seaside post-cards), and smuggling in a sly allusion to the comic disparity between his disgraceful potency and his physique. Although, of course, the official point of the story was to insist on our claims to gentility, which daily decayed.

I acquired a juvenile tramp's knowledge of the reliable bushes to shelter under when it rained hard and the farmers' wives who were good for a cup of tea or hot Bovril. Whenever I could, I got out of number 4 The Arowry, for I refused to feel at home there. There was no room. It wasn't just that the house was smaller, nor that Grandma crowded us. It was a case of emotional claustrophobia. There's something cloying and close about living in a proper family that has always brought out the worst in me and it started back then. I had never known my parents together, as one, when I was small. When my father was demobilised they had become lodgers in the vicarage, an attic bedroom their only private space. The fact that I somehow belonged to them, and with them, had been obscured for me in my grandparents' divided dominion. For a husband and wife to get on together, *gang up with each other*, seemed strange and unfair. (Perhaps this is why people dream back with nostalgia to the extended family? Not because you get more parenting, but because you get less? Who knows, perhaps we secretly long to avoid being eggs in just one basket, which is what you get if your parents build a nest on just one branch of the family tree.) My baby brother Clive's birth and the move to the brand-new house not long afterwards reordered the domestic world. Clive was the child of our parents' reunion and of their married life together. Indeed, I was free to 'run wild' outdoors precisely because so much of their attention was focused inwards and on him.

There must have been envy behind my tomboy transformation and sour grapes (if they didn't want me, I wouldn't want them), but it didn't seem like that at the time. Boys were better in theory, I knew that. Grandma, though, thought maleness in general a mistake and for a while it looked as if events would gruesomely prove her right. My small brother engrossed our parents' attention mainly because he was dogged by illness, for all the world as if there'd been a bad fairy lurking at his baptism to cast a spell. Boy babies are more vulnerable: Clive flamed up with erysipelas (St Anthony's Fire) shortly after he was born in 1949; next, before he could talk, he was rushed into hospital tortured with a 'twisted bowel'; and then, when he was two and a half, he contracted polio.

It was a fearful word that conjured up visions of survivors encased in iron lungs like sarcophagi, with only their heads sticking out, being plucky for the newsreels. At the least, you imagined having to wear iron braces on a wasted leg for the rest of your life. 'No matter how it is called,' says the *Science News Letter* (1955), cited in the *OED*, 'poliomyelitis, infantile paralysis, or polio for short, it is a scourge that has long been a crippler and killer.' Any envy I'd nurtured was promptly repressed. If that was the price for being the centre of attention then I was lucky to be left out. In fact, it was during Clive's illness that I first became truly addicted to the glum pleasures of plodding about alone, for I was quarantined – vaccinated, and kept home from school to see if I would come down with it too. I wandered aimlessly around the plashy fields, producing aches and pains by the power of suggestion. Even I didn't believe in them, though: I was mobile, I plodded on.

Clive, who had only just learned to run, lay prone on a cot in the living-room, hemmed in by the three-piece suite, the dining table and the piano. Dr McColl stuck a pin in his foot

and he felt nothing. Nonetheless he recovered, thanks to a rigorous programme of exercises, with father as physiotherapist. 'Infantile paralysis' turned out to be less terrible than its reputation in his case, because he *was* an infant: it was most devastating in adults. In a few years the general terror of the disease would abate, since the end of the great post-war epidemic was in sight, conquered by mass vaccination – although the major souce of infection (polio is passed on through sewage) hasn't been eliminated to this day.

Once our particular all-absorbing present-tense crisis was over, there was time to put two and two together and to realise that Clive had almost certainly picked up the virus at the seaside. On our trip to South Wales that year we'd stayed in Porthcawl, which had a marvellous beach with rock pools to paddle in, called Rest Bay. An additional delight was the wreck of a Greek oil tanker, the *San Tampa*, perched high on the cliff – as improbable as a ship in a bottle – deposited there by a great storm. One man with an acetylene torch sparkling in the sun crawled over her hull cutting her up very slowly for salvage. The sand was still invisibly clotted with gobs of oil, which stained your skin and clothes, and had to be cleaned off with methylated spirits back at the boarding-house. Equally invisible, but a lot more dangerous, was the untreated human waste that came in with the tide as the Atlantic rollers rushed merrily along the Bristol Channel.

Grandma was adamant, however, that polio was a Hanmer sickness that had no connection with sacred South Wales. She was still in the vicarage as the raw year turned to winter, blissfully unaware that she was going to have to move into the council house as well, so for the moment I was the only inter-loper in that new nuclear family with the cot in the living-room. On dark afternoons I could see them there in the lamplight because, unlike the other houses, ours didn't have net curtains, an act of impropriety which showed from the start that we didn't know how to behave in our new life. Everything about our situation felt exposed, it was somehow safer outside. And although very soon the council put up concrete posts and a chain-link fence to mark out our garden, it wasn't a boundary you could believe in, and I had the freedom of the winter lanes and fields as soon as I left the house. It snowed a lot, and I discovered the pleasure of adding my tracks to those of birds and rabbits, dogs and foxes, on the white ridges of ploughland, and squatting down by a hedge to pit the snow with yellow pee, as the animals did, too.

I found out that most hedges were made of hawthorn, 'bread and cheese', you could chew its leaves but not until spring. For now there were only icicles to suck on. But they were delicious and came in different flavours, depending on whether they hung from the rusty guttering of a barn or the green edge of an overflowing water-butt. When puddles and ponds froze over, you could bounce on their creaking, elastic ice. More than once I went through and had to empty the slush out of my wellies and trudge back to a telling-off and very likely a beating when my father got home. For my mother, although she wanted me out of the house where I was miserable, whiney and under her feet, warned me always not to 'wander off', and became hysterical when I came in late and filthy. I was supposed to be out of sight but just around the corner so that she needn't worry, but of course I wasn't and she did, and once we'd moved I was always in trouble indoors.

So in my memories of that first council-house year, which must have been two years in truth – the year I turned nine and Grandpa died, and the year I turned ten, which was the same year I stopped sleeping and passed the eleven-plus – I'm on the outside looking in, through glass that's frosted by my breath (I'm out of breath, I've run home by some slushy short cut). The view is wintry, and smeared over with tears and phlegm, but it's not unpleasurable although it is unhappy. That whole period seems to have a frosty film over it, but that is its character, something that belongs quintessentially for me to the early 1950s.

My cold comfort has joined a world of *then*, a time with a new texture to it – like the brittle plastic of those new raincoats that closed with stiff press-studs, and that cracked and turned yellow; or like the opaque greaseproof-paper bags in which Smith's Crisps reappeared once the relaxation of wartime rationing allowed. I couldn't at first understand my mother's delight in these crumpled fossils with chewy grey bits (they must have used frost-bitten potatoes back in the beginning as a concession to austerity) although I saw the point of the blue twist of salt from the first moment: it was a matter of luxury, having portable food you could play with. Crisps were for eating between meals and spoiling your appetite, and you could blow up the packet when it was empty and burst it with a bang. But the most important and telling of these new, ephemeral 1950s things were the light bulbs, which came both see-through and pearl. Every council house had one central overhead light in the living-room. Some people enshrined it in a mottled glass bowl hanging by chains and had standard lamps in the corners as well. Once the power was switched on, dateless darkness was in retreat, change was at hand.

Even outside the slow spring came, and with it coltsfoot, snowdrops, primroses, cowslips and ragged wild daffodils. We composed 'Nature Notes' about them in school for Miss Daisy – those of us who could write at all – with new biros that made even more blots than the old dip-pens. And we presented her with gallons of frogspawn which duly turned into tadpoles, which ate each other until there were just a few fat cannibal monsters left, all black belly and no sign of legs, who got poured down the sink. This perverse development wasn't recorded in 'Nature Notes', which after all were meant to reflect the universal order of things, not what actually happened at school. Outside school, tadpoles turned into frogs with no trouble, as we well knew, for the countryside was so wet we more or less shared their element.

Everywhere round Hanmer there were streams and field drains and ditches gurgling away, and water stood around in puddles, ponds, pits and meres. This nature wasn't as 'natural' as it was supposed to be either, however. Hanmer was a most picturesque place from a certain distance, but close up its substance was heavy and strange. In the spring the ground sucked at your feet; with every step you could savour the pull of the mud. This was what I liked so much about tramping around the fields, this stubborn resistance in every sticky clod: you could hypnotise yourself with it, just putting one foot in front of another was so absorbing. This way you could lose yourself until you slowed to a dazed standstill and seemed a very passable village idiot, content to sit for hours in a thicket unseen, waiting for nothing in particular to happen. Quite a few people were doing this at the time around Hanmer, including solitary patients in blue hospital uniforms from a wartime camp at Penley a few miles away, mostly Polish and suffering from TB. Juvenile Hanmer lore had it that they were Germans and when a gang of us got together we'd bravely jeer at them for losing the war. They took no notice, just wandered on, staring sadly into space. Then there were the tramps left over from pre-war days and two or three full-grown village idiots, who talked to hedges and gates, and had trousers tied up with string.

Try as I might to lose myself in the landscape, however, I was still only an apprentice misfit and self-conscious in the part. Other kids who hung about at all hours turned out to have errands – big brothers or sisters to fetch, a message to carry to someone working down the fields, or to Dad in the pub. You loiter with a lot more conviction if you've even the shadow of a purpose to neglect and that I lacked. And the truth was that often no amount of trudging would get me to the state of dreamy abstraction I craved. Then I was simply lonely. I wanted friends desperately and, as it happened, the move to The Arowry held out hope, for it gave me a second chance with two girls from school who'd had nothing to do with me when I'd lived in the vicarage – Janet Yates and Valerie Edge, who were now neighbours. Valerie, brown, rosy, curly-haired and tall for eight, lived at the first council house to be finished, which already had a proper garden with dahlias in the borders. Janet – slighter like me, but unlike me, neat and tidy – came from a smallholding down the lane, with a bush of pungent, grey 'Old Man' at the gate and a path made of red-and-blue bricks. Gates and gardens figured large in our friendship because we spent at lot of our time together leaning or swinging on one or other of our gates. With Valerie and Janet you didn't wander off, not because they weren't allowed to, exactly, but because they were too grown-up, they saw no point in it.

They were busy being big girls, practising for real life, which meant not so much mothering dolls or playing house or dressing up (although we must have done all these things), as whispering in a huddle, sharing secrets, giggling behind our hands and linking arms around each other's waists. It was like a dance, a dance of belonging with no private space in it, all inside-out intimacy, and I found it euphoric, intoxicating. And then we would quarrel, for the magic number three is a formula for dissension: two against one, two whispering together, turning away and giggling, the third shamed and outcast. It's obvious now that this was the real point of the whole elaborate dance, its climactic figure, but back then, of course, each quarrel seemed a disaster and I'd run home, tears streaming, and howl on my own back doorstep for hours. My mother, dismayed in the first place by my obsession with such ordinary (if not common) little girls and even more put out by the intensity of my grief when they turned their backs on me, would say, 'It's not the end of the world.' But she unwittingly provided me with exactly the right words. That's what it was, the end of the world, every time.

I cast myself as the odd one out, but in truth it wasn't always so at all. The real shame that sticks to this memory comes when I recall the pang of pleasure I felt when Valerie and I shut out Janet. Our emotional triangle was a very good rehearsal for the world, the mimic anticipation of group psychology was perfect, even down to the fact that Valerie was never excluded.

She was more sure of herself to start with and she remained innocent of the needy jealousy the other two of us suffered, so became ever more blithely, unconsciously cruel, our unmoved mover. Valerie for her part adored her mum.

Mrs Edge, who came from a large family, had like many Hanmer women of her generation broken that pattern, hence the council house. She lived in hers with style, not only were her net curtains whiter than white, but the whole space, and the whole shape of the day, had an elaborate decorum. She changed her wellies on the back step for carpet slippers with fake fur round the tops, or hid her curlers under her turban, or combed out her hair and put her lipstick on, to a regular, reassuring rhythm. And she supplemented her husband's wages with money she earned by making wreaths in the backyard (holly for Christmas, chrysanths and carnations for funerals) and doing flowers for weddings. Once I went with Valerie and her mum to gather moss, which she used for skewering the flowers into, on the frames of the wreaths, with sharp wire. We went across the fields on footpaths and finally no paths at all until we came to a weird wood or copse where all the trees stood in spongy moss, dead and leafless, and – this was the unforgettable, magical thing – when you jumped up and down, their skeletal trunks waggled against the sky and the whole wood shook.

It was Valerie's mum's example that inspired a game that was not – for once – part of the dance of rejection. True, it just involved Valerie and me, but Janet was away for the summer holidays, staying with some auntie or cousin, not a shadowy rival waiting in the wings. This game – *Doing the Flowers for the Dolls' Wedding* – developed a mimic reality and depth our other games lacked. It didn't seem like play at all, in fact, that was its charm. We planned for weeks, discussed exactly what the dolls wanted, made lists of the different bouquets and sprays we'd need for the bridesmaids and matron of honour, as well as the bride herself (who'd ordered flowers for her hair too) and priced them all, including buttonholes for the families, strictly graded in order of kinship and importance, with mothers top. We were confined to wild flowers mostly, and of course we had to miniaturise everything for the dolls, but these additional problems only enhanced the busy, anxious pleasure of the whole thing. In the days before the big day we picked our flowers and ferns, and put them in separate jam jars ready to be made up into bunches of different sizes and splendour, which was something you had to do at the last minute.

We even arranged to borrow a camera, to take a group picture of the happy event, in order to immortalise our handiwork, although I don't think we managed to take one, for I never remember seeing it. Perhaps it was an overcast day, or possibly no one would lend us a camera – for they were expensive, temperamental, grown-up toys back in 1952. Nonetheless, although the wedding itself hasn't left much trace, it was a great success, for it was the background *Doing* of the flowers over all that time (we were only nine, it must have seemed an age) that counted. So much so that neither the dolls nor their clothes figured at all prominently in our professional calculations about how to get things exactly right – although the dolls were all the wrong sizes and baby-shaped (we were pre-Barbie, let alone Ken). This was fantasy at work, with the emphasis on work. And the other thing that made it idyllic was that we plotted and staged it all on my back doorstep, since Valerie's mum didn't want us under her feet.

For most council-house kids were shooed out of the house, although they didn't take off across the fields. When I played with Valerie I knew where I was for a change and so did my mother; I didn't wander far; I wasn't late back. But Valerie's habits – the Edges kept regular hours – didn't rub off on me, when she wasn't around I was still out of step. The Arowry idea was that children came home to eat and sleep. From the start I'd been bad at coming home and now, some time during that first year, I stopped sleeping once I was there as well. Part of the reason was that I'd developed an illness of my own, although not such a glamorous one as my little brother's – chronic sinusitis, which meant a permanently blocked nose, headaches and faceaches, and made it very difficult to breathe, especially at night. This I compounded by lying awake in the dark crying, which made my symptoms a lot worse and other people's nights hell too.

Eventually, Dr McColl was summoned to see me one morning when I was particularly puffy-eyed and wretched. He was a visitor from the past, just as I remembered him, mauve-skinned, and smelling reassuringly of Scotch and cologne, and he gave me that very day a prescription for how to survive at number 4 The Arowry. Not medicine – that was minimal, aspirin for the headaches and some aromatic stuff to inhale – but books.

When he turned up I was learning something off by heart for school, and perhaps that gave him his clue, for he quickly discovered that I knew a large part of the hymn book and even quite a few of the more bloodthirsty psalms by heart as well. He said he thought I might find more interesting things to read. He also told me that I should consider myself lucky, since I had much more time than people who slept; and he told my mother that she should let me have the light on all night. So he gave me – gave me back – the company of Tarzan and Alice, and William and Sherlock Holmes and Masterman Ready and the Princess and the Goblins ... It was an unheard-of indulgence to use up electricity in this way, but doctor's orders prevailed. Dr McColl had won me space in the council house, a lighted box of my own. Remembering his magic words, I'd look out in the dead of night across the countryside, where not one other light was burning, and practise feeling pleased with myself.

Bit by bit the council-house space that had been designed for a model 1950s family took on a different shape, with a hint of vicarage about it. By the time Clive was ready to move into his own room with its nursery curtains, Grandma was squatting there, and he had to share mine and learn to sleep with the light on. The planners' conspiracy against disorder gave way before the shift system we improvised. We never really shared the open-plan living-room and never sat down to eat at the same time, so the table was only laid at one end, and the rest was used for ledgers, homework and wind-up racing cars. At night Grandma would stay up late and have the whole space to herself, while upstairs I read myself into a dawn doze just in time for my mother to come in and draw the curtains, and recoil from the fat moths my light had lured in.

The atmosphere indoors was tense, still. No one had enough private space, certainly not my parents, with all those war years of separation to make up for. When we first moved house Clive absorbed their attention, but as he recovered and started school, they turned back to each other. The first time I really saw them this way, saw through the mist of my own making, was on the day the eleven-plus results came out. Mr Palmer sent me running home mid-morning with the news and, when I arrived, I found my mother and father sitting alone together in the living-room at the homework end of the table. This was all wrong, my father never came home in the day, but there he was, wearing his old battledress jacket, his arm was round her shoulders and she'd been crying. I was breaking in on some secret crisis, she'd been taken ill, the doctor had just left (how often sickness spoke for us), she was all right now, she had thought she couldn't swallow, that something was stuck in her throat, but it was all just nerves . . . My news fell flat before this revelation. For a moment I could see them as just two, the couple they'd be without the rest of us – strangers encamped in that windy field, trying to make a new life for themselves.

VIII

A Proper Marriage

Like many who'd married in the war, my parents were finding
it hard to survive the peace. This wasn't because they had
discovered that they didn't love each other once their life
together wasn't spiced with constant separations and the threat
of death. Far from it. But they had chosen each other so much
against the social grain that they were tense, self-conscious,
embattled, as though something was supposed to go wrong.
Their families didn't like their marriage, nor did the village.
Hanmer still lived in the era when most engagements were
really contracted between legacies and land, abutting acres,
second cousins twice removed, or at least a tied cottage and a
tea service. The mythically egalitarian spirit of the Blitz only
visited Hanmer in rumour, like the returning rumble of the
odd bomber a bit off course on its way back from flattening
Liverpool Docks. A marriage between the vicar's daughter and
the local haulier's son, who did his rounds in black face (Stockton & Sons hauled coal pre-war, mostly), was dangerous to
decorum. You might think that if the haulier's boy went off
to the wars a conscript private and came back a captain, this
changed things. My parents' story could have been read as the
triumphant progress of the sort of clean-cut local lad and
younger son who does so well in folk tales. He falls in love
with a dreamy virgin in thrall to her corrupt, spellbinding

father; he goes away, wins his spurs in Normandy and the Ardennes, comes back to rescue her from the sterile, vicious vicarage and carries her off to realms of real life – the virtue, order and daylight decency of a proper marriage, and wholesome children. I think in some ways that's how they saw it themselves. However, Hanmer thought differently.

It was bad enough that my parents had gone out with each other in the 1930s, as teenagers. (This would have been a year or so after the Marj episode, Grandpa and Grandma were too busy rowing to care.) If they sat together into the small hours in the parked car he'd managed to borrow, that was further scandalous evidence of my grandparents' indifference to propriety. No matter that these young people, Valma and Eric, deplored vicarage ways and were determinedly chaste; that – if gossip had credited it – would have been further evidence of their nonconformity. And the wrongness of it all was only compounded by my father's army career. The energy and ambition that took him to Sandhurst — where he learned to his astonishment that the upper classes weren't cleverer after all — were suspect in Hanmer and so were warrior virtues, come to that, for this was largely a community of non-combatants and if you were unlucky enough to get conscripted, you kept your head down, joked with your mates and waited for it to be over.

This was what my father's elder brother Albert had done in North Africa. Almost the only leftover signs of Albert's sojourn in the desert were the beret he wore to deliver the coal and the belt he wore to hold up his trousers. Albert was an admirer of Winston Churchill, judging by the framed photo above the roll-top desk where he kept the sooty receipts, but he never talked about blood, toil, tears and sweat. Whereas for my father the war, the Royal Military College, his rise from the ranks, was an experience that remade him. He talked about his adventures on active service compulsively. He always maintained that

he grew two extra inches, at eighteen, as a combined result of army PT and stopping carrying hundredweight sacks of coal for his father every day, as he'd done from the age of fourteen. It was a symbolic story. The army fathered him anew: he sprang full-grown out of the war. And he and my mother married in 1942, just before he got his commission.

He seemed an outsider after his years away, but in fact he was a native. His family lived in Horseman's Green, a hamlet just down the lane, where they owned a pretty square house, that had seen better days, called 'Ferncliffe', with a front garden, a farmyard where lorries left oily puddles and a couple of fields. He didn't seem much at home when we paid visits to his widowed mother (his father had died in 1943, not long after I was born) and Albert and their younger sister Binnie, and he probably hadn't been even before the war, when he'd had the assurance to start courting my mother.

When he was a boy, during the worst of the Depression, his parents had sent him to live with an aunt, while the other two stayed at home, and this separation had left its mark. Later he'd been reclaimed, but not in spirit, although he laboured loyally for his father once he'd left school. A. Stockton & Sons had muddled along, carrying and delivering coal, sometimes cattle, sometimes labourers' worldly goods (giving the truck a hosing-down first) and doing a bit of farming or renting out a field on the side. At one stage they'd had a small shop, too. When he and Albert came back from the army they inherited the remnants of this shapeless family firm and became partners. However, their attitudes to the enterprise were radically different. Uncle Albert, after the Sahara, was looking forward to muddling on as before. For my father muddle and compromise and inefficiency were the new enemy. A. Stockton & Sons became his peacetime 'company' and very soon he was giving the orders.

This did not mean that he wore a suit and sat in an office, although he called himself a haulage contractor. A. Stockton & Sons was after all nearly non-existent by 1946. In order (as he said) to Knock the Business into Shape he had to work all hours and do nearly everything himself. He became a driver, a mechanic, a carpenter and welder (making and mending truck bodies), and did the accounts and sent out bills as well. This was the price he paid for a post-war job in which he could Be His Own Boss: being his own exploited workforce too. Albert, meanwhile, following orders, also worked hard, but never so obsessively as my father, for whom the Business rapidly became a devouring myth, a vocation. With the Business he could make his own place in a Hanmer world that had no place for him now – and that made it all worthwhile. In the service of the Business he could redeploy the practical skills he'd perfected in his rise through the ranks (he'd been a transport sergeant at one stage) and the tactical gifts that had served him so well as an infantry officer in the field. He was tirelessly ingenious when it came to fitting together small farmers' orders – two calves here, a barren cow there, three heifers and half a dozen sheep somewhere else – into one truckload on its way to Oswestry or Whitchurch or Malpas market. And he was absolutely in his element faced with a breakdown in a distant ditch on a freezing night.

But when it came to the human and social and commercial aspects of Running the Business he was endlessly thwarted and baffled. As he acquired new trucks, he needed drivers and it was very hard to find men who would play the part of other ranks to his satisfaction – except for ex-servicemen. And even they wouldn't Look Sharp, or Jump to It, in quite the way he was always exhorting them to. He was a paternalistic employer and would never dream of laying off men in slack seasons, so felt correspondingly outraged and betrayed when they wanted to be paid union rates. Easygoing Albert was a lot better at labour relations and also at passing the time of day with customers. He knew the social map of who was related to whom, and exactly how, like the back of his hand, and loved to gossip about weddings and funerals and wills. Whereas my father, literally and metaphorically, Had No Time for that Sort of Thing. In any case he was never sure what tone to adopt with the farmers, most of whom were pretty obviously not officer material. And he had very little taste for the competition, under-cutting and backhanders that would have given him an edge over his rivals: no eye for the main chance. He thought that the best man should win and indeed would win in some ultimate shake-out presided over by the just God of Private Enterprise, Who would congratulate him for Playing the Game, and count the Corners he didn't Cut.

So the Business grew and magically never prospered. But that wasn't its function. Its main purpose was to support the myth of my father as his own man – the Small Businessman, the Realist. In the late 1940s and early 1950s realism was turning into everyone's watchword. My mother's brother, Uncle Bill (who'd been a radio operator in the RAF, but on the ground), was a socialist realist and there'd be a Cold War atmosphere when he came to visit. For Bill, nationalisation was a first feeble step in handing over power to the people, whereas for my father it stood for Red Tape, a brigade of Pen-pushers and Yes-men who Had No Incentive to work or Stand on their own Two Feet and Pull their Weight, and who, if anything went wrong, could always Pass the Buck. He himself was the man of practical vision, the boss-on-the-factory-floor. He knew what it was to get his hands dirty and yet carried the responsibility for the whole enterprise, just as he'd once humped coal.

He was triumphant when the Labour government decided not to nationalise cattle haulage because it was too local, complicated and messy, and anyway embedded in the culture of the Tory shires: for him this proved that nationalisation was inflexible, inefficient and unrealistic. Looking back, however, one can see that he'd have made a splendid regional manager for British Road Services if A. Stockton & Sons had been engulfed and devoured, and would doubtless have risen through its ranks. At least he wouldn't have been carrying those hundredweights of mythic realism about with him every day of our lives. There was no escape from the Business in The Arowry, Dad *was* the Business. His characteristic tone of voice was a sort of self-righteous yell and even when we got a phone to take the orders he yelled down that every evening too, at Albert, the equable and unregenerate enemy within, demanding always a Straight Answer to a Straight Question. Which luckily he never got, so realism survived to fight another day.

He knew who he was when he was working. He wore lace-up boots and brown one-piece overalls over his trousers and shirt when he drove the trucks to market or dived under their bonnets (which was most days) and came home covered in a glaze of filth made of motor oil and manure. It was understood around the house that he had a monopoly of practical virtue: outside was man's work.

My mother, perhaps in deference to this view, had mysteriously forgotten how to ride a bicycle now that they had a home of their own. She would reminisce about her rides in pre-war days (when she sped so sexily through Grandpa's secret diary) as though they belonged in a different universe and boasted too that she'd cycled to the station at Bettisfield to catch the train to Ellesmere to do her war work as a clerk in the Food Office, even when she was very pregnant with me. This was now unimaginable, so timid had she become. But her new-found helplessness didn't seem as odd as it might have, since this was, of course, the time when married women, having been sent back home en masse, were encouraged in every possible way to stay there – first demobilised and then immobilised. Working in the world was only for Queens and the commonest of commoners, and movie stars, who all had in any case to pretend that they would much prefer domestic purdah, given a chance.

My mother's acquired ineptitude fitted this post-war pattern. And she did, as the propaganda said, try to turn herself into a housewife, although she was very bad at it. Quite how bad only became clear once we'd moved to the council house, for vicarage ways were ingrained; she couldn't be expected to make much impression on that Gothic grime and disorder. But in 'her' brand-new house full of light and hard, washable surfaces (even the window-sills were tiled) she was horribly exposed. According to the people who'd planned these houses, and to the advertisers and the social psychologists, housework was her calling and she simply couldn't do it; she had a kind of genius for travesty when it came to domestic science.

And yet – for all his talk of discipline and efficiency – my father never yelled at her for this blatant shambles. Instead, he accepted it without a murmur and even seemed tenderly gratified. He was her protector, you see: he'd rescued her, and her dependence was perfected by her distaste for her role and her failure to turn number 4 The Arowry into her separate sphere. Many a house-proud Hanmer wife might order her husband not to make a mess 'on my nice clean floor', but never my mother. True, she would complain about the mud we brought in on our boots, but that was a ritual lament, mopping floors never achieved anything, she knew, although she was sentenced to it. If she guarded her threshold it was against prying eyes.

Women neighbours were never allowed in, nor were their daughters, who were suspected of being fifth columnists, housework spies who'd run home and tell their mothers we didn't clean behind the sofa.

She despised those women who did, all the same. Like having pierced ears, wringing out a floorcloth with conviction was the sign of a coarse-grained nature. She just wished – out loud, quite often – that the housework would do itself. In the same spirit she cursed cooking and as she dumped our plates in front of us on the eating end of the table she would announce that we could take it or leave it, and that she wished we could all live on pills. In the beginning it was mostly stew, shreds of grey, nameless meat and lumps of carrot and turnip floating in salty water, with a surface shimmer of yellow fat. This was what I had at school, too, so there was nothing special about it, except for the spice of her revulsion. But as the days of rationing receded, and you could buy a joint of lamb or even a chicken for Sunday dinner (roasting chickens were rare birds back then) her fear of food grew and grew. All meat had to be made safe by boiling, or by simmering it in a lake of spitting fat in the oven for hours, and even then it was dangerously full of knots of choking gristle and shards and spikes of bone, which she'd warn us against with a shudder. She herself could seldom bear to eat any of this nasty stuff, although occasionally she would daintily dissect a sliver on her plate and observe – which was true – that even the boneless bits were tough and stringy.

You might have mistaken her for an aspiring vegetarian, but in fact the thought that we were eating the very lambs that went bleating to market in Dad's trucks didn't move her at all. She didn't care for farm animals. And if anything, she thought vegetables even more dangerous and difficult to subdue. They had to be cooked all morning, particularly green ones like sprouts, which got very salty and stuck to the pan as their water boiled away, and came out in a yellow mush. Potatoes got the same treatment and her ritual Sunday lunchtime cry, as she lifted the saucepan lid – 'They've gone to nothing!' – became a family joke, an immortal line that later converged magically in my mind with the smartest 1950s intellectual slogans. *Gone to nothing* was wonderfully Absurd, a phrase of existentialist and sub-Beckettian power. As for my mother, she should be so lucky was her meaning – if only those wretched roots full of eyes *would* go to nothing! But no, there was a grey sludge left at the bottom of the pan (we never needed to mash our potatoes) which had after all to be spooned resignedly on to our plates.

Dinner on this scale only happened once a week, although since it was a custom that survived into the 1960s, I can still recall my mother's recipe for lumpy gravy. You take the pan of fat in which the meat has been frazzled, add water from the vegetables (and since there's never enough left, top it up with cold from the tap), then add flour, and cook for quite a while, pursuing the lumps into corners with a spoon and crushing them to make more. Then add Gravy Browning so that there's no mistaking them and serve with a sigh.

Luckily no one lives by Sunday dinners alone. The real revelation of the ending of austerity, for us, was ready-made food, the whole rich list of things that needed no cooking at all, which you could eat at any old time. For instance: ham and tongue cut into see-through slices; sandwiches of meat-paste or fish-paste or bananas; canned corned beef, luncheon meat (Spam in civilian clothes), pilchards, sardines, salmon, baked beans and spaghetti; tinned peaches, pears and plums, and fruit salad with mauve 'cherries', and condensed milk. These goodies

– eked out with cornflakes, puffed wheat, digestive biscuits, cream crackers, crisps and sweets – would constitute our staple diet. We actually called them in leftover language 'the rations' and they were delivered once a week by the village grocer in his van.

In the matter of food, in fact, market forces were on my mother's side. Beefburgers and tinned rice pudding and processed cheese and even sliced bread itself were all just the kinds of things she wished for, pills under various guises. I have a persistent but suspect memory that she was somehow involved in consumer-testing fish fingers and infallibly foresaw their future role as everyone's 'rations'. Surely Hanmer couldn't have figured in such a survey? I must be remembering the satisfaction with which she greeted their advent. Fish was to her possibly nature's most nightmare offering – covered in scales and fins, full of bones and very nourishing, so that you were obliged to struggle with it. In fish fingers nature was grandly snubbed and outdone. Their very name mocked the unreasonable design evolution had come up with for fish; and their bland and boneless insides left her nothing to worry about. They didn't need gravy, either.

So food got easier as time went by. Not all our meals aspired to the condition of fish fingers, but there wasn't a lot that could go wrong with (say) baked beans on toast. True, the beans were stewed (with extra water) to be on the safe side. And toast could be tricky (I was quite grown up before I learned that you didn't have to make toast by burning the bread and then scraping off the black bits) but on the whole, even if you allowed for sharp crusts and crumbs that could go down the wrong way, it did solve the problem of what to put in front of us.

The question of what she could bear to swallow was another

matter. It was a lot easier for her to quiet her anxieties on our behalf than to overcome her own revulsion. She didn't starve, but she snacked and picked her way through each day, mostly in private, edging round some secret, shifting system of taboos. Just occasionally she'd develop a compensatory addiction, and binge on something pungent and improbable, like pickled onions, which gave her agonising acid indigestion, or extra-strong peppermints, which ulcerated her throat. She could not simply take food or leave it at all, for it was the sign of a larger, unfocused fear. Her home wasn't her own territory, the daily domestic business of sustaining life made it a battleground, and made her long to get out and away.

But – here was the catch – the world immediately outside the door was also threatening, far too unprocessed, too shape-less, too suggestive of bone and gristle to provide her with any solace. The fields were full of menace: bulls, barbed wire, water, snakes, insects, nettles. The countryside was raw and meaningless, she had no way into it (she'd forgotten how to ride a bike), it was outside, but not *out*, not in the sense she meant when she longed to 'get out of the house'. Her fear of food, which was a fear of the outside getting in, was a key to her character as a wife. Although she so spectacularly lacked domestic skills, she was nonetheless profoundly domesticated. A sort of virginal vulnerability and a fear of intrusion walled her in.

So family outings were charged with huge meaning as a result. The time for going out was on Saturday afternoon, when my father would be persuaded to stop working for once. He'd do this with great reluctance, however, so that by the time he came home to eat and to wash off the mire and motor oil, and change, we would all have been ready for hours, and my brother and I would have had plenty of opportunity to untidy ourselves and spoil our good clothes. This meant tears from my mother, who was in any case seething with impatience, and even more delays as we were told off and sometimes smacked by my father, and washed and tidied yet again. Eventually, after we'd waited for Grandma if she was coming – she was never ready until the last minute no matter how long she had – my mother would damp down the fire (a layer of slag, a layer of coal-dust and water from the kettle) and we'd set off in the car.

Sometimes we'd go to the cinema in Wrexham or Shrewsbury, but at others we'd go to Chester to walk on the Roman walls in fine weather, or in the Rows when it rained, or visit the cathedral and straggle along the gloomy side aisles hung with tattered, bloodstained regimental colours, or to the museum to look at Roman remains, Egyptian mummies, stuffed animals, armour, weapons, old costumes . . . It hardly mattered what, for my mother, so long as it was old and redolent of long-ago lives. She loved castles with dungeons and battlements; threadbare tapestries, mullioned windows and portraits fed her hungry imagination so that she forgot for a while her weekday dissatisfactions. Indeed, the most exotic thing about these outings was not the oubliettes or the stuffed lions, but the fact that we could all sit down and eat in a teashop, my mother included. So long as there was oak furniture and a spinning wheel in the corner, she let go her fear of food and even – although she'd sometimes pick through her Welsh Rarebit for bones, out of habit – seem to enjoy it.

Perhaps it was just as strange, if less striking at the time, that we quite often went out to look at beauty spots that were hardly any different from Hanmer: villages with black-and-white cottages, or the lakeside at Ellesmere, or Llangollen's mountains (these, admittedly, on a more grand scale). But this was scenery, the picturesque, food for sentiment, all transformed by the glamour of distance. My mother felt – and she was surely right – that a landscape is something quite different from the gristle and barbed wire of the actual country. She was a devotee of pastoral prettiness. When all the village children were urged to put on fancy dress for the Coronation Day parade in 1953 she dressed me (with great difficulty, for she couldn't sew) as a very passable shepherdess complete with black laced bodice, floral panniers, a straw hat and a crook tied with ribbons. There I stand in the black-and-white photos of that famously rainy day – along with Valerie, who came in a patriotic red-white-and-blue crêpe-paper crinoline, and Gail in white and gold as a drum majorette – smirking with pleased self-consciousness, my mother's tribute to pastoral romance.

Fancy was her department. She rounded out her role with daydreams: being impractical was not just a negative thing but

a positive attribute. If my father was man the realist, she was truly his other half and complement, she did the work of feminine fantasy. The absent and amorphous aspect of her daily self – 'miles away,' she'd say innocently, not apologising – gave her in addition the air of a child wife, the daughter of the house. Perhaps this was why my father didn't object more strenuously to Grandma's presence and why it seemed in an odd way appropriate. Grandma may never have lifted a finger, but she did support my mother in the character of perpetual daughter, always about to make her entrance into the world. Marriage had fixed her in this part, perhaps even made her more timorous (witness the bike-riding), but she had begun to mislay her confidence around the time she was sixteen, the year of Grandpa's affair with her friend Marj, when she took Grandma's side and turned away with revulsion from all he represented – from the vices of smoking and drinking, from lust, from bookishness . . .

She'd left school without her School Certificate, lost interest in her studies, taken desultory just-about-genteel jobs ('sales lady' in Dudleston's, the old-fashioned draper's in Whitchurch), all this long before her marriage. My father's earnestness, his distance from *his* family, his rage for order, his protective gallantry must have seemed a refuge indeed. She was fiercely monogamous, as if she thought there was only ever one other person you could allow into your intimate life: certainly that was her experience and she disapproved of any hint of promiscuity in others, even the sort implied in socialising. If she and my father were displaced people in Hanmer terms, she almost welcomed the isolation in which they lived.

They made no close friends in those early years. Their union was exclusive and inward-looking. Later, as they settled down, they found social and public roles – he in the British Legion and the Road Haulage Association, she in the Women's Institute drama group, of which she became the leading light. But they would never dilute their own relationship by mixing as a couple. Man and wife, realist and dreamer . . . in truth they were more than one flesh, they had formed and sustained each other, they had *one story* between them and it wasn't at all easy for me or my brother to inhabit it. I regularly cast myself in the part of the clever, unwanted child who's sent out to lose herself in the forest, but manages nonetheless to find her own way, being secretive, untruthful, disobedient, and so on and on, as they never ceased to complain. The children of violently unhappy marriages, like my mother, are often hamstrung for life, but the children of happier marriages have problems too – all the worse, perhaps, because they don't have virtue on their side.

IX

Sticks

Where were we? We'd only once had a geography lesson at Hanmer school, one sunny morning when Mr Palmer with a flourish draped a cracked and shiny blue-green-brown map over the blackboard next to his desk and sat surveying us, tapping his pointer gently in the palm of his left hand. Geography was a game. He'd call out a name – Manchester or Swansea or Carlisle – and one by one we had to walk up to the board and point at it. Any straying finger got a sharp rap from Mr Palmer's stick. Naturally most of us got it wrong, since we'd never seen a map of the British Isles before. The only way to win at this game was to approach very slowly and see if you could spot your town in time, but since most kids couldn't read very well (or at all) this didn't help a lot. I did all right with something beginning with B (Bolton or Blackburn or Birkenhead or Birmingham) but I cried anyway, I always did. Although we may not have found out much about geography that day, we were being taught a lesson, the usual one: to know our place. Hanmer wasn't on the map and Hanmer was where we were. Most of us, according to Mr Palmer, would be muck-shovellers. Two or three of us, equally pawns in the game, would be allowed to get away with it – this time.

Hanmer school's best moments had been the times when no one pretended we were being taught, when fun was decreed with no forfeits – like the warm-up session for the Christmas party when Mr Palmer, a beaming ogre, led us in carols and nonsense songs, ending with an ear-splitting, hysterical chorus, 'Ooooh, the Okey Cokey! That's what it's *all abOUT*!' Or the summer PT lesson when we ran up a bench propped against the churchyard wall, round some gravestones, through the bind-weed and nettles – this corner beetling over the schoolyard hadn't been used for a century – and down another bench into the playground again. Or the day of deep frost one winter when the big boys were sent out with buckets of water to make a slide on the field below the bike shed and we all took turns, marvelling at the long green grass trapped flowing in the ice under our feet like seaweed.

My brother had already started on his school career and would in time be promoted to carrying coke for the cast-iron classroom stoves – perhaps in fulfilment of Mr Palmer's theory of hereditary roles, for Clive was in everyone's eyes much more a Stockton. His time at Hanmer school would leave him with a legacy of fiery temper tantrums. In my case its frustra-tions, mystifications and menace made me chronically shifty. You learned at Hanmer school to keep the world of grown-up authority out of focus, to look askance, to stare stubbornly at an invisible point in the air between yourself and them. You learned to seem dull and stupid. I was no exception. Mr Palmer may have massaged my results to match my vicarage IQ, but I was far too scared of him to feel any complicity. And – although I didn't know it at the time – Miss Myra and Miss Daisy regarded me with special distaste, as the granddaughter of the old devil who'd corrupted their niece Marj. My being bookish hadn't brought me any closer to my teachers than any of the other children.

The blank stare came in handy outside school. I gave my

parents, particularly my father, this treatment, which he interpreted quite rightly as a form of insubordination. Shy and sly
were close. I had acquired from Grandpa (bad blood!) vanity,
ambition and discontent along with literacy. I didn't know my
place. And although my parents were in public proud of me
for getting into grammar school so precociously, they were at
the same time, in private, convinced that my addiction to print
was part of my general delinquency. This was particularly
galling, because they couldn't object to it, indeed had to pander
to my whims, leave the light on all night and buy me a school
uniform. Other kids' parents had promised them extravagant
rewards (a watch, a new bike) if they passed the exam. Mine
promised me nothing, they knew I was bloody-minded enough
to call them to account.

Neither a watch nor a bike would have been much use to
me in any case. I couldn't tell the time, although I kept this a
secret. The involuntary sulk that I lived in included clocks:
just as I couldn't meet people's eyes, I couldn't look a clock
in the face. I squinted at them so hastily and at such a weird
angle that they made no sense. And I covered up this odd blind
spot by allowing myself always to know vaguely whether it
was something to or something past the hour, and usually what
hour it was. The church clock struck and alarm clocks went
off, too, which helped. My lateness in coming home from my
morose wanderings was connected with my clock problem –
it wasn't that I was late because I couldn't tell the time (after
all, there aren't many clocks in the fields and woods), more
that I couldn't tell the time because I resented and avoided any
occasion that meant turning up for inspection.

There was a shadow of satisfaction in my ineptitude. By
contrast, not being able to learn to ride a bike was altogether
shaming. My mother must have passed on to me something of

her own recently acquired phobia. Certainly she always prevented me from messing about on other kids' bikes in the vicarage square when I was six or seven years old. The square had no traffic, but she was convinced I'd pedal straight into the road out of perversity and get run over. By the time I was ten, however, it was an embarrassment to everyone that I was such a wimp and my father undertook to teach me – which turned my lack of confidence into a full-scale mental block. He was systematic and elaborately patient, and very soon exasperated. Under his eye I fumbled, abashed, my arms and legs felt stiff and rubbery at once, my hands were slippery with sweat, and the bike would fold over and collapse as soon as I touched it. I'd emerge from these sessions in tears, covered in scrapes and bruises without having cycled an inch. My father, disgusted, said I was a Member of the Awkward Squad – no Physical Co-ordination, no Sense of Balance.

No watch and no bike, either, just the prospect of Whitchurch Girls' High School, which was where my mother went back in the past, another scary blank to me. *Getting on in the world* seemed impossible. I was at a loss, at a loose end. It was like being inside one of the books I devoured. You could feel the momentum of the plot carrying you along, but you couldn't tell what came next and the sensation of powerlessness was horribly baffling. Since I couldn't skip to the end, I averted my eyes, changed focus, looked somewhere else. Before I got out of the sticks, I would get further in. I found a place to hide.

Just opposite us, but sidelong to the road, looking indifferently away from the council houses, was Watsons' farm. Your first sight of it was the milk stand, a raised platform of planks from which the Milk Marketing Board lorry picked up full silver churns early every morning, leaving empties behind. Most days when it wasn't raining the milk stand was the favourite seat of one of The Arowry's other outsiders, too lame to wander far, the pale twenty-year-old son of our quietest council-house neighbours, who was dying of the TB in his bones. Sometimes I'd sit beside him in silence, kicking my legs, but more and more I ventured through the rutted gateway into the Watsons' farmyard. It was a muddy enclosure, only partly paved, with their house at one end, the rest bordered by cowsheds, the haybarn, a selection of stores and stables and lean-tos, and a manure heap in the far corner. In this yard lived a busy claque of hens, some semi-stray cats, an old collie-dog called Trigger, who'd seen better days, and the queenly cows who came back to be milked. They had names like Mabel and Rose, and knew their way to their stalls by heart, although they were lodged in different, odd corners, since Mr Watson had no shippon big enough for all twelve of them.

I hung around and made friends with Trigger – who was short of friends, since he was smelly and had a festering wound on his face from a rat bite that wouldn't heal. The Watsons' hens, more feral than free-range, laid in cunning gaps between bales of hay or behind old cartwheels in the tractor shed. Soon I was collecting the eggs in a broken bucket, sweeping up shit and straw after Mabel and her court, and chopping up roots for their winter feed in a kind of monster cast-iron mincing machine, with a handle I had to turn with both hands. Mangolds to the mangle, mangel-wurzels, the roots of scarcity, rock-hard and bright orange on the inside. This was wordless work, with no recompense save for the sense of something real to do. Mr Watson would hail me in a joshing, coaxing voice, as if I were some stray creature myself, and I wasn't required to answer beyond a grunt or nervous giggle. I turned up, he let me stay – always outdoors, however, there was no question of entering

Mrs Watson's domain, although she'd hand out hot, sweet tea at the back door, where her pet guinea-fowl pecked around with their freckled feathers ballooned against the raw weather.

The particular bliss of Watsons' farm was that it combined the reassurance of routine with the freedom of wandering off. They had no wish to take me in. They would have been in their late forties, they had grown-up children of their own, only their son Edgar was still in the process of leaving home. Edgar milked the stubbornest cows and once, when he caught me loitering in the corner, squirted warm, sweet, sticky milk in my face. He made me feel suddenly, agonisingly, too close for comfort – needy and 'nesh'. When he wasn't around I was allowed to try to milk an easy cow myself. I wasn't much good at it, my fingers weren't strong enough and I couldn't begin to get the rhythm you were supposed to, with the milk pinging gently into the bucket. But I did learn how to buckle leather straps on to the back legs of the two cows that liked to kick, one of them known jokily as Jezebel. I did penetrate that far into the mysteries of milking.

Because Mr Watson was easygoing and didn't mind me being clumsy, I was a lot less clumsy around him. He labelled me a 'funnyosity' when he found me sitting in the hay with my nose in a book (too much reading was well known to send you daft) and so suffered me gladly. He worked hard, but at the same time the pattern of farm days was loose and wide-meshed, there was a desultory quality about it – unlike the Business, it didn't have to be reinvented from scratch all the time. Mr Watson gave the impression that the farm ran him, rather than the other way around.

It was gently running down, that was why. Watsons' had about thirty acres all told, but the disorderly carve-ups and amalgamations of Hanmer tenancies over the years meant that

133

the fields were dotted around the neighbourhood, not one of them adjacent to the farmyard. Most of this land was used for grazing or growing crops for feed – hay, bitter kale, stony mangolds and millet. I followed in his wake one day when he sowed millet like a man in a parable, walking up and down scattering seed from a basket by hand. Millet-seed is fine and black, and I went home looking like Uncle Albert after his coal round, which so tickled my mother that for once she didn't tell, except to make a joke of it. The whole episode appealed to her taste for the picturesque.

However, Mr Watson's methods were generally less romantic and more mechanised. He had an ancient Fordson tractor, bought forty-second-hand to replace the carthorse that died shortly after the war, whose tackle still hung in the shed. The Fordson was juddering, deafening, temperamental, filthy with oil and dust, and moved very slowly. Mr Watson and I would ride out on it to the more distant fields, me perched on one of its huge mudguards, holding tight and bundled up in scarves. It was very exposed, with no cabin to shelter in, but the two of us were cosy all the same, enclosed in our capsule of fumes and noise. Impatient cars and trucks had to queue to overtake us, we wouldn't alter our stately pace. Couldn't, in truth – but that made us all the more like a force of nature.

Riding on the tractor and feeling its hammering engine in your bones was better mesmerism than trudging through the mud. You could steep yourself in essence of Hanmer, for hours at a time you were fully occupied going nearly nowhere – to the field, then up and down the field, then back to where you started. Farming life seemed a perpetual-motion machine, or an effect of gravity, something cyclic and unstoppable. Actually, it was because this kind of small-scale tenant farming was vanishing that the impression of stubborn persistence was so strong. Ways of life have been dying out in rural England time out of mind, at least for the two hundred and fifty years since the great wave of eighteenth-century enclosures. It's the sense of an ending that's timeless. The best symbol of this version of pastoral is a rusting and discarded piece of farm machinery in the corner of a field. Well, almost the best. When, a bit later, I encountered Thomas Hardy's wry verses 'In Time of "The Breaking of Nations"', I realised he'd described exactly the pull of a world endlessly coming to an end.

> Only a man harrowing clods
> In a slow silent walk
> With an old horse that stumbles and nods
> Half asleep as they stalk . . .

The poem's official message is that life on the land goes on despite supposedly 'historic' disasters like world wars. However, there's an ironic twist, since this minimal, anonymous existence has no more respect for individuality than the obscenity in the trenches. It's a scene that might well itself have been scoured by battles. Such quiet landscapes are graveyards. 'Portion of this Yew / Is a man my grandsire knew' Hardy writes in a jollier variant on the same theme.

Hanmer wasn't on his patch, of course, but you could picture the Maelor district as a mini-Wessex, less English, less fertile, lacking a writer to describe it. The local dialect did make a lot of the syllable 'Ur' that he singles out in *Tess* to stand for the ancient burr you can hear in country voices. In Hanmer grammar 'Ur' or ''Er' was the all-purpose pronoun used for men, women, children, cattle, tractors. It implied a kind of levelling, as though all were objects, and you could use it for a tree or a stone, too. In my memory it's always associated with negatives – 'dunna', 'conna', 'wunna'. You kick a gate that's warped half off its hinge: "Er wunna open,' you say without surprise. Everything had its own sullen, passive power of resistance.

At harvest times there was a carnival quickening in the air. The hay harvest in June was often a frantic race against time and weather. People lent a hand after work late into the light evenings to get the hay stacked and thatched or piled loose into a barn. But the corn harvest at the end of the summer was the event the parish ritually celebrated. As Grandpa noted in his diary, the way Harvest Festival packed Hanmer people into church along with their fruit and veg and sheaves showed just how pagan they were. Not everyone grew corn – Mr Watson didn't – but it had a shared significance, and some rackety field sports were attached to it.

For instance, each field's crop was cut so as to leave a small plot of corn standing in the middle. Then, when the combine harvester had done thudding, everyone, the labourers' families, kids and hangers-on, would converge on this corn island with hoots and yells, sticks and pitchforks, and murder the mass of voles, mice and rabbits that had taken shelter there as they made a last mad dash for safety. If you finished off a rabbit it was yours to take home. I never managed it and couldn't have taken my prize home if I had, for a bloody rabbit still warm in its fur would have been the very embodiment of my mother's food horrors. Soon no one would be eating rabbit, in any case, for myxomatosis reached Hanmer late in 1953. The whole countryside stank for weeks of decomposing rabbit flesh, sweet and foul, and unforgettably disgusting. And everywhere on the roads and paths rabbits staggered about dying by inches, blind, their heads swollen and fly-blown, so that it was a kindness to kill them quickly. Those cruel harvest games were good prac- tice, it was useful to know how to knock a rabbit on the head.

Local people didn't know (or didn't say) that myxomatosis

had been introduced deliberately to destroy the rabbit population and save millions on the crops they plundered. Although dramatic, this act of viral warfare was all part of the drive towards efficiency – the breeding programmes, the intensive use of pesticides, fertilisers, hormones – that would put farms like Watsons' out of business. It would also drastically reduce job opportunities for muck-shovellers, for all Mr Palmer's confidence in the unchanging order of society. Many Hanmer people had cause to sympathise with the rabbits. Even Sir Edward Hanmer, who was a well-known stickler for tradition, wasn't so blind to self-interest that he didn't see that labourers were becoming dispensable. If you were his tenant in a tied cottage, it was always very hard to get him to mend your roof and only dreamers expected him to modernise the plumbing. But now when cottages fell vacant, they'd be promptly bull-dozed, leaving only a lilac bush or flowering currant looking lost in the middle of an empty field to mark where someone's garden had been.

Nonetheless, for the moment, Watsons' went on existing as though it always would. I'd fetch up the cows in the afternoon from whichever field they'd been grazing and feel ineffably useful, caught up in the saving sameness of the days and carried along. They knew their own way, you simply had to amble after with a stick of office pulled from the hedge for show and shout 'Hey up!' if they stopped to snack at the roadside. They moved in a cloud of flies and gnats, and their tails were constantly in motion whisking them away, except when one or another dropped a line of khaki-coloured cowpats along the road, when she'd raise the first few joints of her tail at a dainty angle, like a lady cocking a little finger as she lifted her teacup. They conferred dignity on their minder, these big, calm, pre-occupied animals, and power too – so that when cars came, you could stare indifferently into space and make them wait before chivvying the herd to one side and letting them through. This was better than riding the tractor, especially the times when Mr Watson borrowed the bull, and I could watch drivers' double-takes as they spotted the ring in the nose, the loose chain dragging along the ground, the slouching gait, the red eyes . . . Surrounded by his harem, this bull was a weary and docile beast, but strangers didn't know that and I'd enjoy their alarm when they realised that I was the only one in charge. I'd chew thoughtfully on my straw and bask in being a yokel, a bumpkin, a hick from the sticks.

I'd turned into a tomboy travesty of my mother's little shepherdess, orphaned and anonymous, and utterly absorbed in the world outside. The repetition of farm days made them seem a backwater of time where the future was safely accounted for. And you were superior to those – like my father and mother – who were so anxious about who and how to be. Why not just lose yourself, lose your way but find it too, in among the cows and hedges and ditches and gates that needed kicking? "Er wunna move.' Stick in the mud, why not? I was well on the way to tacking together a sort of nature religion to make up for Grandpa's defection, an apotheosis of the back of beyond, in which I was just another thinking thing, neuter, drab, camou-flaged. There'd be sermons in stones, and books to read in the haybarn, for ever and ever. Amen.

But even if you were very good at not telling the time – and I was – you couldn't not see the signs that Hanmer was after all located in the world of the nervous 1950s. Hicks from the sticks would be very much a part of the new post-austerity scene, they were grist to the mill, the very material of recovery. In the land of the 1950s you were meant to be socially mobile, but personally conformist; self-made, but in one of the moulds made ready. You mustn't miss the boat, but you mustn't rock it either. Older Hanmer generations might stay put, mine wouldn't be able to even if we wanted, for better and for worse we were redundant on the land, we'd be moved on and groomed to start over as good consumers.

Among the signs of change was the trivial but telling matter of clothes after coupons. Suddenly you were spoilt for choice and yet constrained, not only by money, but by the rich variety of sumptuary laws concerning fashion and decency, from which kids were by no means exempt. Girls could wear trousers, for instance – but not generic trousers, not mere pants, nothing that captured the magic neutrality I was after when I tucked my pigtails down the collar of my windcheater and chewed my straw. Instead, the glossy clothes catalogues offered slacks, trews, toreador pants, capri pants, ski pants, pedal-pushers (a particularly bad joke on me) all in bright boiled-sweetie colours, tartans, checks, stripes and spots, announcing loudly that girls wore trousers only in play, in order to look more girly than ever. Girls' pants were cute and tight, made of stretch fabrics or with darts and high waistbands to emphasise your curves. There were jeans, true, but they were cut in the same way, and so elaborately equipped with turn-ups and decorative studs that you looked like a cowgirl in a musical. And – the crowning glory of difference – they *all* had side zips or buttons, never an opening that could for a second be confused with boys' flies, there was to be no hint of gender-bending, nothing loose or baggy or greyly ambiguous. You were a lot less conspicuous as a girl in a skirt.

All the neutral stuff belonged to boys and men, and so should jobs like fetching up the cows. Mr Watson made an exception for me, but when I strayed to other farms this division of labour was obvious. At Hunts', along the road, my favourite tasks fell to the son, Terry, a sturdy boy a bit younger than me. Mr Hunt was training up Terry for his role with curses and cuffs round the ear, and completely ignored me – partly out of contempt, but also because it was a well-established Hanmer rule that (school apart) you weren't allowed to batter other men's children, and violence was Mr Hunt's main language. Once, when Terry tipped over a heavy wheelbarrow full of manure, his strong young father picked him up and sent him flying face-first into the midden and we had to wash him off, shivering with shock and humiliation, in the old horse trough.

Terry was very clumsy and very shy, with a terrible stammer, and his father was always in a temper, red-faced and laying about him. Hunts' was a bigger and more modern farm than Watsons', with milking machines and an echoing cement-floored shippon you could hose down, but its ways were barbaric. We'd hear Mrs Hunt cry out from her kitchen, peer in and see Mr Hunt bending her over the kitchen table with his hand twisted in her hair. And we'd creep away, Terry and I, not knowing what we'd seen – sex or just hurt and was there a difference? – and cuddle each other uncertainly in the hay, whispering, mystified. At times like that, farm life didn't look like a refuge at all, but chaotic and brutish. At least, back in the council house, you were court-martialled before being beaten.

Did Hanmer's remoteness breed cruelty, was it part of the time-honoured pattern? Perhaps men like Mr Hunt were more hysterically tyrannical because they sensed the world changing around them. He wasn't a lone monster. You didn't have to look far for split lips and black eyes, and all sorts of weals and bruises. Either women and children in Hanmer were especially accident-prone, or it was a routinely violent place. You learned not to pay much attention. There were many wives who lived like Mrs Hunt, my own Aunt Binnie, my father's sister, for one, although we didn't know – managed not to know – until years later. Even if you were in love with the notion of life in the sticks there were stories you couldn't not ponder, though.

Mrs Parker, who was the agent with the Technicolor clothes catalogue and used to call at our house every week to collect our payments, often looked the worse for wear. She and her husband had half a dozen children, two of them said to be fathered by their neighbour, George Fitch, a brutal, thick-set man who lived in the next-door cottage with a cowed wife and a tribe of kids of his own, and whose tell-tale red hair those two Parker children inherited, rather than their official father's mousy colouring. This sort of thing wasn't unusual around Hanmer, particularly when people lived in an isolated huddle of houses like theirs. However, Mrs Parker, a handsome, big-boned, quiet woman, *was* unusual in taking on the agency for the catalogue and keeping her family, whatever their provenance, better-dressed than most.

Then, one day, she didn't appear to collect the money, and the day after that everyone knew that it was because she'd killed herself by drinking rat poison. Why, exactly, was never known. Perhaps she'd had secret plans that came to nothing, perhaps she was pregnant again by George Fitch and couldn't face the rows, or perhaps she was simply pregnant again . . . It would have been melodramatically satisfying to imagine thwarted passion, except that it was hard to think of her relation with George Fitch as an 'affair', more likely it was a matter of occasional rape (we wouldn't have used these words back then, but we could picture the thing clearly enough).

Mrs Parker's end caused a brief scandal. Her despair broke the mould of passive resistance, she wouldn't be kicked any more. It made an impression on me, but at the same time I treasured up my experience of the other life of Hanmer, the easygoing life on small, dying farms, ways of being you didn't have to make up as you went along. Not mine. Perhaps not anybody's for much longer, but certainly not mine. I was off across the border into England, to school in Whitchurch, all of six miles there and six miles back on the bus every day: a world away.

X

Nisi Dominus Frustra

Without the Lord, all is in vain said the Whitchurch Girls' High School crest on our blazer pockets. And how right they were, although it was not the Lord but His language, Latin, that was my salvation. Latin, the great dead language that only existed in writing, would compensate for my speechlessness, vindicate my sleepless nights and in general redeem my utter lack of social graces. Latin stood for higher education, still, in the early 1950s, a kind of litmus test for academic aptitude – you couldn't get into university without an O-level in Latin, it was the sign of being able to detach yourself from here and now, abstract your understanding of words, train your memory and live solitary in your head with only books for company. So it was meant to be hard, but I found it wonderfully easy, for just these reasons. I fell in love with Latin. It was the tongue the dead spoke, *ergo* Grandpa's language, of course. I could hear his show-off exasperated tones and his preacher's style in every tame declension and conjugation.

Nisi Dominus Frustra was mumbo-jumbo for the mind's ear. The motto my new school truly believed in, however, was *mens sana in corpore sano*, a healthy mind in a healthy body, and team games, religious knowledge and 'domestic science' figured large on the curriculum. The high school cultivated the air of being somehow still fee-paying, it was designed to produce solid, disciplined, well-groomed girls who'd marry local traders and solicitors like their fathers. The eleven-plus had let in a leavening of out-of-towners and outsiders, but that had only made it more vital to insist on sub-public-school mores – uniforms, 'houses', and an elaborate hierarchy of prefects and deputy prefects whose job it was to remind their juniors to stand up straight, and send them out to run up and down the playing field at break in wet weather instead of huddling in the cloakrooms. So, in falling in love with Latin, I was obeying the letter of the school's law rather than its spirit.

The high school liked girls with rounded characters, loyal, outgoing, serviceable girls who made the best of themselves. Even the communal fantasies were well groomed. Quite a lot of girls back then dreamed of becoming air hostesses. Being an air hostess hadn't yet been revealed as waitressing-in-the-sky, but was somehow connected with team spirit, patriotism and the WAAF officers who mourned the pilot-heroes as they pushed mimic planes about in headquarters bunkers in war films. In peacetime there was more chance of marrying a pilot; or a first-class passenger might at any moment intuit from the way you poured his coffee that you had the sterling spirit and the poise to play his helpmeet on solid ground somewhere in Surrey.

Meanwhile, Whitchurch was a self-satisfied little Shropshire market town that took its character from retailing and auction-eering and accounting. The cattle market was on Fridays and half-day closing (religiously observed) was on Wednesdays. Whitchurch had missed out long ago on the great local events of the early Industrial Revolution that had created Ironbridge, although there was Smith's Foundry still and Joyce's Clock Factory (the wartime voice of Nazism on the radio, Lord Haw-Haw, a.k.a. William Joyce, was a cousin), and a stagnant wharf where a disused branch of the Shropshire Union Canal came to a quiet end. This cul-de-sac stood conveniently for the town's position.

It was rumoured that once upon a time Whitchurch was nearly picked instead of Crewe as the site for the great railway junction of the region, but some visionary reluctance on the part of the town fathers had saved it for rural commerce. The present station was sleepy, just one of the stops between Shrewsbury and Crewe, although it did have a doomed line that ran due west into Wales to Aberystwyth and another to Chester, and a coal depot. Otherwise, there was a cheese factory and a new Silhouette corsetry factory where bold women in curlers made the armoured (padded, circular-stitched, rubberised, boned) bras and girdles that would mould all those rounded characters.

The town's own fat navel was a three-way road junction slap in its middle called the Bull Ring, the original site of the cattle market. High Street, Green End and Bridgewater Street crowded with shops – ironmongers, grocers, outfitters, stationers, drapers, seed merchants – met there in a knot. But perhaps the most distinctive feature of Whitchurch (which had a total population of about fifteen thousand) was the number of pubs, more than thirty of them, ranging from 'hotels' like the Queen Vic, where the prosperous farmers lunched while their cattle and hogs went under the hammer, to spit-and-sawdust snugs like the Back Street Vaults, or Grandpa's old haunt the Fox and Goose, where the lower orders lurked. Whitchurch was a hard-drinking place every day, not just on market days, a tight little town was its reputation, in more senses than one.

Sundays were particularly busy, since Wales was dry on Sundays. Then the same blue bus that I caught to school turned into a drinkers' shuttle ferrying thirsty Maelorites over the border into England, where on the Whitchurch town boundary stood the huge Highgate pub, tiled like a public convenience, proudly boasting on its sign – depending which direction you approached from – that it was 'The First/Last Public House in England'. Not that everyone drank there; they distributed themselves around the town until the witching hour of 10.30, when they converged on the bus once more. Going home, they'd snore their way past another sign of lacy ironwork with only one side to it, and no electric light, that said *Croeso i Gymru, Welcome to Wales*.

On Monday mornings the bus smelled of Wem Ales and Woodbines: selaW ot emocleW. None of us spoke Welsh, but we had broader Shropshire accents than Whitchurch people, marking us out. Then there were our own social strata: the bus served three schools, the secondary modern (mixed), the boys' grammar school and the girls' high school, and it had an elaborate unspoken seating plan.

The back seats were reserved for big girls of fourteen and fifteen who went to the secondary modern, but only just. They had perms, boyfriends and jobs lined up, and they wore their school uniforms in a sketchy, customised way, with extra bits and bits missing, and nylons whose ladders they fixed showily with nail varnish. They had a lot to talk about and laugh over in private. They painted their nails on the way home and picked off the varnish the next morning, although sometimes they passed around a bottle of remover that smelled headily of pear-drops. They didn't have homework, but kept changes of clothes in the shopping bags they used for satchels; school was for them a last concession to other people's picture of childhood, for in the country girls were grown up at fifteen.

The secondary modern boys were younger for their age and scuffled about in the middle seats, playing at being wild, priding themselves on the filthiness of their ties and wearing spare cigarettes behind their ears. Although they sometimes looked up girls' skirts and told dirty jokes, they were second-class passengers, the bus was girl territory, the real tearaways among the boys didn't stoop to catch the bus, but biked to school on the days when they weren't truanting.

And the grammar school boys and high school girls, a conspicuous and shifty minority, distributed themselves around the front seats as they boarded. Grammar school boys stood out sacrificially in bright purple blazers and caps. At least the high school's navy blue matched the majority – although only at a distance, there was no getting around the stigma. The very first time I caught the bus I committed the terrible solecism of sitting next to a big girl who was saving a seat for her friend in the next-to-back row. She very soon – with a kind of matronly contempt – let me know my mistake. Those first few months I ended up more often than not next to a real pariah, Gilbert, a pale and soft-spoken grammar school boy whose mother had once complained to the bus driver when a rude boy stole his cap. In any case, sitting next to someone of the opposite sex meant you were nobody.

In theory we who'd passed the eleven-plus were supposed to despise the secondary modern kids for being common and thick. In practice we envied them for knowing how to be outsiders and as we grew older we aped their style: caps and berets balled up in pockets, greased and lacquered quiffs of hair, secret lockets and chains with rings on them under their shirts. When rock and roll and rebels without a cause hit Whitchurch they were ready with the right look and so were we. In time my old Hanmer school enemy Gail and I would even form our own girl gang and inherit the back seat. But for now being bused just felt very lonely. In my oversized gabardine raincoat (with hood), over the top of my cardboard-stiff blazer, over the top of my oversized gymslip, with my new beret and badge and my imitation-leather satchel weighed down that first morning with my shoe bag and plimsoles and indoor sandals, all marked with my name in indelible ink as instructed, I was like an evacuee or a displaced person. The bus picked me up every day from The Arowry corner at 8.15 and dropped me off again at 4.30, and in between it was just me and all sorts of Latin.

The days went by dreamily, for I was high on sleeplessness and often feverish from sinus infections that made my cheek-bones buzz and my eyes droop. The words, maps, lists and diagrams in my textbooks were to me classic ciphers, empty and O-shaped – obedient, open, waiting to be filled with mean-ing. I'd get light-headed over the simple, blissful fact of alpha-betical abstraction; the thought that the smudgy marks I made shared the same powers as the ones printed in books was a continuous miracle. Numbers were harder, they were more tied to things, but once we got on to algebra I felt safer. This was the letter of the law: suddenly I was doing a right thing. I'd always been a speed-reader, and now that reading was regarded as work I was industrious to a fault and used up my third-form miscellanies in no time.

Extra tasks were a godsend. I especially relished one in particular, making a geography scrapbook, sticking in pictures divided by country and colony. Applying scissors and glue to the vicarage collection of *National Geographic*s gave me an excuse for annexing more of the ledger end of the table at home; it also suited my own mental geography, which was all cut-up and collage, a mimic empire of signs. I imagined my memory as a series of rooms full of old coins, stuffed snakes and dried, flat flowers. I learned verse by heart with ease and hung it on the walls like tapestry samplers. With a small extra effort I could store in imaginary cupboards and call up before my mind's eye whole pages of biology textbook, or French irregular verbs. But Latin set texts themselves were my best trophies. '*Gallia est omnis divisa in tre partes* . . .' Caesar's *Gallic Wars* exuded the most detached and conquering confidence. All books were like pop-up books to me back then and Caesar especially. His were words you could marshal like armies of lead soldiers.

But I lacked the courage to put up my hand in class to volunteer answers and, when forced to read out loud, I slurred the words and scrambled red-faced for the end of whatever folksy and supposedly musical lines from a play or poem we were 'elocuting'. 'Up the airy mountain, / Down the rushy glen . . .' I longed to put the noisy nonsense out of its misery and dissect it in private. I didn't know how to pronounce half the words I played with on paper, of course, and was too humiliated to take in what they were supposed to sound like when helpful teachers corrected me. Saying anything in French was out of the question, self-consciousness stopped my mouth. '*Je m'appelle* . . .' My name wouldn't go into French and I always mumbled it anyway, so that people thought I was called Laura.

In class, the only progress I'd made since Hanmer school was in stoicism: I learned to swallow my tears. Nonetheless, thanks to written exams I came top in nearly everything at the end of the first term. This gave me great pleasure, for surely it meant that my private currency had value in the world outside. I hugged myself. My triumph was tinged with vengeance, too. That'll show them, I thought. I meant the other girls and the teachers who'd suspected me of having someone else who did my homework. But mainly I meant my parents and particularly my father. He'd taken me aside the day before I started at the high school and told me that I should not expect people there to find me clever, as they had at Hanmer. He just wanted me to have a sense of proportion, to get things into perspective, to take a balanced view, to be realistic. That'll show him, I thought, carrying home my end-of-term report: it's not like telling the time or riding a bike after all. It's Latin *and he doesn't understand it.*

He had to take comfort from the abysmal marks I got for physical education and especially gym, which *was* the bike-riding fiasco over again, pretty exactly. I could play leapfrog and climb trees. I could even 'vault' a five-barred gate if I started from the third bar up (I was too short otherwise): then, one hand on the top, the other on the second bar down on the other side and over you go! But faced with a vaulting horse I was abashed, I faltered and ran out of conviction long before I landed on the so-called springboard and collided in slow motion with its hard leather flank. On the wall bars I suffered from vertigo. I couldn't climb ropes at all, my arms became quite strengthless and I shook with my fake and useless efforts. No amount of encouragement did any good and very soon the gym mistress came to regard me with real distaste.

My wretchedness made me unteachable, I had no spontaneity, no openness, I couldn't be helped. For her I was an unhealthy child in the moral sense, a natural malingerer. She'd haul me over the horse with gritted teeth, she didn't like to touch me, you could tell. But then she was the one – since she was responsible for our deportment and 'hygiene' – who had to send my parents notes about the lice in my long, untidy hair (which I still wore in pigtails) and the one who had to try to teach me to walk without slouching when I went up on speech day to collect my prizes, crossing the stage first as the youngest and (as she said) giving such a bad impression at the very outset. I was the sort of girl who let the side down given half a chance. Nonetheless she soldiered on and refused to leave me out of her lessons, even when I persuaded my mother to give me notes saying I had a headache. I wasn't surprised she wasn't convinced, for I thought I was cheating. But perhaps my blocked sinuses did have something to do with how bad I was at gym, perhaps after all I did lack balance? At the time, both the gym mistress and I took my passive resistance personally, as a trait of my character. And it was true that I could stand on my hands when no one was looking.

I couldn't sing a note even if no one was listening, though – and my tone-deafness was a great disappointment to the music mistress, who had taught my mother twenty years before. Several of the older spinster teachers remembered my mother for her prettiness, her acting ability and the sweetness of her singing voice, so I wasn't for them quite the forward peasant the younger ones took me for. Although it was obvious I didn't take after her, at least I had a mother with some accomplishments. But in music lessons I'd doodle in my jotter and Miss Macdonald would send me out for fidgeting, more in sadness than in anger: why couldn't I sit still and listen? If I'd been able to explain myself I'd have said that music, being unintelligible, scrambled my thoughts like static, so I had to shut it out. When we sang in assembly I'd use my Hanmer church choir trick and mouth the words silently. Most of the hymns I knew already and some I loved for their association with vicarage dark corners: 'Immortal, invisible / God only wise' always cheered me up, *that* was a style of mystery I felt at home with.

For speech days the high school had a school song of its own, dating from its 1920s heyday, a kind of hymn to hockey, with a rousing chorus – 'There's many a school in Britain / And schools across the sea / Where girls may be as happy / As clever and as free . . .' No one quite knew whether to be proud of the song or not, since it sounded very dated by the 1950s and not even Miss Macdonald's prize pupils could manage the setting with grace. It got higher and higher until it ended on a drawn-out squeaky crescendo: '. . . just the *schoo-oo-ool* for me!' The music had been written by a friend of the then headmistress, herself a Somerville graduate. He was called Montague Phillips, composed 'light operas' and must have had some very light 1920s sopranos in mind for the high point of the chorus. The verses in between called for less vocal gymnastics, so you could concentrate on the words ('by Miss S. Bostock'), which are wonderfully redolent of the ethos that shaped such schools:

> From the lonely farms and homesteads
> We gather in its walls,
> Thro' early morning's golden hours
> Until the soft dusk falls.
> Just a merry little kingdom
> Which is our very own,
> A wondrous little harvest field
> Where varying crops are sown.

The Arcadian simplicity of Whitchurch is a perfect setting, we're *almost* a boarding-school. We'll set our girls apart with the same ease as we turn (watch!) harvest into a metaphor. Verse two is in many ways the best, a virtuoso variation on *mens sana in corpore sano*, somatic weather:

> Sturdy of limb and quick of eye
> The hockey runners go,
> When keen across the playing fields
> The wintry breezes blow!

But when the smiling summer sun
Looks down from azure skies
The straight ball spinning o'er the net
Like wingèd lightning flies.

Perhaps Miss Bostock had a rather different picture of the girls from Mr Montague Phillips, for these sporty types sound too hoarse to have reached his high notes. She's more interested in solid virtues (that 'straight' ball says a lot, no curvy underhand strokes); although she pays her own tribute to decorative convention with 'e'er', 'wingèd', and 'azure', so poetically wrong for damp, cloudy Shropshire. And note the deftly transferred epithet in 'keen': we're so keen this vile wind from Wales is just a breeze to us. Verse three is about military hero Sir John Talbot, who stands for Britishness – we'll face any threatening 'shadows' (very vague these) with his courage. But the fourth and final verse puts it all together, team games and virginity pitted against the forces of darkness 'out there':

When we leave our little kingdom
To seek a wider world
And embark upon life's ocean
With snowy sails unfurled . . .

In my generation we crudely interpreted this line as a warning against 'going all the way' with boys, but we were underestimating Miss Bostock, who was also talking in code about the Empire and exporting the values you'd learned as a half-back to India or Africa, or at least chastely producing sons who would. This was the far-off mythic origin of the air hostess fantasy, although we didn't recognise it. Perhaps the fact that the dreadful chorus was set to follow inexorably yet once more helped blur Miss B.'s grand perspective on the wide world: Back to schoo-oo-ool.

Joining in the chorus without a sound, I was on my own. In my first high school year I had no friends, I was mostly invisible as well as inaudible: small, grubby, uncouth, a swot and no good at sports. Then there were the bugs. We finally bought the lethal shampoo from Boots and applied it, and they died, but not all at once, and for a while afterwards I went on scratching out of habit.

And – worse, much worse – during that first winter I had braces fitted to my teeth, top and bottom, a mouthful of complicated shiny wires. Now that it's almost a stigma *not* to visit an orthodontist and a metal grin is sexy, like having multiple earrings or a stud in your eyebrow, a licensed young ugliness, it's hard to believe how grotesque my braces seemed back in Whitchurch in 1953. No one else I knew had them. It was an outlandish deformity, like having a very, very bad squint, a squint so awful you had to wear an eyepatch; or having a purple birthmark; or a leg-iron. Even wearing glasses made you vaguely repulsive and absurd. Sometimes I'd comfort myself that at least I didn't have glasses *as well*, but it was no good, my shyness had taken on this terrible, visible life of its own. I was truly tongue-tied, locked in my scold's bit, and most people tried not to look at me nearly as hard as I tried not to look at them.

The braces were the most agonising part of my rite of passage into the land of Latin and they hurt physically as well – each time they were tightened my jaws were racked. But my actual visits to the dentist became an adventure. Teeth had to be very crooked for the National Health Service to pay for 'cosmetic' work then and mine were. I had been referred to a scholarly consultant on Liverpool's Harley Street, Rodney Street, who showed me 'before' and 'after' plaster casts of other patients to encourage me, and said that people were very often assigned the wrong teeth.

You inherited them from some ancestor who'd had a quite differently shaped jaw and they simply didn't fit, but stuck out and were squeezed sideways like mine. Mouth-breathing hadn't helped either, but that interested him less than the vision of genetic mayhem in mouths through the ages.

He was fascinated by teeth in an impersonal way and finding me teachable, he talked to me about his work in flattering detail. According to him my teeth weren't really mine, so I needn't feel embarrassed and I didn't in his surgery. This was also partly because – although we never, never mentioned it – he himself was very small, almost a midget. I was taller than he by the time the treatment was over and I'd reached the height of five foot one. His littleness lent a magic to our appointments. His 'before' and 'after' casts in their glass cases, and his lyrical descriptions of the perversity of teeth and the heroical project of righting them, all fitted together with the stages of human evolution we were doing at school – millennia of prehistory in one dental chart. Like Dr McColl handing me my sleepless nights as a present, the Liverpool dentist made my miserable mouth into an emblem of progress. Each appointment meant a visit to the big city, too.

We'd approach from the other side of the Mersey, past Lever Brothers' enormous works at Port Sunlight, where they made yellow Sunlight soap, Persil washing powder and Lux toilet soap, and the air was heavy with an animal stench of tallow and fats, overlaid with carbolic and topped off with chemical gardenia. Then came the Mersey Tunnel, and just before its entrance a new set of smells from a slaughterhouse and tannery, hides and hooves piled bloodily in carts along the road. Then the Tunnel's smooth tube of cement and on the other side Liverpool, cratered and pocked with bomb-sites.

It was in Liverpool that I saw in reality the cityscape of the newsreels – the remains of blitzed tenements, wallpaper, fire grates and private plumbing exposed, clinging to walls which were buttressed with wooden props while they waited for demolition. Not far from Rodney Street stood the huge new Anglican cathedral, round about it a great emptiness where swathes of streets had been razed to the ground. We'd walk its echoing aisles if we arrived early enough, for although my mother didn't like its newness it was a monument of sorts and paid tribute to the Gothic past. Then we'd move on to my dwarf consultant's cavernous waiting-room, with its solid pre-war furniture and landscapes in oils, the ante-room of 'after'.

Fixing my teeth was mainly my mother's idea: it was part of her pursuit of prettiness and her dream of a different life. She didn't want it done because she aspired to middle-class decorum, it was something born of her absence and brooding, like taking so long to deal with the lice in my hair. It was a *vicarage* thing at bottom, personal to her and fantastical, with a buried logic. Her own front teeth were crowned, because they'd been smashed when she was sixteen, and had fallen downstairs in the dark, running to separate Grandpa and Grandma who were fighting like fiends in the kitchen. The crowns looked false, she thought, and she hated them. She must have associated them with Grandpa's vileness with her friend Marj, and the disgust and self-doubt that had spoiled her own concentration at the high school. So she wasn't only saving my looks but – as she said often and bitterly later – giving me the chance she never had. Not the chance to be pretty (she was pretty, the teeth didn't show, really), nor the chance of school, she'd had both, but the chance to be whole. Her parents' selfishness had broken her, she and my father had mended me, I could have the career she didn't – that was how her thinking worked.

And in the long run she was right, although not in the way

she meant or wanted. As I grew I found I could lead a double life: one life in my looks and another in my head, boys and Latin for short. And this in turn would buy me a kind of popularity with my high school peers. I'd be forgiven for not being a rounded character because I had a pretty face, precocious breasts and I started my period when I was eleven (a great status symbol). But my mother and father saw me turning into Grandpa's creature. She could have mended her own mouth, but some paralysing memory stopped her; I was supposed to live this for her and be different, and here I was, some kind of moral throwback.

But as long as I was top of the class I could get away with spiritual slyness. I worked very hard to stay up there. It was a pleasure, but also a matter of survival, for exam results were my alibi. This was understood between my parents and me: my academic performance was taking place on a kind of high wire; so long as I could keep it up my lack of moral balance didn't count, but if I slipped and fell I'd be revealed in my true colours, as conceited, unrealistic, self-centred and sick. If I once slipped I'd have to start all over again, to learn how to be neat, obedient, outgoing and open, a good girl. I thanked God for Latin. *Nisi Dominus* . . . Our school motto comes from Psalm cxxvii – 'Except the Lord build the house: their labour is but vain that build it . . .' Its message is that you shouldn't be proud of your own efforts, because you can do nothing by yourself. 'It is but lost labour that ye haste to rise up early, and so late take rest, and eat the bread of carefulness: for so he giveth his beloved sleep.' In my sleepless nights I turned this doctrine heretically upside down. If I'm getting on so well, I thought, it must mean that I'm well connected, and that the powers that be are secretly on my side.

157

XI

Family Life

My mother told on me, but I liked secrets, so I never told on her when I chaperoned her on her visits to Mrs Smith, who kept a clandestine little clothes shop in town. We'd do our real shopping first (the grocery 'rations' would in any case be delivered), then we'd make our way casually up towards the quiet end of the High Street, away from the bustle of the Bull Ring, open a door that rang a muffled bell and slip into Mrs Smith's stuffy den. Mrs Smith was 'exclusive'. Although there were always a couple of items in her window – a tailored suit, maybe, and a smart three-quarters coat, displayed on legless, armless, headless dressmaker's dummies – they had no price tags and were hardly visible, thanks to a thick film of orange cellophane stuck to the glass. Mrs Smith herself stood guard inside; she was plump, corseted, unctuous and made up in matronly fashion with powder, rouge, pencilled eyebrows and a pursed, lipsticked mouth. Her hair was done in an iron perm and she too favoured tailored suits, which she wore with costume jewellery and expensive scent. Mrs Smith didn't encourage people just to wander in and indeed we nearly never found anyone else there, although there was a chair in the corner to sit on while you waited.

I waited a lot, for my mother's dealings with Mrs Smith were delicate and involved a lengthy ritual of seduction. At home, we leafed through the clothes catalogue in public and paid up by instalments. Those clothes displayed their attractions quite frankly, along with their prices. They arrived and you wore them, and wore them out. Here everything was much more intimate, 'classic' and mysterious. Mrs Smith's very name sounded false, she had a black-market air, as though once upon a time she had been involved with dubious dealings in clothes coupons. What her posh accent and her breathy whispers really sought to hush up, however, was the fact that most of her stock – perhaps all – was second-hand. These were genteel cast-offs, hardly worn at all, not for a moment to be associated with jumble sales. They were the real thing, at a fraction (quite a big fraction) of the cost. When Mrs Smith insisted on the quality of the cloth and the superiority of the cut, she was addressing my mother as a class casualty and a dreamer, some-one in danger of getting stuck in a council house at the kitchen sink, unless she had a good suit, or a really *dressy* dress.

My mother would go into the back room to try things on and survey herself in the floor-length mirror with an embar-rassed but pleased smile, while Mrs Smith smoothed and patted and murmured. Sooner or later she'd have to ask the price, and then there'd be head-shaking and sighs; but Mrs Smith would say with a simper how well it suited her colouring and her build, why didn't she put it aside for a tiny deposit and come back and try it on again next week ... Often we came away with nothing, but still a transaction would have taken place: my mother would have paid something off her account and something down on something 'new', and more often than not paying a bit off doubled as a down-payment, so that her debt to Mrs Smith grew and grew. The new thing would stay in Mrs Smith's back room for a few weeks, before being brought home to be hidden at the very back of the wardrobe until she felt able to bring it out and wear it – that is, until she could be supposed to have afforded it. This was tricky and sometimes she'd be reduced to passing off her Mrs Smith purchases as her own old clothes, something she'd found in Grandma's trunk.

Money, as usual, was the domestic sticking-point, the disputed territory between fantasy and realism – that is, between her and my father. Money was a minefield. She was supposed to be dreamy and impractical, but she was also supposed to be dependent, trusting and in a way transparent, a bit like children were supposed to be (and I wasn't). Of course my father knew about Mrs Smith, but he was never quite sure what my mother's dealings with her amounted to – either in terms of hard cash, or in terms of sentiment. Was she being unfaithful with Mrs Smith or not? The Valma of the pretty clothes and daydreams was the one he'd fallen in love with. But deceit, mystification and personal debt (the Business Overdraft was quite another thing) were vicarage vices he'd saved her from. Then again, wasn't her longing for clothes we couldn't afford a criticism of him, as though she regretted her life and was still dreaming of a different future? Did she feel cheated, a Cinders who'd married the coalman by mistake? Was she sorry she'd married him? No, no, she'd protest, and turn her face aside, as he produced extra cash to pay off Mrs Smith (cash which would turn into a tiny deposit on that frock she'd been trying on for weeks). He was on to something, I thought. After all, Mrs Smith was always saying how slender and young my mother looked, how hard it was to believe she was married and the mother of a big girl like me.

Did she regret her marriage? I certainly did and hoped she did, and so did Grandma, who said so under her breath often. But my mother believed that marriage made you one. Like those ceremonies in the movies where a cowboy and an Indian slashed their wrists and bled into each other, it created a bond as ineluctable and intimate as biology. This infuriated Grandma, who hated my father all the more for alienating my mother's loyalty and daring to tie her to a red-skinned Hanmer tribe. She had a whole list of grievances against my father, and used his name 'Eric' as though it was a swear word. Eric had a dirty job and a loud voice. Eric was always making a song and dance about money. And worst of all, Eric couldn't seem to grasp what a privilege it was to chauffeur us to Chester or Shrewsbury.

But although my mother would acknowledge these short-comings and would join in when Grandma abused men in general for being beastly and deceiving, she would still make an exception for my father. Stubbornly she stopped short of denouncing him as a monster. Worse, she continued to sleep with him and not only because there were no spare bedrooms or attics in the council house. She could at least have stayed up half the night, Grandma felt, to make sure he was sound asleep before joining him in bed, but no.

Grandma had to content herself with more minor signs of betrayal. And Mrs Smith was an ally. That private, perfumed little box of dressing-up clothes was reminiscent of the room over the shop in South Wales where Grandma and her sister Katie took hours getting ready. This was their mother's terri-tory all over again. Mrs Smith might be venal, but her insinuat-ing voice still held an echo of the dead woman with hair the colour of a sovereign. It was my mother's need to feel mothered that drew her back to be fussed over and flattered by Mrs Smith, as much as any fear of losing caste.

For it seemed that nobody inside our family wanted to be mother, everyone was a daughter in perpetuity. You could have children of your own and still stay a mother's girl, as Grandma's example daily demonstrated. My mother, too, carried on the tradition, although she could hardly remember her grand-mother, the mythic maternal figure at the start of the line. She was insecure in her girlishness, however, as Grandma and Katie never were, shamed and tired out by her own incompetence as a homemaker. Grandma – who added considerably to her dom-estic burdens by demanding a lot of fetching and carrying and toasting of teacakes at unsocial hours – fed her discontent by reminiscing about the rosy days of her own youth, all hair-brushing and treats. Grandma's example, though, suggested no remedy except dressing up to go to the pictures. (We had no television yet and in any case 1950s TV was brisk and service-able, you couldn't dream the day away on a diet of soaps and old movies.) Grandma had revamped her marriage in order to support the style of life she preferred. She took a new vow to hate Grandpa in sickness and in health, blackmailed him for an income and refused to touch him with a bargepole, as she often proudly recalled. But my mother, since she loved my father, cast about for some other expedient that would enable her to wear the clothes from Mrs Smith and to pay for them.

This was how she hit on the idea of getting a job – which she described, suppressing Mrs Smith, as a means of getting out of the house. It's a measure of my father's pride in her as superior and 'different' that he didn't oppose her plan, although perhaps he foresaw all along that it couldn't come to anything. Received opinion was certainly against it. Women who were neither working class nor qualified professionals (we'd heard of women doctors and lawyers, but never seen one) were sup-posed to stay at home, or do good works if they felt restless. But my mother was no longer securely middle class enough to take on voluntary work, she wanted the money. There *were* ladylike jobs that were just possible: you could be a receptionist, or the kind of secretary who didn't type. Such positions, however, could not be found in Hanmer; she would have to commute to Whitchurch or even further afield and to do that she would have to learn to drive. The logical first step, then, was to buy L plates and take lessons with my father . . .

But after each lesson the verdict was more discouraging. It turned out she was too nervy, too highly strung, to pass the test. My father was a lot kinder than he was to me about my failure to learn to ride a bike. My mother, he said – and she agreed – wasn't down-to-earth enough to drive. So the job receded into the realm of unreality and there did its work as one of her repertoire of daydreams; and the clothes from Mrs Smith stayed hidden at the back of the wardrobe for long weeks and months at a time, before being slyly smuggled into the light of day. And we went on visiting Mrs Smith. In fact, the whole idea of my mother going out to work – or rather, its failure – confirmed my parents in their separate worlds, his the outside world of reality, hers the castles in the air and council-house frustrations. Not driving became another sign of her sensitivity. Like not cleaning and not cooking, it showed (in a mysterious way) that she was meant for better things, a life that wasn't confined to home – and that in turn was part of her impractical charm as a wife.

She did, however, sometimes talk with bitterness about my father's sister, Auntie Binnie, who'd started to drive during the war when there were no tests and who was surely just as nervy. It was well known that Auntie Binnie could only drive to places she'd driven to before, along roads she knew by heart – although it was never explained how she had driven anywhere for the first time. And she couldn't park anywhere smaller than a farmyard. Nevertheless, she had a licence and my mother sometimes felt that, but for an accident of timing, she too could have driven Binnie-fashion and worn her smart suit to work.

It was not to be. What would domestic life have been like if she had deserted us? Who would have cut off Grandma's crusts, and given the kitchen floor a lick and a promise? Not me, certainly; I was a dunce at domestic science. But we'd have managed somehow, a bit more mayhem wouldn't have mattered; we'd have lived on sliced ham and sponge cake, and scorched our own fish fingers. And in terms of the household's psychic economy it would have been a blessing. My mother's timidity and her dread of confrontation meant that it was horribly easy to defy and bully her and so we did, Grandma, my brother Clive and I. Although, since Grandma had the excuse of her age and diabetes, and Clive was still only small, I was her chief tormentor. When I wasn't at school or at Watsons' farm, I wandered off and went missing, driving her frantic with worry; when I was forced to take Clive with me he came back the worse for wear (once I made him touch the Hunts' new electric fence); and in the house I sulked, whined and nagged, and threw temper tantrums when I couldn't get my maths homework to come out right. I shouted at her, I may even have hit her. And when my father came home she told on me.

He'd be late back himself often, smelling of cold and cowshit, and full of unfinished Business he'd yell about down the phone to Uncle Albert — One Damn Thing After Another, Fed Up to the Back Teeth — before going into the kitchen to wash his hands at the sink. My mother would follow and, while she warmed up his take-it-or-leave-it tea, she'd weep and recount my offences. I'd worried her sick, she couldn't cope with me and she *couldn't stand rows*. It was always this last line that did the trick. Rows meant the old vicarage misery, he was honour bound to save her from its clutches. What had I to say for myself? I'd pretend to be doing my homework, but he wanted a Straight Answer to a Straight Question, and when I lied and wouldn't look him in the eye he'd lose his temper. By now it's a set routine, there is no way back. I'll shake, snivel and look guilty, he'll shout that he's going to Teach me a Lesson I won't Forget in a Hurry – this too is code, school isn't the Real World – and put me across his knee and smack me until I say I'm sorry, I won't do it again.

This is where my mother wrings her hands and pleads with him not to hit me too hard, and I howl and writhe with humiliation. It's all happening in the open-plan living-room, with Clive and Grandma looking on. Clive is smug but frightened, Grandma trembles with excitement, she loves rows and loves to see Eric reveal himself in his true Hanmer colours. I promise not to do it again. But I will. I'll slouch upstairs to rest my swollen eyes with reading and make resolutions to lie better. I'll read and read, while Clive twitches in his sleep across the room, and my mother and father murmur together in bed. May they rot in hell, I'll say to myself. Grandma will visit in the small hours, to hiss that all men are brutes. But it's my mother who has taught me the lesson that divides me from the daughter line. I won't be like her, there are too many children in our house.

One red-eyed night when I was poring over the romance my name came from, *Lorna Doone*, it was suddenly not myself but my mother I saw in the fey and queenly little girl who's so out of place in dark Doone Glen, and my father in the character of honest John Ridd, the farm boy who grows up to be her stout-hearted yeoman lover, and who tells the story his way. It's a stirring tale: John rescues Lorna from the anarchy of her clan (we're in the wild West Country in the years of the Monmouth Rebellion and Judge Jeffreys's Bloody Assizes, the Doones are outlaws on nobody's side but their own) and discovers that she's not a Doone at all by blood, although she's still a lady and above him: 'She drew herself up with an air of pride . . . and turned away as if to enter some grand coach or palace; while I was so amazed, and grieved, in my raw simplicity . . .' But the author is only teasing. Despite dazzling the court in London Lorna is constant to John. He is knighted for services to the Crown and, after a marvellous scene where snarling Carver Doone shoots Lorna in church at her wedding (if he can't have her nobody will), John worsts the forces of darkness in single combat and our couple settle down to a happy ending at Plover's Barrow farm.

I can see now why I was so struck by Lorna Doone's likeness to my mother. It's because her Victorian creator, R. D. Blackmore, an Oxford man who had previously only 'translated from the classics without attracting very much attention' (as one biographer puts it), had dealt with the difficult but best-selling business of how to have his heroine marry 'down' without being suspected of lust for honest John (who is over six feet tall and the local wrestling champion) by making Lorna skittishly chaste and childlike throughout. Blackmore had hit on a deviant formula for romance, where heroines – like Jane Eyre twenty years earlier – usually married the master. If the hero is not socially powerful then his masculine mystique comes into full focus, although the Victorian heroine mustn't know where to look. *Lorna Doone* innocently anticipates Lawrence. This John, like Lady Chatterley's lover, is a great believer in the natural order of things between the sexes and also speaks with a bit of a burr when he remembers to. For instance:

I know that up the country, women are allowed to reap . . .
But in our part, women do what seems their proper business,
following well behind the men, out of harm of the swinging-
hook, and stooping with their breasts and arms up they catch

the swathes of corn, where the reapers cast them, and tucking them together tightly with a wisp laid under them, this they fetch around and twist, with a knee to keep it close . . .

Although this is just an aside on country customs, it suggests the sort of preaching about proper positions Mellors goes in for. Blackmore's heroine wouldn't be seen dead in a cornfield – after all, we are dealing in symbols: John Ridd's charm for Lorna resides in the firm authority underlying his deference. She can stay a young girl for ever. It wasn't at all a perfect allegory of my father's relations with my mother, since John Ridd has cosy Plover's Barrow and *his* mother to mother his child bride when he gets her home. But you can't have everything.

What I like to think is that Grandpa had been inwardly seething like Carver Doone at their wedding, marching his daughter to church and handing her over to this honest John,

and that's why the name popped into his head when I was born. Like Carver, he'd have wickedly despised my father's John Riddish combination of conscious virtue, modesty and manly prowess. Eric was a natural for the role of responsible adult when he came back from the army after the war: Grandpa was eager for him to take it on, too, since it mainly meant my father trying to balance the vicarage books out of his own pocket. Grandpa could still clutch the skirts of his clerical dignity round him and appeal to his higher Authority. After his death, my father had not even this shadow of a rival for the part of patriarch and, young as he was (thirty-three in 1952), his army training predisposed him to take it very seriously. On the Home Front everything conspired to make him a martinet.

We 'other ranks' were chronically insubordinate. We didn't want to be part of his outfit, we weren't even sure (except for my mother) that we were on the same side. Sensing this, he was on the lookout for signs of disrespect, edgily insistent on his authority – all the more so since it was under such pressure in his business dealings with customers and employees. In the army, if you'd come up through the ranks, they never sent you back to your old regiment after giving you a commission, you joined a different regiment where your brand-new role as a leader of men wouldn't be questioned. But when my father returned to Hanmer, where his only pre-war command had been in the Boy Scouts, he found himself having to establish who he was almost every day.

At home he was certainly the only grown-up, there was no other court of appeal. The Buck Stopped with Him, was how he saw it. The army years had inserted a ramrod into his personality, along with the shrapnel lodged next to his spine in Normandy. War gave him a vocation, peace took it away, but left its ethos behind. He didn't identify with the officer class of the peacetime forces, cold-warriors of snobbery who drank gin and tonic in the mess and chatted among themselves. Fitting in and staying on was out of the question. However, he voted Tory in 1945, for he had come to think of himself, quixotically, as hierarchy's champion. He *missed* the war, it was his worst of times, his best of times, the time of his life. It was his university and his Grand Tour, and very nearly the end of him. He was surprised to find himself alive. But in some ways it was as though the big picture was over and life itself had shrunk in prospect. The daily 'debriefing' rant at Uncle Albert about the Business was therapy for this form of shell-shock and so was telling war stories.

Whenever the shadow of an occasion presented itself – and a cloud passing over the sun *could* do it, a casual remark about the weather – my father would recount his experiences to whoever would listen. Caen, Liège, Düsseldorf, Hamburg, Genoa, Trieste, Pola ... Kayesselleye only resolved itself gradually over the years into the initials K-S-L-I, the King's Shropshire Light Infantry, the regiment he joined a week after the war started in 1939 and left behind when he was commissioned. The foreign names were a familiar litany. Soon he'd be scoring the tablecloth with the wrong side of a knife blade, lining up the pepper and salt and the sauce bottle, and making maps of where he was wounded, where Jerry nearly overran them, where he won his spurs. Arise, Sir John Ridd!

My father was a prisoner of war, although he was never captured. He would retrace over and over again obsessively all his life afterwards the steps by which he'd come through to the end, when so many had not: muddy bootprints across the summer of 1944, tracks in the snow in the winter of 1944–5. He'd get a faraway look in his eye. Sometimes he'd shake his head in a kind of mimic bafflement. The 6th Battalion of the

Royal Welch Fusiliers, to which he'd been posted as part of the July reinforcement wave of the Normandy invasion, lost eighteen officers and two hundred and sixty men (half its officers and a quarter of the other ranks) within forty-eight hours west of Caen. This was when they made him a captain. The next thing he knew he was badly wounded (on 16 August) and shipped back to England. He'd lasted six weeks at the front, a lot of the time in trenches under heavy shelling. His stories weren't about the heroism of killing, but about the resolution, coolness and luck it took not to die. They were tales of survival with honour, which seemed to belong more to the First War than the Second.

There was even a story about going over the top into no man's land, although it was set in Germany. Casualties weren't so heavy when he rejoined the Royal Welch in the Ardennes, but it was there that he did the worst patrol of his life. The Germans had been in a pine forest on the other side of a steep valley, but were they now? He was sent with a sergeant and four men to find out. In between was a slope of virgin snow leading down to the stream at the bottom. The quickest way was to run down the slope: if they were fired on they'd know the answer. 'So we went over the top of the ridge here . . .' The rucked-up tablecloth turns to snow. They divide up, the sergeant and his two men about five hundred yards to the right, and run zigzagging down the slope in deep, soft snow, feet clogged and sticking; and when they're about three-quarters of the way down the Germans lurking behind the teapot and the sugar bowl open fire, and the sergeant's hit. He lies still, his men scramble back to the top, my father and his two, carried on by their momentum, reach the stream, take breathless cover under a bridge and wait for night, before trudging back. Mission accomplished. It had been done in broad daylight, with no cover and no snow suits. 'We were expendable, really,' he'd say without bitterness, drumming his fingers on the table. 'We were sent out there to see, sitting ducks.' The sergeant survived, he played dead and was taken prisoner. In this story my father, the sergeant and the men were all equal targets. In another story he carried a sub-machine gun when they were advancing through the Reichswald forest, because snipers in the trees picked out the profiles of officers armed only with pistols. In fact, he liked to think of himself as a captain with an NCO's saving sense.

It was in the woods that he was wounded the second time, carrying ammunition across a clearing (they'd overrun the range of their own guns and had to move their mortars back): a shell landed, two men were hit quite badly, but he was lucky, the piece of shrapnel that went through his teeth necessitated nothing worse than a session with the dentist after they'd delivered the ammunition – 'penicillin and anti-tetanus jabs and a few days living like a king with Divisional Staff'. By now it's nearly over, although there are some nasty moments in Trieste and Pola where he ends up peacekeeping among warring Yugoslav and Italian factions. Playing policeman isn't to his taste, exactly, but it's part of being a servant of law and order, command is a burden he bears. Although he is not, of course, a blind follower of orders like the abjectly obedient, heel-clicking enemy.

He speculated about this distinction a lot, for Germans, when he actually encountered them, were disconcertingly recognisable – square-set, fair, ruddy-faced, blue-eyed and relieved to be alive. One of his jobs as part of the occupying forces had been to supervise the herding of all adult Germans into the cinema to be shown films of the concentration camps. However, he'd found it hard himself to believe in their reality and to credit that his 'opposite numbers' in the Wehrmacht had known what was going on. Like many in the British Army he'd thought the worst reports about wholesale extermination of the Jews were Allied black propaganda, until he saw Bergen-Belsen for himself. But then, he'd reason, perhaps there was in the German character a penchant for abstract and mechanical solutions, something inhuman, fanatical. Whereas the British were in the best sense amateurs, chivalrous and independent-minded . . . Man versus machine. So his stories led him back to the present – getting up, stretching, putting on his overalls – with a renewed confidence in the sanity of home-grown realism. Memory only made him more intransigent. How I yearned to grow up, so that I could muster my own stories and fight him in the reality wars.

Family life drove me back to books and schoolwork with a passion, and gave my wanderings in the fields a guerrilla feel. When I was twelve my father stopped hitting me – not because I learned obedience, not even because I lied better, but for reasons of decency. My adolescent breasts and curves were beginning to give the whole performance a compromising, sexual savour. After all, spanking was a popular motif in 1950s films, a taming-of-the-shrew mating ritual. John Wayne spanked Maureen O'Hara particularly memorably in *The Quiet Man*, but it was happening on all sides. In romantic comedies, costume dramas, Westerns, grown women were being spanked as a form of foreplay. No wonder Dad was embarrassed.

At about the same time Uncle Bill (the socialist realist) sneered sideways at me round the wet end of his Woodbine and remarked that I was turning into the poor man's Brigitte Bardot. Then he made a grab and I shoved him into the frogspawn on the edge of Hunts' pond (we were on a country ramble) and tramped home. The radio was playing a love song, and I remember thinking disgustedly, so that's what it's about, Uncle Bill's greedy fingers. And so I told on Bill . . . No I didn't. I liked secrets and I kept my own counsel. I wasn't a child, I was definitely growing up. Leering Bill and my virtuous father both registered it in their different ways, even if they didn't have much idea what went on in my head.

XII

Family Life Continued

Any minute now I would be a teenager. My clock would strike
thirteen almost exactly in time with Bill Haley and his Comets,
the peremptory thud of that nice noise would rattle around in
my head at all hours, like blood beating in my ears. My parents
would complain and jeer at my sudden, slavish (and of course
tone-deaf) devotion to rock music, but at the same time they
were relieved. I was behaving as I was supposed to for once.
Rock'n'roll made the separation of generations official, teenagers post-1955 were a tribe apart, they marched to a different
rhythm. Being a teenager let me off the hook too, in a way, I
wasn't so conscious of my parents' obsessions, I paid them less
attention. Their 1950s was a different place.

And for the moment I was still lodged there, in pre-teen
limbo, loitering resentfully inside their lives, looking on. My
mother would take me along with her to meetings of the
Women's Institute in Hanmer parish hall, where large ladies
(true to Hanmer tradition, one was actually called Mrs Large,
another Mrs Cheers) organised charity draws, staged cake-
decorating contests, and politely listened to visiting speakers
spreading the word of Constance Spry on flower-arranging and
managing without help in the house. The WI song was William
Blake's 'Jerusalem', whose words ever after for me conjured
up that rickety village hall with its splintering floorboards and

jagged lines of folding chairs, where the old blackout curtains doubled as draught excluders: a temporary shrine to the matronly spirit presiding over whist drives and garden fêtes for five miles around.

Bring me my bow of burning gold. Bring me my arrows of desire sang the WI, dreaming of stainless-steel spatulas and electric whisks. Their tweeds smelled of damp and camphor, their jowls trembled under a coating of powder, their lipstick ran up into the cracks under their moustaches and their blue eyes watered from the fumes of the coke stove. They never took off their hats (felt, feathers) even when they shed their jackets to pass round tea and sandwiches. Most of them were older than my mother, or seemed so. They were substantial people of a kind we never saw except at church – better-off farmers' wives, wives and widows of professional men and their spinster sisters, interested in cards, gossip and competitive baking. My mother could contribute nothing under any of these heads: she didn't socialise, she was no good at all at cooking, or eating for that matter, so seemed entirely out of place. But she wasn't: she had her established role, her part to play, for the WI had a drama group which put on a play a year, plus a variety of entertainments which toured the other local branches, and in all of these she starred. This was where *her* arrows of desire were aimed. Her performing talent made up for her lack of local ties and her shortcomings with batter and marzipan. She was volatile, shape-shifting. Even her voice was foreign, she had kept her South Wales accent and its lilts and trills – let alone her sheer swiftness of delivery – sounded dramatic in themselves compared with the slower burr of Hanmer speech.

The solid WI matrons all petted her, but I regarded her amateur-dramatic doings with a revulsion that made me writhe and seethe. Every time she got on the stage – or even when she was learning her lines at home – I'd feel so angry it made me sick. It must have been partly vicarious embarrassment at seeing her habitual timidity and lack of confidence (wasn't I horribly shy myself?) transformed in this public exhibition. Or rather *not quite* transformed, for the particular awfulness of amateur acting is that you can always see through the disguise to the actual person underneath. My mother's acting seemed to me like a monstrous display of bad faith, she was pretending to be outgoing and self-possessed when 'really' she was helpless. Or, even worse, on the stage she was revealing the way she *always* pretended, for the helplessness she put on in real life was an act too . . . Her performances scared and repelled me, although I could see that she was much the best local actress and everyone else was applauding. Secretly, she was *doing this to me*, exposing *my* shyness as she indecently revealed her own frustrated longings for a more glamorous life.

And over the years it got worse, for the drama group gradually admitted the impossibility of roping in men to play men and the unsatisfactoriness of the Mrs Larges in drag, and concentrated on all-woman playlets, dialogues and monologues. Although some time in the early 1950s, perhaps in the patriotic afterglow of the coronation, they'd put on Noël Coward's *This Happy Breed*, later my mother was able to shine with Joyce Grenfell-style soliloquies – virtuoso tragicomic acts of self-exposure all *about* embarrassment, embarrassment squared. I raged. *Bring me my chariot of fire . . .*

I sang 'Jerusalem' silently and inwardly, taking its words away from the WI, wiping off the throaty voices, putting the letters back in the book and replacing the book on its shelf in the library in my head. Another great offence involved in acting was that it turned words into so much breath and spittle, and made them mix in company, whereas I wanted to savour them in solitude. When we built Jerusalem in England's green and pleasant land it would be, so far as I was concerned, a city of separate towers where you could retreat to commune in private, probably at night, with imaginary friends who'd step out from between the covers. Impersonating characters on the stage was a cruel assault on the whole race of unreal people.

I was privately contemptuous and disapproving of the very idea of performance (my stage fright shamed me, but that didn't mean that acting mattered). I had hundreds and hundreds of lines of verse by heart, which I paraded past my mind's eye as though in a way they were mine. Reading was already a kind of theatre, 'live' theatre was its literal-minded travesty. In fact, I read plays in private, too, not only set-book Shakespeare and Marlowe, but Shaw, Synge, Eugene O'Neill and even Coward and Terence Rattigan, whose works I borrowed from the library and who struck me – the last two – as the last word in smartness. I thought them quite unperformable. Their worldly characters were *ineffably* chic, they suffered from some kind of doomed yearning for perfection.

Ennui was a word that fascinated me, all the more because I had no idea how to pronounce it. Its foreignness was not French but fantastical, it belonged to the elsewhere I roamed in my avid, aimless reading. For although I read indiscriminately I edited out prosaic or realistic stuff, I didn't want to meet *lifelike* characters, I preferred characters who carried off their unreality with conviction. All my favourite books were poetical even when they weren't in verse and their authors – Rafael Sabatini, Rider Haggard – sounded like invented heroes of romance themselves. Not that I was very interested in who wrote what.

Books didn't belong to a particular time or place of origin, their contents all mingled and transmigrated. They were all one book, really – and indeed, I owned a book that could stand for all the rest, inherited from the vicarage and exiled from the public bookcase in the open-plan living-room because it had lost its spine and covers. This was *Poetry for the Young*, a fat School Prize anthology published in 1881 and much reprinted, a treasury of heroical and sentimental verses culled mostly from the Romantics and their Victorian followers, particularly Mrs Hemans and Longfellow. *Poetry for the Young* had murky engravings of castles by moonlight, shipwrecks and birds – the only form of wildlife ethereal enough to carry its message, for although it was packed with rhymes about nature's busy doings (storms, torrents, tides) it was absolutely silent on animal appetites and contrived to confuse love with waving goodbye to one's native land. Its real subject was death: death in infancy, death in the far corners of empire, death at sea on the way there – and just plain old death. Death was *Poetry for the Young*'s great prize. Dying, anyone was elevated to the condition of poetry: Blake's chimney sweep, Byron's gladiator 'Butcher'd to make a Roman holiday', the boy on the burning deck, the minstrel boy, Somebody's Darling, Ozymandias, Poe's Lenore, Lord Ullin's daughter who rhymed with water, the Forsaken Merman, the Solitary Reaper, Simon Lee the old huntsman, Gray's mute inglorious Milton, and Lucy like a violet by a mossy stone even while she lived, which wasn't long. This world was 'the bivouac of life', the mere 'suburbs of eternity', in Longfellow's memorable phrases. The last words in *Poetry for the Young* went to Shelley: 'O World, O life, O time, On whose last steps I climb . . .' Bliss. Ennui.

I'm digressing, wandering away from my mother's world – but that was always exactly the point of the books, you could escape into them. No one followed after to investigate my reading habits, for although my mother carefully preserved the vicarage books and even dusted them occasionally, she never opened one, not ever. She read only play scripts from French's, *Woman's Own* and the reports on local amateur-dramatic events in the *Whitchurch Herald*. She had resolutely turned her back on reading when she was betrayed by Grandpa – it was as if he lurked inside the books, along with his promiscuity, duplicity and self-indulgence. Obviously this wasn't spelled out. In theory my mother thought reading a good thing, but you could tell from the small shudder and sniff with which she said that she didn't have time for it that she was keeping herself pure. And I knew that she was right, the books were haunted. The bookcases not only had a bad case of vicarage woodworm, endangering the new council-house three-piece suite, they were a graveyard, you could bury yourself in a book and slip away into anti-social, delinquent ennui. Grandma may have lived with us in the flesh, mumbling sponge cake and wheezing, but Grandpa was still around too. He emerged like a genie from a bottle whenever I communed with the dandyish and despairing characters in his leftover library. Didn't my mother wring her hands and say that he'd spoiled me?

I was so secure of my own monopoly on transgression that I simply didn't see that when she went on the stage *she* was his girl too. But the large ladies certainly saw him in her. The WI seemed so wholesome, matronly and respectable that it never occurred to me to make the connection – even though I had the example of Nurse Burgess before me every day – but in fact more than one of those tweedy spinsters had had an affair with Grandpa. They saw in my mother's acting talent a glimmer of his bitter, needy eloquence, no doubt. Just when I thought I had his ghost safely solipsised, there he was, true to form, still philandering in others' memories. I identified him with the books with the blacked-out titles, there (I thought) I had him to myself.

The only person who knew what was in the books was my mother's brother, Uncle Bill, and he affected to despise them. He said that fiction was a waste of time, the opium of the bourgeoisie, that you had to get a real grip on the facts of life. He had books of his own and even a shelf of his own in the bookcase, since he was always flitting from one bedsit to another and liked to travel light. There he lined up books on evolution and fat teach-yourself tomes with no-nonsense titles like 'Mathematics for the Million' and 'Science for the Citizen'. However, he'd also added quite a few volumes to Grandpa's collection of unrealities: *Gone with the Wind*, *Forever Amber*, *King's Row*, *The Werewolf of Paris* among them. These I read too, enchanted by their news of forbidden love, civil wars, corsetry through the ages, incest and necrophilia. Uncle Bill's rejected collection of escapist classics looked and felt different from vicarage books. This was not only because you could read their spines, but also because he'd bought them in Canada, where he was stationed at the end of the war, and they exuded North American profligacy in their very bindings and their extravagant use of paper, at a time when English books were printed close and meanly. This difference was impressed on my sensibility for ever the night I finished *Gone with the Wind*, reading in bed, no one else awake: as I neared the end, speeding on, I could feel with my right thumb the reassuring thickness of the pages left to turn and *knew* there had to be a happy ending. And then – nothing! Just a mocking set of blank pages left over by careless binders. I cried and cried. After that, for years, I used to check automatically when I started a book what the end pages looked like. Uncle Bill introduced me to the material nature of culture without even knowing it.

Bill's born-again fidelity to hard fact wasn't entirely consistent. There were collections of cod-anthropology on his documentary shelf – *Strange Customs of Courtship and Marriage* was one I pored over. It offered titillating and vague descriptions of traditions like 'bundling', which seemed to involve nothing more exotic than pre-marital sex between courting couples in the chilly north. They were probably clinging together for warmth. Of course, at the time (when even married people in the movies couldn't be shown sharing a double bed) this was dynamite. I knew these *Strange Customs* were supposed to provide illicit thrills, but I couldn't get on the right wavelength, I read the book again and again out of sheer bafflement and disappointment.

That was more or less my reaction to Uncle Bill, too: he proved a lot less of a kindred spirit than he seemed, despite his rows with my father about Business. He was realistic too, in his own way – at least he loathed idealities and took a suspicious amount of pleasure in stripping truth bare. Hunger was real, sex was real, and money was more real than either since it enabled you to satisfy these other wants. Bill would rock from his heels to his toes with his hands in his pockets, grinning impatiently and rattling his change while he made his demystifying speeches. He was small and wiry, and always looked rather hungry himself, although he preferred smoking to eating. He was certainly sex-starved, he'd boast with a bitter snigger, marriage was a mug's game, buying and selling was all it was about: private property in women. Without money you had to make do with what was going and not be too fussy. He didn't seem to mind that I'd rebuffed his advances (the poor man's Brigitte Bardot), he was doing me a favour by introducing me to the brute facts, as I'd find out for myself in time. Our educational walks didn't cease altogether, or at once, but I kept at a suspicious distance; I felt mocked, he didn't take me seriously as a fellow reader.

Bill was and wasn't a member of the family: he was an outsider, a self-declared black sheep, which I had imagined when I was small as one of those sheep that roamed the slag heaps in the Rhondda, stained with soot and rummaging through dustbins, and in a way I wasn't far wrong. He was resolutely urban and regarded Hanmer with contempt. He'd moved after the war to Wolverhampton and worked with someone he'd met in the air force as a sort of freelance handyman, patching up and painting factory buildings; he was not (as he led me to suppose) a worker on the factory floor. He also went to night school since, like my mother, he'd dropped out of school in his teens when Grandpa and Grandma were too busy tearing each other to shreds to notice. He had an idea of studying to become an architect, although he mainly went to classes, he said, to pick up women and save money on the gas meter. Anyway, he was too restless to stick at anything, and took pride in his rootlessness and indigence. Come the revolution the solid folk would find out what was what.

Meanwhile he relied on casual labour and handouts from Grandma. Billy (as she always called him, he was her boy still) was entirely exempt from her otherwise universal hatred of the male race, he could do no wrong. She saved up her pension and stinted on her contributions to the council-house budget in order to bail him out when he ran short, as he so often did. Perhaps this was why he turned up at all – although he was an addicted wanderer and scavenger. He kept a pair of bicycle clips in his pocket in case someone might want to lend him a bike.

His visits could be relied on to create an atmosphere you could cut with a knife. My father's air of conscious virtue would become more pronounced than ever, since although he 'rowed' with Bill about politics, it was just symbolic sparring; he never let himself go about the money, in deference to my mother's feelings. So far as I was concerned, Bill steadily dwindled in importance. Far from turning me into a fan of fact, he actually reinforced my conviction that imaginary beings were *more real*. My scenarios of revolution were acted out by quixotic figures in period costume, he was seedy, implausible and one-dimensional by comparison. I was still alone in my head. More so, in a way. It was round about now, just in this pubescent moment between childhood and licensed teenage moodiness, that I found you could sometimes be more satisfyingly separate in the company of your family than on your own.

Saturday afternoon outings to the pictures with my parents took on a new meaning. Acting on the cinema screen was blissfully free from the alienating personal dimensions of drama in the parish hall. The great thing about the stars was that you felt they had been assumed entire into the heaven of immortals. Kirk Douglas and Jean Simmons may have showed through their roles in *Spartacus*, for instance, but they themselves – 'Kirk Douglas', 'Jean Simmons' – were safely larger-than-life and quite unreal; *they*, not the feeble fictions they put on, were the heroes and heroines of the Hollywood Big Picture. They were always themselves, her eyes always soulful, her lips tremulous, her smile sweet and impulsive, her ankles thick; his teeth always gritted, the dimple in his chin as improbable as Popeye's. The stars could mingle with the people out of my favourite books with no difficulty. Watching movies with my family, I was transported, my mother and father and bored Clive would vanish into the stuffy dark until they were nothing but a rustle of sweet papers.

When we left the cinema I'd loiter to delay the moment of facing the grey light outside and to commune with the framed portraits of stars in the foyer. I would sneak glances at myself in the mirrors, seeking a reflection of their dreamy, pancaked finality in my own face, finding for a moment a touch of glamour in the heavy-lidded eyes of my sleeplessness. All the Odeons, Gaumonts and Majestics back then had whole sequences of curving, carpeted foyers and corridors, which acted like airlocks or green-rooms, antechambers to fantasy. When we walked out past the queue for the second house, I kept slightly apart from my family, imagining strangers' eyes on my face. Perhaps they'd realise that I didn't belong to these people at all, that I moved secretly in much grander company.

But on the way home from Wrexham or Shrewsbury I was regularly carsick, headachy and hung-over from the combined effects of the airless excitement of the cinema and the fish and chips afterwards. Sometimes we stopped for me to be sick in a lay-by, more often I'd swallow the rising bile, lapse into a groggy doze and replay the film on the inside of my eyelids with the drone of the car engine for soundtrack. It was hard, though, to sustain the illusion. Our cars were noisy, their exhausts and silencers were semi-detached from bumping over farmyard potholes, their engines coughed and rattled. Cars came after trucks in the Business order of priorities and my father tinkered with them hastily to keep them going. The car often needed repairs en route and he kept an old oily pair of overalls in the boot for routine emergencies. When he couldn't get it to start at all, we climbed into the cab of a truck in our best clothes, Clive and I squeezed between my mother and my father on the gearbox. So our outings threw us together. Even in the car (unless Grandma came, which she sometimes did, although she would never, never have condescended to ride in a truck even if there'd been room) we felt like a family business, a human limited company. The car was one of us, it played a part in making us one at all, the 1950s nuclear-family model:

two parents and two-point-something children travelling along life's highway, socially mobile, their own private enterprise.

Clive and I, in the back seat or sandwiched between our parents in the lorry, were made to know our place. We were the passengers, they were in charge. Except that it was all tied together with string. Once, on a winter Saturday, coming back from Wrexham in the dark, my mother from the passenger seat – always in character, fanciful and far away – said dreamily what a pretty pattern the headlights were making, flickering on the hedge as we passed. My father had started on an indulgent reply (how like her, how impractical, just as well she didn't drive) when he suddenly did a double-take and braked hard. The engine was on fire. We all scrambled out and stood shivering at the roadside while he first opened the bonnet and then hastily shut it again when the flames leaped out. He made off at a sprint to a garage a mile down the road, and we stood in the circle of firelight and watched the car burn. It wasn't until another passing motorist stopped and shooed us away that we realised our danger. It might blow up: this was a more serious breakdown than usual. But then my father arrived with the garage breakdown truck and a fire extinguisher, and eventually we were ferried back to Hanmer, leaving our Standard Vanguard on the forecourt covered in foam.

After that we went out in the lorry for a while, until my father acquired a new second-hand car to work to death. The car-that-went-on-fire became a family story in which somehow my mother's fey remark supplied the comic point, not my father's sketchiness as a mechanic and definitely not our narrow escape from being barbecued. Our family life may have been a fragile construct, my parents may have been making it up as they went along, but they were good at improvising – at least so far as their story went.

They always closed ranks and pretended that everything was solid, normal and natural. Here we have the family of the period: self-made and going places. Only when you look more closely can you see that this housewife is pathologically scared of food, hates home, is really a child dreaming of pretty things and treats; and this businessman will never accumulate capital, he's still a boy soldier, going over the top again and again. Their obsessions had met, fallen in love and married; they completed and sustained each other. In the pictures of their austere wartime wedding, he has only just grown a moustache in order to look old enough to give orders and she is smiling like a star. Their insecurity and hopefulness are disarming, if you think of them as a couple. But I didn't, back then. They left *no room*. Family life was the open-plan living-room, the family car. It was like a nightmare council house on wheels.

Still, Grandma gave the lie to the notion that marriages were made in heaven; Bill too, with his *Strange Customs*; and my mother's friend from before the war, Ivy the divorcee, was compounding her offence by seeing a new man and planning to marry again. Ivy did more than anyone to liberate me from domestic claustrophobia, for reasons of her own, for she needed somewhere for her daughter Gail to go in order not to cramp her style. And so Gail, my old Hanmer school enemy, came to be included (by arrangement with my mother) in some of our Saturday outings.

Gail was admitted into our family circle, while everyone else was kept out, because she was in no position to inform on us and her mother was in no position to criticise my mother's housekeeping habits. I remember looking across at her with a kind of wonder one damp afternoon, as we sat on stones in the mountains at Llangollen sharing our soggy banana sandwiches, while my parents and Clive sat veiled by condensation in the car. It seemed so improbable that she was really there, as though she'd stepped out from behind a mirror. Her hair was fawn, mine yellow, her eyes green, mine blue, her skin pale olive and moist, mine pale pink and dry, but she was seething with resentment and that was why we recognised one another. Tentatively, we talked our way on to common ground. She loved animals, I loved books, but her animals were mostly phantasms – the pony her mother couldn't afford, the dog she couldn't have because local farmers shot pet dogs on principle, the iguana she couldn't have either because you only saw them in the reptile house at the zoo.

Learning to swim was the first important thing we did together. Gail was good at gym and athletics, but like me she'd been put off swimming by high school excursions to Whitchurch Public Baths – small, steamy, stinking of chlorine, with cracked tiles and deafening echoes, the gym mistress counting to three and pushing you in. Now, in the summer holidays, she and I went down to the mere like other Hanmer kids (who didn't much speak to us since we'd passed the eleven-plus), changed on the bank among the goose and duck droppings, and fooled around in warm water that smelled of rain until we found we could float and then swim – although in a style that horrified the gym mistress when we went back to school. Even now, if I say to myself 'dog-paddle' I can see Gail's head sticking up out of the soupy mere water in her rubber bathing hat, her eyes hard as pebbles with determination, her eyelashes glued together with the wet, while she paddled furiously and hardly moved at all. I kept pace and did the same, we both learned to dog-paddle and soon it was easy to swim whole lengths, even in the horrible baths.

Being disaffected daughters brought us together and, once together, we could leave our parents to take care of themselves.

Just before she was thirteen Gail was a bridesmaid at her mother's Register Office wedding and this seemed to us both a rite of passage. She and I now formed a kind of miniature generation in ourselves, we were furiously impatient to be teenagers. I could never have thrown myself into the part with such conviction without her. She did away with the defects of loneliness, not its private intensities – which I suppose is one way of describing how friendship works.

Swimming was wonderful after failing to learn to ride a bike and climb ropes. And I could do it alone, too, as part of my communings with Hanmer's muddy essence. Lying to my parents, I'd claim a date with Gail and make off down the fields to swim all by myself. Once, wrinkled brown Mrs Jones, who lived in one of the oldest Mere Cottages, where the floor was made of earth and she'd sit by the fire with a swan on her lap for company, came out and shook her fist at me, and threatened me with drowning. I trod water and waved back. Poetry for the Young.

PART THREE

XIII

All Shook Up

Whenever I went round to Gail's house, her mother Ivy was on a stepladder with her hair in a scarf and a cigarette in the corner of her mouth, expertly manoeuvring the edges of the next pasty sheet of wallpaper into place, matching up the neoclassical scrollwork or the groves of bamboo. Now that she was married again Ivy also had a council house, at Horseman's Green. Here she set about home-making with restless idealism. She redecorated the whole place with embossed wallpaper in different pastel patterns, and she enjoyed doing it so much that as soon as she'd finished she would pick away at a corner, strip a room and start all over again. Gail's new home was always making, never made and that suited her fine, for she had been an only child with a single parent much too long to take kindly to this new set-up.

Her stepfather pretended she didn't exist. He was called Mr Ward, a quiet man with a blue-collar job who kept himself to himself. His passion was breeding budgerigars in the back garden. Gail crossed budgies off the list of living things she loved – although she had a bit more time for the sleek black mynah bird who lived by the back door and could imitate to mocking perfection Ivy's smoker's cough and the infant lisp of her new little sister Denise. 'Mummy'th thilly', the mynah would whisper if you got very close to his cage. Gail agreed.

She was one of those child stars who find it hard to grow up. She'd been an unqualified success as a little girl, with her ringlets and her pretty clothes and physical graces; now she set about being an awkward adolescent with redoubled zeal – she wouldn't be reconciled to losing top billing.

We were made for each other, born again as best friends. Together we were teenager incarnate. When we were torn apart at night we attuned our psyches via Radio Luxembourg and held our breath on the Top Twenty countdown to number one in case our idol had been toppled by some saccharine trash left over from before the revolution. We hedged our bets. Out of pin-ups and clippings we pieced together a composite hero – a monster of narcissism to match our discontented dreams. He had ennui to spare for me, animal passion for Gail, softness and hardness, pale suede skin and a heavy dark mane, and vacant, hungry, wolfish eyes with bambi lashes. His knees buckled with lust when you let go his strings and he clung to the mike or (was it?) his guitar for dear life, keening, 'Jus' take a walk down lonely street, jus' put a chain aroun' my neck an' lead me anywhere, don' be cruel . . .' He was mostly Elvis, but then Elvis was nobody, anybody's. His slack mouth, his lewd, fat tongue and that flickering sneer were all spoken for, long before the *Zeitgeist* stuffed him full of tutti frutti and he was crowned king of kitsch.

Elvis's sort were shiftless, driven not by ambition but glands. They slouched, spasmed and moaned about fevers and chills, and comedians made jokes about apes that were code for the wrong colour. Elvis was from the wrong side of the tracks, and even more Jerry Lee Lewis, with his ecstatic Southern Baptist last-days babble (Great Balls of Fire!) – poor white, white trash, the sort that blurred the black–white line. What we saw was country boys with *carpe diem* written all over them.

We want it now. They came from the back of beyond with mud on their souls, they were heroes of outside. When Elvis travestied himself on the screen in *Love Me Tender*, stumbling after a horsedrawn plough behind the credits – and we fell about laughing, for who could resist? – we still saw that the sentimental lie was telling the truth. There was one particular publicity 'still' we treasured, posed behind the scenes during the making of that first awful movie: Elvis in denim lolling on a canvas chair among tangled cables, looking like one of the crew rather than the star. He had a Coke bottle tilted to his lips, his hair was spiky with grease and sweat, and his other (right) hand with the signet ring hung loose from the armrest, long fingers idly splayed.

I describe this picture as if I had it before me, although it's forty years since Gail and I clawed it to bits with our new long nails. This was the Elvis we loved, the muck-shoveller manqué, and we scorned his clean-cut wholesome rivals – particularly Pat Boone, who was tanned and scrubbed, with a parting in his fair hair and what my mother called a nice, light voice. One memorable day when Ivy and the stepfather took us for a trip to Southport, Gail and I spent all our time and pocket money dashing from one jukebox to another to make sure that Pat Boone's chaste hit 'Love Letters in the Sand' would be drowned out all over the windswept town by 'All Shook Up'. The one was sweetness and light, the other inarticulate, insidious bump-and-grind. 'Please don' ask me what's on my min', I'm a little mixed up but I'm feelin' fine . . .' All the Elvises groaned and whimpered at once, and the waves rushed in and obliterated Pat Boone. And we clung to each other in a shelter smelling of orange peel and piss on the promenade, and shrieked with glee, like the Bacchae who dismembered Orpheus.

The tide only came right in a couple of times a year at

Southport, but our euphoria supplied the rainbow spray. *Nothing lasts* was what we meant. Rock's idols were prodigal, noisy with nothing, jumping jacks who wanted the world, but most of all to be wanted, so that all their frantic, restless energy drained away and they were yours. Their existence was brittle as a seventy-eight, two-dimensional as a picture, we had to make them real. We wanted to eat them all up, what big eyes we had, if we swallowed them whole we'd take on their powers, they'd be ours, they'd be us. When Jerry Lee arrived for a British tour with his fourteen-year-old wife who was also his cousin, the sin the lost boys sang about came out into the open. Shake, baby, shake. Sex for kids now. 'Go away,' Mrs Jerry hissed at the reporter from the *News of the World*, through the crack of the door of their suite at the Ritz or the Savoy, 'Go away, Jerry and I are in bed.' Instead, they were packed off themselves, drummed out of the country for their hillbilly customs of courtship and marriage. There was a lot of huffing and puffing and moral panic over their lack of shame, their backwardness. They didn't know any better. We imagined her bouncing on the five-star bed in her Baby Doll pyjamas. 'I just wanna be yo' teddy bear,' Elvis sang.

The sex in the songs was a second chance at childhood. In Hanmer and Whitchurch, in theory, you couldn't afford the time to be a teenager, you were supposed to go out to work at fifteen, or if you were still at school you had your sights fixed on the future. A few intellectual tearaways at the boys' grammar school talked about jazz and existentialism, but they were practising for university. Rock was slumming – a dangerous game in the sticks, although from the start it was contained and packaged.

In one of the earliest rock movies, *The Girl Can't Help It*, there's a scene where Fats Domino, seated at the piano, sings over his shoulder about the holiday joys of Saturday night to an all-white, twitching, bopping audience, some of them in their bow ties and Peter Pan collars no more than thirteen years old at most. Beaming Fats himself is already about sixteen stone, plump-faced and also very young, but as knowing as hell, he comes from a place where time is different. In *The Girl Can't Help It* black and white performers never appear on the stage at the same time, and black and white actors never share the same shot, except in one scene where Jayne Mansfield's black maid can't resist kicking up her heels and rolling her eyes to the rhythm when white-but-grubby Eddie Cochrane appears on television. This gives the new teenage music the seal of authenticity but it also maintains decorum: we *know* we're slumming, just playing. Watching this film was like getting lost in the fun house. There were the boys being cuddly and hysterical, all shut up in playpens. Jerry Lee and Mrs Jerry – Myra was her name – were miscegenating fact and fancy.

There was a great mystery here: did being a teenager mean you grew up faster, or slower? Were Gail and I tense with excitement or bored stiff? Or both at once? We crackled with emotional static. As we waited for the bus, or dawdled Whitchurch streets, we held hands to earth ourselves – not gently or sentimentally, but squeezing hard as though we'd fall or float any minute and only our interlaced fingers kept us grounded. We regarded Hanmer mores with scorn and went off into gales of contemptuous giggles if avuncular Hanmer types asked us when we were going to start courting. *Courting!* Nonetheless we scrutinised the Young Farmers (*young!* some of them were pushing thirty, waiting for their red-faced fathers to die or retire) looking for any sign – sideburns a little too long, a dark glance – that they *knew*. But knew what? Something we knew, or something we didn't? The world teased us with possibilities. Even the tame boys who played ping-pong and drank warm pop at vicarage socials could take on in three-quarters profile, in the right shadow, a louche look. We talked for hours – to each other, not to them – speculating, reading in the symptoms of suppressed want.

It was a thankless and perverse task, particularly with vicarage 'do's', for the new order in the vicarage was peaceful and bland. Mr Hopkins, my grandfather's replacement, was a mild-mannered man – mildly snobbish, mildly well-off (his children went away to school) – not given to showy sermons or excesses of any kind. There were no dark corners left in the vicarage, it had been thoroughly spring-cleaned. Mrs Hopkins let it be known that the house was in a scandalously dirty state when they moved in and she was understood to refer to moral hygiene as well. Now it was light and open to inspection, and Mr Hopkins held his blameless ping-pong parties in the attic and confirmation classes in the parlour that used to turn dusty blind eyes to the square.

The confirmation classes, as it turned out, provided more of an occasion for sin than the table tennis. After a couple of sessions the old vicarage spirit of place, so ignominiously turned out of doors, prompted me to take a stand. I stayed behind when the others left and announced that I couldn't be confirmed because I didn't believe in God. This was true: a combination of *Poetry for the Young*, Shaw, Hardy and my grandfather's defection had turned me at thirteen into a believer in Universal Mortality and Pitiless Nature. Mr Hopkins, however, was not interested in the state of my ideas. He seemed weary and embarrassed by my apostasy, and said that he thought I should anyway be confirmed because if I wasn't it would look odd and my parents would be upset. I was outraged by his superficiality and worldliness, and at the same time hugely gratified.

I took his advice and extorted from my mother a pair of new white shoes *with heels* to be confirmed in. These had to be worn with proper stockings, which meant I had to have a suspender-belt, which meant that confirmation was in truth a rite of passage. The actual ceremony left me cold – it was the first and last time I ever took communion. Gail, ever avid for sensation, claimed that she felt a definite frisson when the Bishop laid his hands on her head, but she didn't go back for more either.

The magic of the Church no longer impressed us. Our own bodies were more mysterious than the wine and wafers, and the whimsical notion put about by the Mothers' Union that the spell of the marriage service changed a couple's every atom in order that they could make babies had never seemed very convincing in Hanmer, where so many brides went bulging to the altar. The Church's job was more like exorcism, turning the incubus into a husband and provider after the event.

Once, when Gail and I went swimming in the mere the summer I was thirteen, just such a bad boy was staring moodily into the water, sentenced to be married in two days' time. His way home, we knew, took him past the end of my lane and I hung about for a daring hour that evening pretending to pick blackberries from the hedge, hoping he would spare me a desperate word, even a doomed kiss, but he never came by. Instead, the late summer midges gathered round and sucked my blood, and their bites festered and blistered since I'd become wildly allergic to all sorts of new things. My body was over-reacting to every stimulus, from inside or outside, my period came every three weeks in a heavy iron-smelling flood, along with backaches, headaches and cramps. Each time I'd swell, and then lose pounds in a couple of days off school, moping around the house, insulated with aspirin and groggy daydreams.

The metabolic misery had its pleasurable side. I'd writhe in a chair and read, and wrap the bloody sanitary towels in brown paper and poke them into the back of the fire, where they smouldered slowly, like me.

Bad blood, excited blood. My nose bled, too. It seemed that no sooner had I got over my fear of the water and learned to swim than the chlorine in the baths inflamed my sinuses and I had to be excused swimming lessons. This was galling because I had found at last a way of impressing my enemy the gym mistress. I wasn't a fast or stylish swimmer, but I could dive into the deep end. Once you'd taken the plunge, gravity did the rest, diving was a wonderful cocktail of inertia and adrenalin, not at all like vaulting over her headless horse, although she thought it was and looked at me with new respect until chlorine made me a malingerer once more. By then I'd had my long hair cut off, to be sleek in a bathing hat. I didn't really regret it, for I'd always associated my pigtails with the shameful years of bugs. Now I had teenage hair, the sort you endlessly, hopefully, experimented with, in page-boy bobs, with and without fringes, sticky with sweet-smelling eau-de-Nil-coloured setting lotion called Amami and crisped like candyfloss with hairspray. Gail, after all *her* years of ringlets wrapped in rags every night, enjoyed the freedom to make her own mess of her hair even more than I did.

Soon, under orders from the Spirit of the 1950s, we both settled for ponytails, and after that our hair was always halfway up and halfway down, our fringes forever growing in or growing out; we were almost ideally untidy. Hair and nails were our fetishes. We didn't use our clippings to make voodoo dolls, but split ends and bitten cuticles were just as spookily significant as if we'd believed in their magic. They were us and not-us, a sign language which expressed our restless conviction that we meant something new. Nothing about them was trivial. If you changed one part of that language, then other things shifted too.

For instance, ponytails were a particular key because they simply didn't go with school uniform berets. You either had to tuck all your hair inside your beret and look almost bald, or anchor the silly hat on top (more slides and clips and grips) folded flat like a felt pancake. Obviously it was easier, more decorous even, to take it off and put it in your pocket. And at the same time you could turn your school cardigan back to front to look like a turtle-neck sweater (and hide your tie), pull in the belt of your school mac to make a wasp waist and there you were – wearing the Other uniform of the girls who hung around the streets giving Whitchurch High School a bad name. Gail and I deliberately missed the school bus on many afternoons and caught instead the later one that ferried shop assistants and Silhouette factory workers back over the border at five o'clock. This gave us an extra hour in which to chase boys we pretended were chasing us, and sit spinning out plastic cups of grey, frothy coffee as we watched the coloured lights pulse between plays in one or other of the town's curvy new jukeboxes.

Gail had a gift for intentness. She could caress shapeless moments like these as if she was stroking a puppy, until they wriggled into life and sucked your fingers. Even in school she'd people the corners of the day with adventure. She was adept at cultivating crushes on the prefects. She would pick out some gaunt, sporty girl to bamboozle with slavish devotion, following her around, imitating her style of serve, drawing her profile on the blackboard, asking her what was her favourite colour, poring over her horoscope – and then suddenly transfer her allegiance to another, leaving the first wrong-footed, missing attentions she was supposed (according to the rules of this game) to regard with entire indifference. Gail's crushes were so exigent and arbitrary that it was as though the prefects were the suitors, not she. I was her confidante and shared her obsessions, but it wasn't freckled Dina the hockey captain or willowy, double-jointed Jean who inspired my hero-worship. My crush was on Gail herself, I was fascinated by her strength of conviction. She played the part of Shaw's St Joan when we read aloud in class. She was Jane Eyre, she was Cathy ('Nellie, I *am* Heathcliff!'), she was the heroine.

Later, when we actually talked to some of the boy gang from the grammar school who'd noisily ignored us in coffee bars, they told us that they'd known straight away (a) that we were lesbians; and (b) that Gail was using me – dreamier, curvier, blonder – as her stalking horse, to hunt down boys she wanted. We were amazed and outraged, but not, alas, for the right reasons. We should have been appalled by their crass assumption that 'lesbian' meant limbo, the *faut de mieux* condition of females lacking males, and by their inability to imagine that a girl gang (even of two) could generate a frenzy to rival their boy gang rites. But in fact we mostly shared their views.

We too took for granted that it was relations with boys and men that would enfranchise us as real women in the world. Our mutual obsession 'passed' as an unreality, and what made it easier was that apart from holding hands and a bit of grooming – hair-brushing and nail-filing – we never touched, all that kid stuff in the vicarage shrubbery (which anyway she'd never joined in) was lost back in the mists of time. Now, I think: the hands were enough. All our caresses were locked finger by finger into that one. That teenage rite of passage was an end in itself – not a matter of holding someone's hand while you cross the big road, but holding passions past and to be, rejected parents and siblings, ghostly lovers, husbands, children, pens and pets and self-love from the future, all in the palms of our hands.

Gail and I were determined never to marry or have children, thanks to our parents' example. Love and marriage went together like a horse and carriage. Dad was told by Mother, you can't have one without the o-o-ther. We knew better and decreed them absolutely separate in our imaginations. Meanwhile the solid Whitchurch girls at the high school played the game, confident that whatever we said, types like us wanted what they did, it was just that our Hanmerness was against us. My bugs and braces and Gail's mum's divorce and being bused across the border all accounted for the slackness of our grip on the real world, which was doubtless why we clung to each other in that affected way. So we weren't cast as outsiders or rebels. Outside was reserved for the secondary modern kids, who had failed the social test for which the eleven-plus was just a cover.

The middle-class part of the town kept its character by blandly ingesting anyone who didn't fit. One startling example of this was a girl in my form I watched narrowly because she was dangerously clever and certainly would have done better at maths than me except that I slaved over my homework. She was called Jean Evans, her dad had been away in the army during the war, but afterwards went back to work for the railways, and her mother had been a cashier in a proper shop. They'd married early in the war, like my parents, and were colourlessly respectable. Jean was an only child. So far so unsurprising. But Jean was black. Well, dark yellow with a bloom of sooty down and hair that was frizzy where it wasn't painfully pulled flat. Her father must have been one of the GIs briefly stationed near Ellesmere. However, no one in Whitchurch, and certainly not at school, ever noticed or mentioned this interesting fact. Jean was her parents' child and attended the high school, and that was that. There were no black people living in Whitchurch then, of course, which in a way may have helped to make her difference invisible. On the other hand there were plenty of 'common' girls who wore white lipstick and black eyeliner, and curlers in their hair all day long at the factory under their nylon headscarves: they were the ones you needed to draw the line against in those days, the poor whites.

Still, as a tribute to topical teenage angst, the headmistress arranged a make-up lesson by a lady from Pond's. Face paint was strictly forbidden in school, but it was understood that as nice, normal girls we were already dreaming of marrying men like Dad and needed to give off the right signals when we weren't in uniform. After a brief lecture about how to tell whether you had greasy, dry or combination skin, the Pond's lady picked out a couple of fourth-formers, one mouse-brown, one mouse-blonde, and set to work with foundation, powder, eyebrow pencil, eyeshadow, mascara and lipstick to demonstrate how to add make-up to the good girl's armoury. No red, no black, no white, for a start, and *no eyeliner*; instead, pink lips, pale-brown eyebrows and lashes, and blue eyelids. Natural make-up, said Pond's, whipping off their nylon bibs. Which meant more mouse, make-up that made you look neat, presentable, vulnerable; serviceable make-up that once you'd left school would last all day behind your secretary's desk with judicious touching-up; make-up for getting engaged, with pink nail varnish to match the lipstick when you showed off your ring. And above all *prophylactic* make-up. That particular shade of pink lipstick, the hint of turquoise in the awful eyeshadow, were contraceptives. They spelled heavy petting, *waiting*, saving for a semi. The only contraception available to adolescent girls was mythological, back in 1957, so why not Pond's Vanishing Cream?

Gail and I held hands throughout this scary demonstration of Whitchurch sexual *realpolitik*. She curled her lip, which was something she did beautifully – her face was fine-cut and finished, although the rest of her was pre-adolescent still. She would never need to draw lines round her lips and fill them in with pink grease to keep babies at bay. And I drew courage from her scorn when I privately tried out images for my own future self. My favourites were improbable on principle. There was the one from science fiction B movies, with sculpted cheekbones, hair in an immaculate French pleat, wearing a white coat and carrying a clipboard along the humming corridors of a nuclear power plant, with deferential men scuttling behind. Not that we did maths or physics or chemistry at the girls' high school, only something called general science, which didn't even have an O-level attached; you went to the boys' grammar school to take real sciences in the sixth form, if your parents agreed, and that was my private plan. Or one of them.

Another future came out of the past: Kathleen Winsor's best-selling Restoration romance *Forever Amber*, one of Uncle Bill's dirty books. Amber has been fostered by decent Puritan farming folk, but there's wanton aristocratic blood in her veins, and when the Cavaliers gallop back in 1660 she can't wait to be deflowered in the rotting leaves and hitch a lift to London. Amber falls in love with her ravisher, Lord Carlton, at first sight – he's a rake and a privateer, old enough to be her father, 'a man free from bonds and ties' who knows the old world and America, too. So her first sexual experience does it all, turns her into her own woman in one swooning paragraph: 'She was . . . glad with every fibre of her being that it had happened. It seemed until that moment she had been only half alive.' Although he never stays home and has no intention of marrying her, he's now her mentor for ever, and she takes on his rakish resourcefulness to become an actress and a scheming courtesan.

It was a story as mysterious as the Fall in Genesis. How did Carlton pass on his knowledge with one wave of his phallic wand? I pored over the gaps between the lines to no avail, as I did over the tantalising reference to contraception (also apparently entirely in Carlton's power), when Amber finds herself pregnant:

> 'I intended to be careful – but sometimes I forgot.' Amber looked at him, puzzled. What was he talking about? She'd heard in Marygreen that it was possible to avoid pregnancy by spitting three times into the mouth of a frog or drinking sheep's urine . . .

Amber never quite gets the hang of how not to start babies, but since we're in libertine land where you put patches on your plague sores, she has abortions or farms out children with impunity. What she doesn't ever, ever do is lose faith in her Lord. She may be a bad woman, but she's a real woman. Career girls all went to the boys' school. Amber wasn't, in fact, her own property; her very body was on loan.

But that we took for granted. The high school's best swimmer had to ask her parents and the headmistress for permission to use Tampax when her period clashed with a big competition, in case she demystified virginity. But there was little chance of such a thing. Everyone was swaddled in myths, that fourth-form year – perhaps especially Gail and I, who thought we weren't. Actual boys stayed elusive. We missed buses and fed jukeboxes, and in the meantime we had us. At school, every lunch break, on our own in the gym, we would get out a scratched seventy-eight of a track called 'Zambesi', with a jaunty saxophone solo, and practise the quickstep, Gail leading. We said to ourselves we'd rather be rocking, but we needed to know the quickstep for next year's school dance, when the fifth and sixth forms of the boys' and girls' schools would mingle. We could never get the bit with the crossed ankles right twice on the run, however. We were wrong-footed repeatedly and had to take up our positions again each time, holding hands at ballroom-dancing angle, our other two just touching her shoulder, my waist. Perhaps we got the steps wrong on purpose, for the pleasure of embracing each other so formally, so inconclusively. One, two three, back to square one.

XIV

Love–Fifteen

I always lost the first point when I played singles, but when we played doubles she'd be there, bobbing and weaving at the net, ready to savage some unwary opponent's return of my mild-mannered overarm service, and we'd start fifteen–love up. On the tennis court we did play the game the boys suspected us of – I was the decoy, my girly, limp-wristed strokes led people on and set them up for Gail's lightning shots. And if they went past her along the tramlines, or cheated her reach with a lob, I'd be there backing her up, hitting two-handed. I was a feeble player by any conventional standard and nothing would induce me to approach the net. But the things I could do – stubbornly return hard-hitters, place balls wide and deep with monotonous regularity and the occasional slice – looked wonderfully cunning and effective when fronted by her classic flair. She had an elegant, fast, heavy service, her scoops and leaps at the net were bliss to watch, and her backhand was spring-loaded, with no wobbles at all. I felt happily invisible. The court was hers, I only patrolled the baseline, self-consciousness forgotten. As we played we kept up a continuous sub-conversation of congratulatory murmurs, despairing groans and warning hisses ('Yours!', 'Leave it!') which drew us together in defeat and sweetened our victories.

Our finest moment was when we knocked out three pairs

of grown-up ladies in the County Championships before being eliminated ourselves, although we also looked falsely modest when the results of matches against other schools were announced in assembly. The headmistress was gratified: for once we were doing something to the high school's public credit, coming out of our subversive huddle. You couldn't hold hands *and* play tennis. However, we weren't at last learning the joys of competition or the team spirit, as she thought (she was a modernising moralist who hoped for great things from improved personal hygiene and the forthcoming New English Bible), but cementing our union of two.

The double act was the result of hour upon hour spent practising our parts in private, playing *against* each other. Hanmer's only sporting amenity, save for the mere, was a pair of new clay courts a mile out of the village, surrounded by a towering chain-link fence. Like the council houses, they made a squared-off hole in the village's manorial map and they dated from the same post-war era of small breaches in the feudal order. In the daytime in school holidays, when no one had leisure to play except people who had grass courts of their own, Gail and I had sole possession. Love—fifteen. I always lost, every match. I did sometimes manage to break her serve and even very occasionally to retrieve my own, coming from behind, whereupon she'd congratulate me, just as I'd commiserate when she served a double fault, or a smash went out, or a sneaky shot of mine – a return of a return – went past her at the net and I wasn't there on the baseline to look after it. We played ourselves. We played us and we won.

We were never bored with this perverse version of the game, which fitted our differences into each other like pieces of a puzzle. It wasn't simply a matter of Gail having the upper hand (although the will to win was certainly one of her cards), for my passive character exerted its own pull. Every time we played she would ride her bike to Hanmer from Horseman's Green to meet me, then dismount and wheel it beside her on our walk to the court, since I still couldn't learn to ride a bicycle and that she accepted, that was me. Indeed, she could have found another doubles partner at school at any time, someone who could really play tennis, but she never looked for one, she too was addicted to our Hanmer games. You could play tennis and hold hands.

On humid summer evenings the ageing Young Farmers organised easygoing mixed doubles and broke the spell. In their company we lost conviction, for it was gradually dawning on us that much as we didn't fancy them, they didn't fancy us even more. Paired off with one of these ruddy, solid men whose suntan stopped short at his rolled-up shirtsleeves, I'd look across the net and see Gail's glamour dwindle. Her mother's history and her family's plentiful lack of land were entirely anti-aphrodisiac for them, cancelling out the way her thigh muscles were moulded and the strength in her slim, knobbly wrists. And as for me, my family had no acres either, and their fathers, uncles and cousins all owed my father money for taking their livestock to auction, money they paid off at leisure, knowing he couldn't insist (offend one, and you'd have the whole clan conferring and switching their custom next Wrexham or Whitchurch market day). We might jeer at Young Farmers for sprouting hair in their ears or wearing long shorts, but they condescended to us comprehensively. They were down to earth, they had their feet on the ground. The farmer wants a wife, just as we'd sung in the playground under the churchyard wall. No wonder they made us feel insubstantial.

However, mixed doubles didn't do lasting damage to our love affair with tennis. Nor did the clouds of gnats and midges that came out at the same time as the Young Farmers, although I was horribly allergic to their bites, and several times was actually laid up with disfiguring, rubbery, amber-coloured blisters and elephantine ankles that had to be deflated by applying poultices of hot, grey clay. My legs were a source of shame and distress at the best of times – stocky, too short, mottled pink – so these ugly eruptions were almost a relief, an excuse to hide them altogether, adolescent stigmata like the hormone storms of spots that people would cover up with Clearasil. I coped better with 'passing' by now. Gail had given me the confidence to conform and tennis gave me the confidence to play hockey. I was a defender, naturally (left back in the second eleven), and for a freezing season I spent my Saturday afternoons stamping my feet behind the twenty-five-yard line, waiting to tackle tired forwards who had run half the field's length with the ball, passing and dribbling in great style, only to have me hook it aside and whack it back to where they got it from. Often it didn't work out like that, though, and after hockey fixtures my legs would be covered in purple-black bruises, cryptic coloration – like playing hockey itself, which was meant to appease the high school spirit.

I wasn't *joining in*, I told myself, only seeming what they wanted, blunting the distrust and dislike. Even sucking on oranges with the other ten at half-time, when our breath made one mist in the raw air, I was watching the effect dubiously from the sidelines. Still, hockey was a sign of a true difference between Gail and me: she never even played at team games, let alone played them. Apart from tennis, she only really went in for field sports and gymnastics, off the court her repertoire was severely early Olympic. She went her own way, but I lacked moral fibre. I couldn't resist the longing to be liked and accepted, even though it was so transparent its very intensity undermined my efforts. No one in the second eleven was more than dutifully friendly; they were embarrassed by my neediness and wary. Only in her company could I forget myself.

While I wanted to be wanted, she wanted to win her service with four impeccable aces, or break the school's javelin record and see the disbelieving look on their faces when they stretched out the tape, or keep a chimp as a pet, or grow all her nails at once without one breaking and paint them purple, or meet Paul Anka in person and convince him of her undying devotion. Her objects of desire were only just out of reach. They were vivid and particular, and their pursuit was an end in itself, frustration had its own pleasures. By contrast, the character of my wants was shadowy, vague and amorphous, and depended on people I probably didn't even know yet except in books – and except for Gail. I couldn't play games, for I was in deadly earnest, without her. There was only the search for recognition, being reflected back (every eye was a crystal ball) so you could imagine who you were. But people frosted over the more anxiously I peered. The two of us looked forward to our first school dance with very different hopes.

Preparations for making the gym-cum-assembly hall into a ballroom began in November, when Mrs Last's art students cut out stencilled clowns to transform the old blackout curtains into a carnival backdrop and hide the wall bars. It was the high school's turn to provide the premises and hire the band in 1957. We'd have preferred to go to the boys' school – with its picturesque playing fields on all sides and doric colonnade, it was a much better pastiche of a minor public school. There was even a forlorn little band of boarders whose fathers were in the army abroad. But we found it surprisingly easy to pretend that the gym was somewhere new and strange once the parquet floor, as always a little sticky from lunch, was sprinkled with

French chalk, the lights wreathed in pink net and hung with balloons and streamers, the classrooms either side converted into cloakrooms and the lavatories labelled 'Ladies' and 'Gentlemen'.

A couple of weeks earlier, to allow time for it to sink in, we'd been given a special lesson in ballroom etiquette for fifth-form debutantes: discreet mouse make-up; a pastel-coloured frock; *small* heels (nicer, and in any case boys probably wouldn't ask a girl who was taller to dance); eau-de-Cologne not scent; no straps showing, but lots of straps (even if you'd hardly any breasts going bra-less was unthinkable, it would have announced you were some kind of retard, a lack of elastic armour was a sign of moral idiocy like being cross-eyed and slobbering); you must accept if a boy asked you to dance, but you mustn't dance too often with the same boy; no holding hands between dances, you should both return to your corners like boxers when the bell rang; no dancing cheek to cheek; and – a new rule – no jiving, no rocking, no rolling. There were other prohibitions too, but they were too vulgar to bear spelling out. No adding alcohol to the fruit punch, no crude contact (no tongues, no bellies, no genitals, no thighs), no assignations on the dark hockey pitch . . .

And no more 'Zambesi' at break for Gail and me. This was the real thing, boys in the flesh. All the prohibitions, especially the ones that stayed unvoiced, had made boys much more exotic; it was as though we'd never met one. The whole school hummed with excitement and the headmistress's aspect softened with anticipation, for she was about to let the dangerous genie of adolescent sex out of its bottle and tame it. She spoke in veiled, suggestive terms in assembly of freedom and responsibility, and we giggled uneasily – it was all vaguely shocking, like being tickled by a policeman.

On the day itself we were allowed to go home in the afternoon to get ready. My mother and I had compromised over my new dress – her visions of me in floating white chiffon which anyway we couldn't afford, and mine of something cheap in all senses, off the shoulder and tight in the skirt, with a lot of dark red about it, which I'd seen in the catalogue, had converged on a princess-line calf-length frock 'that emphasises your pretty figure' mused the Shrewsbury saleswoman, looking over my shoulder, smoothing it down over my hips for just a little too long. It was Wedgwood blue, with a white pattern and a square nearly low neck, and I secretly liked it, although I complained it was babyish. Then back to school, to the hot, heaped-up 'cloakroom' and a confused smell of forbidden scent, bath salts, talc, hairspray and new-fangled, stinging deodorants, and familiar people transformed with shiny sandals and flushed faces jostling for the one full-length mirror. I thought I'd faint when we got into the gym, the ceiling seemed to have vanished, the room stretched upwards into space, and there were pools of solid-looking darkness on the floor and in the corners.

The awful business of beginning fell to the head boy and head girl, but at least they didn't have to choose, or be chosen. What if no one asked you? You'd gradually sink into oblivion and the dark would close over your head. Boys sidled across the hall, their temples glistening with sweat and Brylcreem, nudging and shoving each other, and suddenly here was one, saying 'May I . . .' Well, yes, the relief was enormous and this was easy, a waltz. Once my first pang of gratitude had subsided, I noticed that my partner was preoccupied too. He seemed to be having trouble remembering the steps, for he was pumping my arm and counting under his breath (one, two, three), and his breath smelled like the open maws of the pub cellars that gaped on Whitchurch pavements on delivery day. Beer. He'd been drinking and, although in theory this was glamorous because forbidden (and he was anyway certainly under age), in fact he was distracted, disjointed and clammy. He stepped on my feet (one, two . . .) and groaned as if his pain was greater than mine, and then it was over and I was back in my corner, my white shoes a bit scuffed, still waiting for the evening's true, occult ritual to start.

Now one of the scatter of sixth-formers wearing dinner jackets would surely pick me out, someone older (teachers only danced with teachers, alas) whose casual touch would unlock the mysteries of the quickstep and A-level physics. But my next two partners seemed just as inept and nervous as me. I wasn't getting anywhere and, as if to rub it in, my first partner was back, more dishevelled than before, his collar unbuttoned, mopping his brow. This time, instead of counting, he talked as we jogged around the floor, into my ear, in a whispered shout over the music: his mother had broken her arm falling from a stepladder in the shop where she worked, where she wouldn't have to work if her sons and her husband looked after her properly, which they didn't, his own bad behaviour was adding to her troubles, no wonder he was pissed . . . He snickered sarcastically and seemed about to burst into tears. This was awful. Each dance with him took me further from my imagined cavalier, he was leaving his messy mark on me – this time it wasn't just the bruised toes and the dirty shoes, there was definitely a damp patch on my dress in the small of my back where his hand had been and my hair felt sticky where he'd leaned on me to tell his story. Who was he? How could I get rid of him?

Back in the girls' corner, they knew who he was at least, he was a distant cousin of one of the fifth-formers, a gangling pariah called Sheila who had wildly protruding teeth and had once tried to befriend me when I was a pariah with braces. He was Victor Sage, his mother's pride but no one else's, well known for clowning, drinking and fighting after hours behind the Back Street Vaults, and they lived in Whitchurch on the council estate and his mother worked in Dudleston's, the drapers on High Street. My head was starting to ache. I went and stared at myself in the mirror in the 'Ladies'. Of course. That was where my mother had worked before the war, with Gladys, who must be his mother. I recalled mutual boasting sessions, once in particular when I'd passed the Scholarship, and so had Victor said his mother proudly to mine, pretending to wrap up some lingerie to borrow time to talk. In fact, my mother had often stopped off on the way to Mrs Smith's to talk to Mrs Sage as she now was, while I kicked my heels and tugged at her sleeve. My tormentor was essence of Whitchurch, then, part of the familiar tangle I so yearned to slough off. And he wasn't handsome either, with that gap-toothed grimace, although that wouldn't have mattered if he'd been the magical mentor I'd looked forward to, the prince of ennui.

Gail had done much better when it came to realising her imaginings. Her eyes shone and she hummed a few bars of Paul Anka's number one hit, 'Diana', about a mythical older woman, which was written when he was fourteen and inspired by falling in love with his babysitter. Against all the odds she'd discovered in Whitchurch a Paul Anka lookalike – same high cheekbones and black, black hair – and although this one's eyes were blue and Paul's were brown (he was 'of Syrian extraction'), they were deep-set and inward-looking in just the right way. He was called Michael Price, a boy like a startled gazelle who refused to dance at all; he was probably as unobtainable as a sonneteer's mistress and that was as it should be. For my part I returned to the floor furious. The deputy head boy asked me to dance, but by now it was too late. When Vic Sage reappeared, as I knew he would, I lost my temper, forgot I was shy, and told him to *go away*. He was shocked and staggered back on his heels for a moment, but it was no good, the last waltz was upon us and there was no time to wait for another partner. So we trudged around the gym one final time in silence, and then I bundled on my coat in the cloakroom, my punctual father in full view of everyone picked me up outside in a cattle truck (the car had broken down again) and my mortification was complete.

That encounter at the school dance would prove fateful, but not yet, not yet. At the time, it just seemed a bad start to the game. Love–fifteen. I was used to starting a point down, however, and I was no more lastingly disheartened by my experience than anyone else. We all – even girls who'd been wallflowers or had to dance with their brothers – developed over the next days before the Christmas holidays an air of being 'out'. Doing our Christmas shopping at lunchtime or after school, weighing up the merits of different gift packs of scented soap and bath salts for our mothers, and socks or hankies for our fathers (aftershave was still judged dangerously effeminate), we were doing a new dance you'd only have been able to see from a spotter plane, partnered by boys who were often hanging out a street or two away. Their steps were nonetheless synchronised with ours and vice versa, so at regular intervals our paths would cross and recross. It was a dance you could do sitting down in cafés or standing at bus stops, too, and included catching people's eyes, waving, making remarks designed to be over-heard and even small snippets of direct conversation, although they were mostly of the 'my friend says your friend told *her* that he saw you talking to me' kind.

Gail would stare Michael Price out of countenance until he flushed hot pink, which gave her a thrill; and we'd cross the road to avoid Vic Sage wheeling his bike along a Green End gutter, or walk past the milk bar if we saw it tethered outside, to please me in my turn. It was all part of the pageant. She and I wrote up private diaries each evening to show to each other next day, detailing our sightings of the various grammar school boys whose names we now knew, although almost always we'd both been there at the time. The point was to heighten and savour every hint of an encounter, the more fleeting the better. I remember that some of my best entries described boys glimpsed through spyholes in the condensation on the steamed-up windows of the bus taking us back over the border.

But there were closer contacts and although the headmistress tried to believe that Gail led me astray – because I was so shy and so bookish, despite my peasant proclivities – I was the one who initiated them. For the dance on the streets you wore school uniform, but on Saturday mornings in mufti you could cross-dress as an adult. This was more exciting than it sounds, for in the 1950s glamour was grown-up and fifteen-year-olds dressed to look like thirty-year-olds rather than the other way around. That winter when I went into Whitchurch on Saturdays I wore a boxy fake-suede jacket, a pencil-slim skirt, a tight sweater and high heels (which, rude realist Uncle Bill explained with a leer, changed women's posture, made them thrust out their tits and bums on behalf of biology). It was a get-up that suited me fine – I had the right kind of shape and a sleepwalker's shamelessness, it was as though such bold self-display was actually a concealment, like the Max Factor pancake that hid my blushes.

In this disguise I'd catch the early-morning bus all on my

own, pick up my copy of *New Musical Express* at W. H. Smith's, and go and sit at the corner table by the window in Edwards's café, above the big old-fashioned grocery that smelled of Cheshire cheese, bacon, brown sugar and the ground coffee they turned into the gritty grey soup they served upstairs. The corner table was a kind of crow's nest or lookout from which you could oversee half of the High Street, and various moody boys and girls (but mostly boys) climbed up to observe the passers-by. Being there, you identified with the boys, but you were also flirting – you might exchange knowing glances when *she* stopped to smile at *him* down in the street, but you were being looked over yourself, too. I found I hardly had to talk at all and could pretend to be reading my paper if need be. Gail would usually cadge a lift with her mother and turn up later, but she was only really interested in looking, not being looked at, and by mid-morning the circle of chairs in the corner had become so wide most people couldn't see out of the window. The café was reverting by then to its traditional function, and was about to serve lunches of meat and two veg with lots of gravy to hungry shoppers. So, after a debriefing in the Ladies when I'd recount what I'd seen and heard, dodging the matrons adjusting their hatpins in the mirror, Gail and I would turn back into a girl gang.

She exerted a contrary pull against the mesmerising compulsion to get boys, almost any boys, to acknowledge my existence, to *make me exist*. But it was a force like gravity, ineluctable. I was desperate to be grown up, I wanted to be haled into a future where I'd be someone and the way of doing it was for now to be no one, blank, masked, wantable. One day that winter another girl at the corner table told one of the boys that it was my birthday: 13 January 1958. How old was I, he asked idly. Fifteen, she hissed and he made a great show of shock

(jailbait!), but he *was* shocked too. Only the white trash from the secondary modern school at Broughall (the Brothel as it was jokily known) flowered so fast, like weeds.

The first boy I actually went out with, just before spring, blond and baby-faced Alan Burns, was in the same fix as me. He too was only fifteen, but he smoked and drank, and was fed up with being so young. For a couple of weeks we went to the pictures together on Saturday nights and necked with such assiduity that my face felt skinned, although I'm sure he didn't shave. The third week he excused himself, telling a friend, who told a friend, who told me, that I was 'too serious'. I told the messenger, who passed it on, that I didn't care and told Gail that really I did, for I felt I should, but I wasn't sure. Our dates had been fraught with anxious self-love, our mouths were dry with stage fright. I thought at the time that he meant I was too serious *about him*, and felt ashamed and indignant. He probably meant in general – Alan had his escape into the future planned. He would leave school that summer after

O-levels, to join the Merchant Navy. I recall running into him years later, in our swinging twenties, and thinking, well *that* was it, he preferred boys all along.

But perhaps back in 1958 I had simply said something that let him see how bookish I was, how much I lived in my head on the quiet. Like all the girls back then I knew that being too clever was much worse than being too tall. Being five foot three, tongue-tied and blonde I mostly passed muster, except that I was so unskilled in small talk that I sometimes blurted big words (hypocrisy, or pretentiousness), which jumped out of my mouth like the toads in the fairy tale before I knew it. In any case, you could cultivate the wrong sort of silence – the sort that implied brooding self-absorption rather than attentiveness. Face to face, I was so distracted by speculation about what people made of me that I didn't really listen to what they said.

It was different with books, I still hung on their every word. The night I finished *Dracula* was a lot more exciting than Saturday night at the Regal. Lying in my private pool of light, with moths ricocheting between the bulb and the lampshade, and the wire from the radio aerial tapping on the window, I drifted into a pre-dawn trance while my little brother (not so little any longer, he was nine) slept soundly across the room in the shadows. Although I protested to our parents that I hated having to share a bedroom with Clive, his unconscious presence heightened my pleasure in my orgies of reading. I was sinning with an undead dandy while innocents wallowed in oblivion. The night was mine and Dracula's. How I yawned at the thought of common daylight's coffin.

That was affectation, though: I was 'out' and determined to sleepwalk my way in the world if I could, and have a career. Boys and homework were supposed to be incompatible but since I was an insomniac I had time for both and hadn't stopped coming top. Books weren't just a solitary vice. Our new young English teacher, Mrs Davies – large, handsome, her dark hair cut in page-boy style, her broad mouth red-lipsticked – smiled down on Gail and me: on Gail for the panache with which she read aloud in class, on me for my untidy, passionate essays. She understood we were a double act, she was part of one herself. She and Mr Davies were a kind of professional couple new to Whitchurch: he taught physics at the boys' school and they had bought a redundant country vicarage, which they were doing up – or rather, stripping down. That summer they invited over some of their pupils, including us, to help dig the garden and limewash the outhouses.

It was in that improbable pastoral setting that I remet Vic Sage. And – since he was so remote from my idea of a boyfriend – told him all sorts of things: that I hated my parents sincerely, not just in a manner of speaking, and couldn't believe everyone didn't; that I of course expected to pass all the O-levels I was taking, the only thing that worried me was what grades I would get; that I couldn't tell the time; that his notion that it was 'fair' that he should be caned by his headmaster for indiscipline (for example, being drunk in the bus on the way back from the school trip to Stratford-upon-Avon) was nonsense, obedience made tyranny; and property was theft. In the evenings, waiting to be picked up by her mother or my father, Gail and I would fit ourselves into one armchair, while Mr Davies (who was older than his wife, and – we took for granted – cleverer in an abstract way) deplored our inability to play chess or even draughts decently, and we questioned him about other puzzles. I still remember his description of how you could reconcile predestination and free will: it was as though God made a documentary film of everything that happened and could watch

it when He chose. This made no difference to the choices we the actors made, our freedom wasn't compromised in the least by the fact that what happened happened and *always had*. In the midst of your life, hacking your way through the jungle, you naturally couldn't see the wood for the trees. That's how the definition of liberty went, I'm pretty sure, that summer.

XV

Sunnyside

Even in the Maelor District, Tory bank-rate cuts and the easing of the credit squeeze made a difference. My Hanmer contemporaries who'd left the secondary modern school at fifteen were leaving the village to find work, because farms were becoming bigger and more mechanised, and used less labour; and the cattle haulage trade was being shaken up too. With the end of meat-rationing and the birth of burgers, cattle dealers expanded their operations from the local markets and so did my father. The Business was booming. Not that there was ready cash, it was simply that the turnover was bigger and he could borrow more. He was still writing 'Please' on overdue bills, then '*Please*' three months later, and it always seemed ominous that the office stationery (which came by mail order) was called Kalamazoo, as though it was designed for enterprises in cloud-cuckoo-land. Nonetheless it was true: we'd never had it so good. In 1959 we moved across the border to the western edge of Whitchurch, where the town petered out and the pavements stopped, to a house called Sunnyside. The rest of this story has a new setting. Well, new in a way.

I'd passed Sunnyside every day on the bus for years. It was an Edwardian villa (stained glass, pointy gables, fancy wrought iron) set back behind a high hedge on a gravel drive, surrounded by laurels, laburnums and lilacs, and obscured from the road by a copper beech. Its warped white gate hung always ajar, and even the 'For Sale' sign soon looked weather-beaten and blended in with the general air of neglect. The Davieses were ahead of their time. No one wanted a big house unless they meant to take lodgers or start a 'Home'. And there was no pressure for planning permission. No private houses had been built on Wrexham Road since the war – the council estate where Vic lived straggled along the bottoms of people's gardens, so this wasn't a smart part of town. Sunnyside was going cheap – the house and one and a half acres of land for £1,800 – and my father saw at once that he'd be able to park a small fleet of trucks down the back garden, and that the stables would serve splendidly as a workshop and garage.

There was more to it than that, of course. I wasn't the only one oppressed by open-plan overcrowding in the council house. Whatever had been my parents' hopes when they started life as a proper nuclear family with baby Clive, they'd been sullied almost immediately by Grandma's advent and my misery, and by now number 4 The Arowry was bursting with frustration. Grandma, more and more frail and housebound, trembling with impotent resentment as well as Parkinson's disease, could hardly manage the steep stairs to the bathroom and Clive ran wild out of doors at all hours just as I'd done. Everyone hated it. What we *should* have done, though, if we'd been decorously upwardly socially mobile, was acquire a neat new four-bedroomed semi with all mod cons. Instead, we were going back to the future. Sunnyside had a heady aura of dereliction and privacy none of us could resist – or none of us except Clive and he was too young to count. We were moving back to the vicarage, but without Grandpa – bliss for my parents, and (even) for me and for Grandma, since despite its bright and cheerful name it was a shady, reclusive house with lots of solidly separate rooms.

The previous owner had ended his days shuffling between just two, the sitting-room and the kitchen opposite, through a green baize door that once divided servants from masters but had dropped on its hinges and was wedged open. In the dust of years he'd worn a path where you could just make out the mosaic pattern of the stone floor of the hallway. Sonny (Sunny?) Foulkes. His family had bought the house in 1919 – the dashing Irish Guards captain who'd built it had been killed in the First World War. It had originally been created for fun, you could still tell, for Sonny had lived in it like a squatter, changing nothing. There was a whole 'wing' with a billiard room and (on the floor above) five tiny bedrooms for the help; cellars with wine racks and meat safes and hooks for hanging game; a cabinet for sporting guns that had been discreetly looted by lads from the estate, although they'd left behind a stuffed greyhound in a glass case; a tennis court hummocky with mole-hills; a sizeable paddock for grazing a couple of horses; an orchard of half-dead cherry, plum, apple and pear trees; rare rose-fancier's roses struggling with weeds and raspberry canes; and a tackle shed neatly stacked from floor to roof with empty Gordon's gin bottles. In the dead leaves blocking the drains there lived elegant pale-yellow lizards. This was a Maelor of the mind, a detached portion of time. Here we'd be once more in social limbo, unplaceable, with plenty of *lebensraum* for solitary fantastical grudges and dreams.

With minimal modernisation – installing electric light in place of the leaky gas jets, replacing the kitchen range, which collapsed in a red cloud of dust at the first touch – and some DIY decorating it would do fine. My mother wasn't dismayed at the thought of the housework, for she suspected straight away that there'd be less of it, since it was in any case impossible to keep such a big place clean. This house had vicarage dirt, not the common kind you could be expected to mop up. To join the dirt, vicarage things that had been in store for years were retrieved, although many of them got no further than tea chests stacked in the billiard room. There Clive and a new friend Jeff, from down the bottom of the back garden, patiently blew them to bits with a toy cannon whose range they'd improved dramatically with home-made gunpowder.

Sunnyside had something for everyone and united us for a brief while, since it enabled us to go our separate ways. The night we eventually moved in there was a moment of rare collusion. Grandma had already been installed, while we'd gone back to Hanmer for some last bits and pieces. Returning, as the car crunched round the gravel of the drive – our drive – we saw her framed in the curtainless bay window, sitting on a tall chair, as if suspended in space. Her feet didn't touch the bare floorboards. She was bathed in greenish light from the television and was shaking her fist at the wrestler on the screen – witchy, grotesque and (horribly) at home. We were hysterical and laughed till we cried. But then it was only fitting she should feel at home, because the £600 that she'd extracted from Grandpa and put in a post office savings account in my name all went towards buying the house. My parents reckoned reasonably enough that it was anyway ill-gotten and that she owed it to them for all the years she hadn't paid her way, and the remaining years she still wouldn't. And as for me, I already knew that property was theft. But although I tried to feel robbed, in fact I wanted the move as much as anyone.

More. I was beginning to think that *I'd got away with it*. Got away with my secret arrogance and hopeless shyness, with counting in cabbages and blotting my copybooks, with bugs and braces and bookishness, with admiring my left profile in the bathroom mirror . . . Sunnyside, where the soul of the vicarage seemed reincarnated in a new body of bricks and mortar, lulled me into a false sense of security. I'd duly collected all those O-levels back in the summer, and although my parents had agreed with the headmistress that (despite 85 per cent in maths) my talent was for arts subjects and I wouldn't be going to the boys' school to catch up on physics and chemistry, I didn't put up a real fight for my right to wear a white coat and become a foot soldier in the space race. I didn't any longer need to go to the grammar school to compete with the boys – fraternise with the boys – since over the first months of the new school year Vic and his friends (who were mostly doing English and history or classics), the bunch from the Davieses, had become Gail's and my co-ed chums.

Or that was the story I palmed off on my parents when they embarrassedly broached the question of what I was up to. I made us sound a bit like the busload of slow developers who, a few years later, would be preserved for posterity in Cliff Richard's *Summer Holiday* – too young to fall in love (because when they *do* they'll be serious), too busy getting the show on the road to brood on lust, too scrubbed, wholesome, bouncy and normal not to appreciate the safety in numbers (They're *all* going on a summer holiday).

On one shaming occasion before we moved house, when I turned up at Sunnyside to get a lift home with my father, who was doing some plastering in the kitchen (a false alarm about foot-and-mouth disease meant business was slack), he started on a meaningful monologue about how important it was to have self-discipline and self-respect and . . . In a panic I shut him up by recycling the school assembly talks we'd been given on freedom and responsibility, and how you had to be free to *be* responsible. I don't think I'd read Milton's immortal words about not being able to praise a cloistered virtue, or I'm sure

I'd have quoted them. Anything to forestall some awful attempt at intimacy and 'understanding' talk about necking, heavy petting and going too far. I took an even loftier moral line than he had and so made it quite impossible for us to discuss what I did or didn't. I lied fluently and plausibly and self-righteously, because I didn't want to know myself, exactly. I *hadn't*, but not for his reasons. It was none of his business, and anyway nothing to do with my private integrity, as he seemed to think.

Perhaps he'd heard gossip about Vic's brother Cyril, who was a lorry driver in his twenties, and who'd already got a girl into trouble and had been before the magistrate for a paternity order. Cyril was quite famous in Whitchurch. He was actually Vic's half-brother: when my mother and his were Dudleston's sales ladies in the 1930s, Vic's mother had been a widow, Mrs Price, and Cyril – who was clever as well as dashing – was generally thought to have turned into a tearaway because of violent differences with his stepfather, which was why he'd run away to live with his grandparents and dropped out of school to drive a tractor. He'd been called up to do his National Service just in time for Suez, too, which hadn't helped: he came back from Cairo spoiling for a fight, and set up as a seducer and a member of the working classes. Still, Vic's mother was an old friend, and so obviously mortified by Cyril's disaffection and bad-boy reputation that my parents couldn't bring themselves to disapprove entirely of Vic. After all, he was staying on in the sixth form and (as I kept telling them) we all hung around together.

It was true that Gail had been the occasion of the first really intense conversation Vic and I had, when we told each other more – and more, once we started we couldn't stop – about our families. We were at a Whitchurch tennis club where Michael Price played and the plot was that we were supposed to help her inveigle him into a doubles match. Instead, we swapped childhoods and sat apart in the shade, and while her courtship advanced hardly at all as usual, we confided recklessly. We boasted to each other about the awfulness of life in our respective council houses and stripped off the appearances with which our parents covered their privacy. The luridness and absurdity of his domestic set-up was wonderfully familiar, somehow. We discovered that we were cursed with craziness. The grandparents were my trump card, Vic's was his father. He came from South Wales too, the next valley to Tonypandy, or as good as – Abercynon – and was short and wide like Grandma.

He'd had a whole career as a sergeant in the regular army until Dunkirk, when he'd been invalided out with just short of twenty years' service and no proper pension. Was he already unbalanced, had he been for years and the army only just noticed, had he been traumatised on the retreat, or was it civilian life that drove him mad? Nothing showed for a while: he had a Civil Service job looking after army stores when Vic was born in 1942 and, although he was high-handed at home and a martinet as a stepfather – Cyril climbed out of the bathroom window at eleven to avoid a thrashing and never came back – that wasn't at all odd for the time. It wasn't until the 1950s that his mood swings got more extreme and he began to give orders with a new peremptoriness. Then one day in the office a typist was insubordinate and he hit her.

While Michael Price served and Gail savoured his grace, I listened spellbound. Vic's father was promptly dismissed from his job and it suddenly became clear to the family doctor that he was unhinged. He was hospitalised and diagnosed as a paranoid schizophrenic. Psychiatrists were very sure of themselves then, once they'd decided you were insane, and in any case his symptoms were classic: he had, it turned out, been receiving secret messages for some while, he was an NCO in some alien Command. At the hospital they gave him a lot of electric-shock treatment and some downers, and sent him home months later without having changed his world picture much.

This would have been around 1956 or 1957, not long before I'd first met Vic at the school dance. They had not been living in the council house for long, in fact, they'd rented bigger and better places before, but now there was no chance of his father returning to work they couldn't afford it. Cyril, who found and lost jobs with lightning speed, wasn't much help and anyway wouldn't live under the same roof, and Vic, his mother insisted, must stay at school – he was her last hope, he must *get on* despite the wreckage. So there they were on Thompson Drive in a house with the same living-room as The Arowry, although already Vic's mum, a loving gardener, was hiding the chain-link fence with rambling roses and filling the borders with hardy annuals. His father had a huge head, a long white beard and glared like an Old Testament prophet. He sat in his carpet slippers in front of the television most of the day, sometimes watching the programmes, at others communing with Channel 13, which was empty buzz and snow to most people, but had orders for him that he listened to with attention.

He wasn't better, just subdued, and still at intervals he made a run for it: cleaned out the joint account, shaved and set out in his good suit with a flower in his buttonhole to Windsor, Sandringham or Balmoral. He kept a very creased picture of the young Queen trooping the colour under his pillow or in his pocket, and from time to time was sent to see her, his not to reason why. Each time he'd be picked up by the Special Branch and returned to Thompson Drive, after a brief spell in hospital. Vic's mother hated what had become of him, but took him back again and again. He'd been so self-confident and dapper when they'd met and married before the war that she felt she couldn't desert him now, although from the lofty perspective of his lunacy he despised her patience and self-sacrifice. He felt her job was beneath him, even though it paid for his keep and the little extras he enjoyed, like the roll-ups whose stray sparks burned holes down the front of his cardigan.

Vic's mum was so stoical and self-effacing, wanted so much to just have an ordinary, decent life, that he too found himself sometimes furious with her. She came from a family of small farmers and took hard work for granted. It was horrible bearing all her hopes; he couldn't resist behaving badly. She praised him to his face, whereas my mother and father were only ever proud of me in public, but both of us had to do well at school. That in itself set us apart, since most of our peers were merely expected to maintain the middle-class status quo: trying too hard was in Whitchurch a sign that you were an outsider and socially shifty. And so our families unwittingly brought us together, although the last thing either of us needed in their view was a boyfriend or girlfriend, certainly not one in the same boat. But it was too late. By the time the sun set on the courts that day and Gail whacked a last lonely practice stroke into the net, he and I had begun to see ourselves as magically alike. Even the trick of inheriting the wrong set of teeth ran in our genes: he'd only had a few second teeth, whereas his cousin Sheila had lots to spare; and I could confess to the same, now my braces were gone.

He was more like me than Gail was – chronically unsure of himself, desperate to grow up and extricate himself from humiliating dependence. His picture of the future was more realistic than mine, although that didn't help him to believe in it, for he was looking forward with incredulity to the job in a bank or the Civil Service that would delight his mother and make him feel honest or at least less guilty. Whereas I was selfishly dreaming simply of running away, probably to university, where I'd meet some fairy godfather who'd teach me everything and make me a woman of the world.

So it didn't occur to either of us that the other was the answer to our problems, it was more a matter of pooling our predicaments, but whatever it was, for the time being we were inseparable. The autumn before the move to Sunnyside, when I was fifteen and he was sixteen, he'd walk me (often Gail too) to the bus, wheeling his bike, we'd go to the pictures on Saturdays and wrestle in the back row, and we'd hold hands. He taught me to tell the time one November day, on the clock in the windy bus station. I persuaded him to resign from the Combined Cadet Force at the grammar school because that was playing into the hands of the past (how could he bear to be *like his father?*) and I scorned to be seen with him in battledress.

I kept the future out of focus. Although I didn't have the blank misgivings I'd felt when I'd passed the eleven-plus, the move into the sixth form and to Sunnyside surprised me with useless regret for Hanmer's patched lanes and spongy fields. Not the pretty bits, but the ground under your feet. I'd wedge myself moodily into a tree and read Wordsworth trying to convince himself that growing away from nature was bearable. Nature at Hanmer wasn't sublime, my solitary childhood tramps hadn't stirred the exultation Wordsworth recalled. However, I thought I recognised his fall into self-consciousness, finding yourself at a loss in a landscape you know intimately, as though it's in a picture and you can't step over the frame. Wordsworth pressed his nose against the picture glass and envied the rural dead like Lucy:

No motion has she now, no force,
She neither hears nor sees,
Rolled round in earth's diurnal course
With rocks and stones and trees.

Reading lines like these I'd grow uneasy, spooked by the sense that the book in my hands was an anti-book. The more you read about Lucy or Betty Foy and her idiot boy or the solitary reaper or the old Cumberland beggar, and the nearer to them you felt, the more being literate seemed a mistake. On the other hand I suspected that in Wordsworth's world I probably *would* have been a lump in the landscape – not quite dead, but not exactly alive either, certainly not doing Wordsworth's anti-book as a set text.

'Nature never did betray the heart that loved her,' wrote Wordsworth. Or rather, 'Nature never did betray / The heart that loved her.' It was thanks to him that I discovered that I had a photographic memory, because no one else in the class could recall where the breaks in his blank verse came, although the line's break was the life-threatening hiccup in its heartbeat. All I had to do was consult my inner eye and I could conjure up the words on the page, which was doubtless why I was an adept at exams.

My perceptions of the real, physical world were less exact, noises and smells and other people's voices broke in, so the present was a blur, like the future. I couldn't make out where I was going. For instance, you were supposed to choose between boys and books, because for girls sex was entirely preoccupying, your sex was *more of you* than a boy's appendage, you *were* your sex, so you had to do without if you were to have enough energy, self-possession and brains left over to do anything else. On this logic County Education Committees would stop a girl's university grant if she cohabited, married, or became pregnant, because it was a waste of public money, although it had probably been a waste of public money all along (many people thought) because the girls would marry when they got their degrees, have families and only work part-time, if that, at jobs they were overqualified for. There were women who didn't marry, but they were unfeminine, unfulfilled, sexless by nature or, the next-worst thing, lesbian, and in any case were only compensating for the fact that no one ever fancied them. Give them half a chance and they'd melt down like those dragon career women in the movies, who purred when our hero took off their spectacles and loosened their scraped-back hair.

Perhaps with this mythology in mind my form mistress would leave a neat pile of hairgrips on my desk as a hint. My hair was long again and all over the place, and I didn't need glasses, either, so I just didn't look the part. I was letting my hair down too early in the plot. But I thought my true notion of myself could stay invisible if I didn't meet people's eyes. Everything said about sex at the time was about separate spheres. We thought Shakespeare's idolatrous sonnets were addressed to a girl, we did *Lady Chatterley's Lover* for A-level in the expurgated edition – but even if we'd had the full text I don't think we'd have worked out that the most sacred and searching act of intimacy between Connie and Mellors was buggery, so loud were the rallying cries of nature and realism that cloaked what people actually did. Difference was ineluctable. Even if you thought you were a free spirit or a bohemian, your female nature meant you were programmed to go round again with the rocks and stones and trees. Our heroes the Beats reinvented the same world. Joyce Johnson, Jack Kerouac's lover, has described how she was typecast:

Could he ever include a woman in his journeys . . . ? Whenever I tried to raise the question, he'd stop me by saying that what I really wanted were babies. That was what all women wanted and what I wanted too, even though I said I didn't. Even more than I wanted to be a great woman writer, I wanted to bring life into the world, become a link in the chain of suffering and death.

It took Joyce almost thirty years to write out this claptrap so coolly. It's galling to realise that you were a creature of mythology: girls were the enemies of promise, a trap for boys, although with the wisdom of hindsight you can see that the opposite was the case. In those seductive yarns about freedom girls' wants are foreknown. Like Lucy, you are meant to stay put in one spot of time.

I recall a flattened patch in the long grass going to seed on the bank of the towpath along the Shropshire Union Canal. It's a hot, bright afternoon in summer, a year on from the time we pooled families, and Vic and I are semi-hidden from the surrounding fields, not from walkers on the towpath or canal boats, although they're very few and far between. It's not safe to undress, we'd be more secure in the dark, but what we're doing isn't part of the timetable for lovemaking, it doesn't count. We're trying to get inside each other's skins, but without taking our clothes off, and the parts that touch are swaddled in stringy rucked-up shirts, jeans, pants. There are no leisurely caresses, no long looks, it's a bruising kind of bliss mostly made of aches. Motes of pollen seethe around us, along with a myriad of tiny moths and flies whose patch this was. We're dissolving, eyes half shut, holding each other's hands at arm's length, crucified on each other, butting and squirming. Our kisses are like mouth-to-mouth resuscitation – you'd think we were dying it's so urgent, this childish mathematics of two into one won't go.

Spots of time. One day when my parents are out we're lying on the edge of the old tennis lawn at Sunnyside, in the weeds, and there's a rapping on the window. Grandma peers out, too short-sighted to register details, but she can see that I'm horizontal and hugging a boy, that's enough. Rat-tat-tat, wake up. I opened my eyes wide and looked at us, and saw that my breasts and his chest were covered in little worms of dirt rolled out of sweat and dust by our friction. That particular day sticks in my memory.

Most days in the summer holidays merge into each other, though. Every morning I sat in the kitchen, in a fireside chair lined with old newspapers (because it was where my father sat in his filthy overalls to take off his boots when he came in from work) and I translated two or three hundred lines of Virgil's *Aeneid*, without using a dictionary, guessing at words I didn't know. Latin was still my favourite subject; despite *Lady C.* and Mrs Davies, it was almost a kind of licensed laziness to sit there scribbling out Rome's epic with old *Daily Mail*s crackling under me. In the afternoons I played tennis on Whitchurch courts with Gail, or we wandered from Edwards's to coffee bar to milk bar, or listened to records, or I went for a walk down the canal with Vic to make a nest in the grass. One day Gail told me that Vic had told a friend who'd told his girlfriend, who'd told her, that we'd gone all the way and that he had a trophy, a smear or spatter of blood on his washed-out jeans, to prove it. She was shocked that something so momentous had happened and I hadn't confided in her. But it hadn't, I protested, truly, or I would have – and he and I had an angry and reproachful conversation about loyalty, betrayal and boasting, because after all, we *hadn't*, had we?

It was so unthinkable that when I felt ill, bloated, headachy, nauseous and, oh yes, my period hadn't come, I stayed in bed and we called out our new doctor, a pale, prim man in his thirties, Dr Clayton. After taking my temperature, asking about bowel movements and looking at my tongue, he looked out of the window at the copper beech tree, cleared his throat and asked could I be – um – pregnant? No, I said, feeling hot suddenly, No. He recommended a urine test anyway. Meanwhile I took aspirins for my aches, but they didn't go away and, although school had started and I'd finished Virgil, I spent days at home. On one of them Dr Clayton turned up again, embarrassed and puzzled. How old was I? Sixteen. He'd heard I was a clever girl, doing well at school, didn't we ever have biology lessons? I must have known what I was up to ... From his first words and his tone, which had weariness and contempt in it, I knew it was true, just as absolutely as until that moment I knew it couldn't be.

I'd been caught out, I would have to pay. I was in trouble, I'd have no secrets any longer, I'd be exposed as a fraud, my fate wasn't my own, my treacherous body had somehow delivered me into other people's hands. Dr Clayton asked if he should tell my mother, but he wasn't really asking. I sat there in my new Sunnyside bedroom, everything falling into place in my aching head, thud, thud, thud. My mother came upstairs and opened the door, her face red and puffed up with outrage, her eyes blazing with tears. She'll tell, this time, no question. For a minute she says nothing and then it comes out in a wail, *What have you done to me?* Over and over again. I've spoiled everything, now this house will be a shameful place like the vicarage. I've soiled and insulted her with my promiscuity, my sly, grubby lusts ... I've done it now, I've made my mother pregnant.

XVI

To the Devil a Daughter

My parents' plan was that I should go to a Church Home for Unmarried Mothers, where you repented on your knees (scrubbed floors, said prayers), had your baby (which was promptly adopted by proper married people) and returned home humble and hollow-eyed. Everyone would magnanimously pretend that nothing had happened, so long as you never seemed to be having a good time or developing too high an opinion of yourself – from now on you could count yourself lucky if they let you learn shorthand and typing. Look where so-called cleverness got you . . .

My father was appalled, but also triumphant. Just as in the old days he'd done his best to beat vicarage corruption out of me, now he righteously denounced me for my scandalous offence against decency, monogamy and my mother. He galloped off on his high horse, chivalrously saving her once again from the horrible past, and she was up behind him, her arms clasped round his shining armour. I wept and sulked, and called up in my mind's eye a rival image of a louche Lord Carlton riding by, but it was no good, he wasn't going to. Nonetheless I swore to myself that rather than go to their Church of England Home I'd hitch a lift down the brand-new M1 motorway to London, ask the way to Soho, and look for a man who'd have a cigarette hanging from the corner of his mouth and a knowing, appraising smile, who'd fix me up with a back-street abortion, so that I could start my career in vice.

Charities didn't take you until you were six months pregnant, however, and they couldn't think of anywhere to send me until then. My mother didn't want people in South Wales to know and my father's aunt in Queensferry was too old, although no one knew me there and she had supervised factory girls who were no better than they should be during the war. For the moment, since nothing showed yet, it was decided I should go to school as usual and tell nobody. There was, after all, a chance I might have a miscarriage. Dr Clayton said that I should carry on doing gym – but I'd long given it up and I could hardly start colliding with vaulting horses again without drawing attention to myself. Judging that I was distraught, he also prescribed sleeping pills, since he didn't know that I never slept much. He gave them to my mother to dole out in case I was tempted to try killing myself, but I wasn't, not even to frighten them. I didn't want to gratify their expectations – suicide would have been an acknowledgement of guilt and despair, whereas I didn't feel guilty at all, only furious. If they were outraged, *so was I* and I wasn't going to give anyone an excuse to send me to a mental hospital.

But I did wonder if I was going mad. How could I have got it so wrong? Such was the irreality of the situation that I'd have been a lot more prepared to find myself pregnant if we'd actually used a condom, since that would have meant I had to know what we were doing (but then I wouldn't have done it). However, French letters, rubbers – the only contraceptives available and only to boys – were, like all other ways of divorcing sex from reproduction, trashed by the myths of the times. Having sex using a rubber was like having a bath with your socks on, boys said nastily, and in any case it was an insult to the girl, because you'd only use one for hygienic reasons. Likewise, mutual masturbation, having sex during a period, oral sex, sodomy were all variously outlawed as dirty, sick, perverse or criminal. Thus everything conspired at once to fetishise and forbid the one true act.

These ideas had penetrated deep into my mind, that was the catch – I scorned virginity as just something 'nice' girls traded on the marriage market for a suburban semi and a car, but I had absorbed the notion that real sex was some kind of visionary initiation involving the whole of you. It seemed until that moment that Amber had only been half alive and according to Lawrence (as we solemnly noted down) the phallos was a column of blood that filled the valley of blood of a woman. That's why I was so sure that I hadn't done it. And even on the most crude system of moral accounting you paid for pleasure, surely, and since I hadn't had the pleasure I shouldn't be paying. It was grossly unfair, like some kind of travesty of the immaculate conception ... The first gynaecological examination I had was my definitive deflowering. I hurt and bled, for I was still partly a virgin – in fact, as opposed to mythology, even that wasn't a question of yes or no.

Contingency didn't count, however. Getting into trouble meant you were certainly bad, which in turn meant you were either pathetic or evil, and it was obvious which to prefer. I'd read and reread Dennis Wheatley's *To the Devil a Daughter* (a 1950s best-seller and another of Uncle Bill's anthropology books), all about how the baser forms of eroticism threaten the very fabric of Western civilisation. The heroine is nice in the daytime, but when dusk falls she dresses up, drinks, gambles, kisses men with her mouth open and shows signs of being able to look after herself – shooting off an automatic, for instance. That's not her true character, though, she was dedicated to the devil as a baby by her father, in return for worldly success. Dad is a self-made man and also therefore an agent of Bolshevism: the Satanists who recruited him are working for the Soviets, plotting to manufacture homunculi to serve Big Brother, and their spies and allies are 'pederasts, lesbians, and over-sexed people of all ages'. Our heroine is saved at the last minute from donating her virgin blood to the evil Empire and is handed over intact by her repentant father to the hero on her twenty-first birthday.

The book's charm naturally lay in the queer behaviour of Ellen/Christina when she was not herself – in one memorable scene she twisted her ankle and asked the nervous hero to help her pull her stocking up: 'the flesh there was like a cushion of swansdown under a taut-stretched skin of tissue-thin rubber', he reported with awe, before taking his hand away sharpish; he was nearly distracted by Satan! Alas, rereading it now, even such moments pale before passages of unconscious bathos like the flashback where Dad is seduced by a devilish vision of a factory with his name in lights: BEDDOWS AGRICULTURAL TRACTORS; or the time when the heroine is asked to tell all she can remember about her daytime good-girl life from the beginning and it takes her the best part of an hour.

In my case the bad blood had skipped a generation. You're just like your grandfather, my mother had said when we rowed over clothes or make-up, but now it was almost too blatant to need saying. Only Grandma didn't regard it in that way. Opposed to my father in everything, she saw my plight as the result of being rash enough to go *anywhere near* a member of the male race and cast Vic as the villain of the piece, while my parents were rather disposed to see him as a mere accessory after the fact, so convinced were they of my devilish duplicity. For the same reason they didn't doubt my ability to conceal my condition from people at school and they were right. No one suspected, not even Gail. I couldn't bring myself to tell her, not because she'd be scandalised, or betray my secret, but because she'd be fascinated by how it felt, curious about every sensation and so make being pregnant more real than I could bear. Although I didn't hold out any hopes for a providential miscarriage – my luck was obviously lousy – it was easier to cope day to day, throwing up in the mornings, feeling faint in assembly, without anyone's empathy. A misery shared is a misery multiplied when nothing can be undone, and I reflected bitterly that mine was multiplying anyway, all those cells splitting and getting on with their lives, whatever I felt.

It was hard work remembering who I was and staying myself, and probably I was a little crazy. What else to make of a couple of letters addressed to me ('Miss L. Stockton') that have survived from that autumn? They are almost identical. This one is from Miss E. M. Scott, the Principal of St Aidan's in Durham:

24th November, 1959

Dear Madam,

Thank you for your application form. I note that you will not be 18 until January 1961, and as I do not normally admit students under the age of 18, I cannot consider your application for admission in October 1960.

Yours faithfully . . .

The letter from St Mary's College said the same. Had I applied because people at school expected me to? But then they would have anticipated this response, surely? Perhaps I was, as we say now, 'in denial', and somehow imagined I could divide into two and one of us could make her escape to the far north. Perhaps I wrote off without consulting anyone. Grandpa had been a student at Durham, 'MA Dunelm' it said on his brass plate in the chancel, although in another version of his blighted career he hadn't had the money to finish his degree. But then he couldn't have been ordained without one. Unless he'd faked it. Whatever had prompted me to fill in the forms, I'd neglected to change my date of birth and Durham wouldn't have me.

Vic, meanwhile, had been wondering whether to run away to sea. His mother was wretchedly disappointed in him for following in his brother's footsteps, her pride in him was battered down and her stoic resignation was hard to take. She was far too decent to think he should get away with it, they couldn't just carry on as if nothing had happened, he'd have to leave school in disgrace – she foresaw it all, straight away, the defeat of her hopes for him. Like my parents, she saw us as juvenile delinquents who'd forfeited our chances. We were as gratuitously criminal as the kids from good homes (rebels without reason) you read about in the papers, teenagers who robbed sub-post offices or stole cars in insolent defiance of the law, except that in our case it was the moral law, which was, if anything, worse. At first we were forbidden to see each other, but there was no point, as my father said (with a disgusted shrug), the damage was done. He loathed the idea of us copulating with impunity, but he needn't have worried. We were ourselves so stunned by this bad magic we'd managed that for the moment we merely huddled together for warmth, each other's only friend.

Small scenes surface: Vic and I sitting together on the verge of the drive at Sunnyside, staring into space, clutching our knees, picking pebbles out of the gravel and chucking them away, which was when I told him the bad news and had for just a second the wild hope that he'd say it couldn't be, although I knew he wouldn't and he didn't. And the two of us, on a bleaker day, walking fast along one of the new Crescents or Ways on the housing estate between my house and his. We're holding hands, I'm chewing aspirin for a headache and we're in earnest conversation, conspiring together.

There'd been no recriminations between us. I hadn't said why wasn't he more careful, he hadn't said I led him on — although those were the days when it was certainly the girl's fault (people even said rape wasn't possible, you had to have let it happen); and although I knew that he was rumoured to have done it with a sad girl called Mildred, a waitress in Eccleston's café, where we listened to records, who had badly bleached, matted hair and was supposed to be a bit soft in the head and hadn't got *her* pregnant. We were innocent. And the more we talked the more innocent we became — babes in the wood, brother and sister, orphans of the storm.

Being sworn to secrecy had cut us off and locked us up together in embattled intimacy, and from cellmates we turned into soulmates. We invented a story for ourselves which started out as a kind of excuse, but soon took on a life of its own. It went something like this: the baby was an accident, but really we knew what we were doing. We were each other's other half, or even closer. We were one and the same, we'd abolished the differences the conventional world assumed between the sexes, we had a union of true minds as much as bodies. Well yes, we were in love, but that wasn't the point. We were *serious*. So the bad luck that had entrapped us (making a baby the first and only time, and without really going all the way) was transformed into a portent. It showed we were meant for each other.

The parents were treating us like corrupt children — we patched together a new, mutant myth out of poems and stories and sheer necessity. Our brainchild. In it we grew up overnight and cast off the mind-forged manacles of Hanmer and Whitchurch ... I led him on this time, for sure. This one I was certainly responsible for, so was he and so were other people who knew nothing about it – including Gail, Grandpa, Sartre and Simone de Beauvoir, Miss Roberts my Latin teacher, and Vic's friend Martin, who'd been asked to leave Ampleforth, done some camp consciousness-raising in the grammar school sixth form and added Wilde to our list of set books.

As the dank, disgraced autumn of 1959 turned to winter we reinvented marriage, for better and for worse. If we got married we would no longer be legally in the guardianship of our parents, we'd worked that out too. Of course, we needed their permission and they very much didn't want to give it. They didn't think we should marry at all – we were far too young and too irresponsible. It was an insult to matrimony. It was also shaming, it would make us look lumpen, real white trash, common as muck. On the other hand if we were bold enough to go to a magistrate for permission we'd probably get it, because I was pregnant and we weren't – they weren't – respectable or well-off enough for their objections to count. And the case would be in the *Whitchurch Herald*.

And what if we ran off to Gretna Green? Reluctantly, gradually, my parents came around to the idea and so did Vic's mum: we'd marry and Vic would move into Sunnyside to start with. It would be postponed until Christmas, however, just in case ... and so that we could leave school during the holidays, a bit less visibly. And then? Well, Vic could take the entry exams for the Civil Service and A-levels, and look for a job; and as for me, my immediate future was accounted for. Dr Clayton told me and my mother that it was well known that as your pregnancy advanced you became absorbed by it, serene, preoccupied, reconciled, round. My mother, I could tell, wasn't convinced, presumably she didn't remember it quite like that. And I was appalled at the thought that he might be right and that I'd forget to be angry. (He wasn't and I didn't.)

I wanted my body back. I'd never until now thought of it as mine, really, now that it wasn't. Pregnant, I was my own prison but you could tick off the days on a calendar; it wasn't a life sentence. Except for the baby, and I imagined him (babies then were nearly always male beforehand, you couldn't find out their sex in advance) playing in a corner, a quiet little ghost of futurity, while we construed elliptical bits of Lucretius. I planned to sit my A-levels as well. No one could prevent me from entering as an external candidate, and unless the dates were wrong and the baby came in June like the exams, instead of the end of May, I could manage both. The mutant version of marriage Vic and I were making up as we went along didn't automatically mean family life as my parents knew it (he the wage-earner, she the dreamer), but none of us said so, we simply went ahead at cross-purposes. We were all temporarily exhausted by the crisis and peace was declared while we waited for the end of the school term.

The more my parents saw of Vic, the more they liked him; he was much less intransigent and bloody-minded than me. My mother, in particular, was gratified to find that he was always hungry. It began with the leek soup. Glossy packets of soup mix had started appearing in the shops and, true to her conviction that vegetables were only edible when denatured, she bought lots and served them with big lumps, gluey on the outside, powdery inside. There was always leftover soup in a pan on the stove and one evening that waiting winter, when he brought me home to Sunnyside, she asked him would he like some warmed up, adding, in case politeness caused him to refuse, 'It's only going in the bin.' He wolfed it down, although his mother was a very good cook and he was well fed at home, for he really was hugely, indiscriminately hungry. 'He polished it off,' said my mother, shaking her head in theatrical disbelief and laughing with amazement, and from then on she never stopped plying him with reconstituted horrors and some frozen things called 'Chicklets' she especially fell for around then, which even my father rejected. In fact, she fed him up so successfully that he developed a kind of parallel paunch and put on weight as I did.

I tried to eat as little as possible, but it didn't work, and by December I was grateful for the shapelessness of school uniform and had swapped my skimpy Silhouette girdle for a heavy-duty version, bones and all. There was only one occasion when I felt close to being found out, but that is etched on my memory with panic's acids, complete with the kind of circumstantial detail that usually you don't store away because it's so ordinary and innocent. The school hall had an upper gallery that served as a corridor linking classrooms, and also as a vantage point for watching gym displays, drama rehearsals and so on. I cannot recall what was happening that day on the floor below, but one of my friends or fans – a fat girl who admired me – had dragged a stool from the biology lab to the balustrade. As I passed by she reached out, put an arm round my waist, pulled me on to her lap before I could escape and exclaimed with what sounded like triumphant malice, 'Ooh! You've put on weight!' In that moment the smell of formaldehyde from the rats pinned out on boards in the lab, and the familiar, claustophobic feel of the closeness of other girls' bodies, inspired such fear and nausea that I was beside myself. I was an outsider, harbouring an alien, an alien myself. Having such a secret was like having cancer – a disease which couldn't be mentioned except in shamed whispers.

Not that anyone ever confessed at the time to thinking like this. Uncle Bill's favourite sex-kitten, Brigitte Bardot, who was now twenty-five and would soon (January 1960) be looking radiant in the newspapers, posing with her husband and their new baby, said years later that she had come to love her son Nicholas with a passion, but then (*'mais à l'époque!'*) it had been like expelling *'une tumeur'*. Even in 1996, when her autobiography was published, there was a public outcry over this passage. True, her whole account of her one experiment with motherhood was provocative. For instance, pregnancy tests then involved the use of female rabbits, and BB – ever the animal lover, Gail would have approved – tells us that she insisted on redeeming her rabbit and taking it home with her. But to admit that she regarded the baby she was carrying as a life-threatening lump was unforgivable in itself, so ingrained still is the notion that nature is bound to adjust your feelings to your condition, unless you're a monster.

Unreconciled and undetected, I made it to the end of term and the school dance. Fear of discovery didn't blight life entirely: I remember that the get-up I wore to that last dance had for me a special, pleasureable, private meaning. I was about to take a step into the dark, so like a heroine of romance I wore a strapless dress, black with midnight-blue splodgy flowers, tight-waisted and full-skirted, and I looked – as I'd wanted to two years before – a lot older than I was, voluptuous, hooked-and-eyed into a ferocious corselette that pushed up my breasts, with stiff crinoline petticoats, dark-blue stockings and spiky high heels: all the trappings of slang glamour. When Vic came round to collect me, with slicked hair and narrow trousers, we stood before the mirror over the fireplace in the sitting-room at Sunnyside and looked at our reflections. The dance would be our farewell to teenage limbo, we were out on our own and the realisation that no one would know it that evening but us was bitter and heady. The flickering firelight held us in a pocket of warmth, not for the first time.

Once, earlier that winter when my parents and Clive were out and Grandma had gone to bed sated with *Sunday Night at the London Palladium*, I'd wantonly used up all the hot water and come downstairs wearing only a bath towel and a dusting of talcum powder to let him in. We'd lain on the hearthrug, melting in the gloom and listening for tyres on the drive. All dressed up for the dance, watching ourselves in the mirror, we both remembered and put on world-weary smiles to match our finery.

Ten days later we were married. I had on my new winter coat, whose fur collar didn't reconcile me to the concealing lines that had attracted my mother. Our shotgun wedding – us holding the gun to their heads – took place on Boxing Day, for my father had found out that the Register Office was obliged to open for business on 26 December, although it was seldom called on to do so. That year we were the only customers. He drove us through the empty early-morning streets to the town hall, where a dyspeptic registrar pronounced the words and we signed the right forms, witnessed by Mrs B. R. D. Sage and Mr and Mrs E. P. Stockton. Then we came out into the cold sunshine on the High Street. No one took any photographs, there was not a soul in sight, the pavements were rimed with frost and salt, and it was so quiet that you could hear the tinsel streamers strung across the road rattling in the air.

We bundled into the car and back to Sunnyside, where the Christmas tree lights were on the blink again and had to be tested ritually one by one by my father to locate the faulty bulb that must be replaced before they'd work. He didn't mind, this was the kind of task he liked to have to occupy the time when he wasn't working and it came in especially handy that day, since we didn't know how to fill in the interval until the cold turkey. It was hardly an occasion for celebration – although over the years it would be added, like New Year's Eve and my January birthday, to the festivals for which the Christmas decorations would also serve. When he'd finished with the blue-green-red-white lights, my father went upstairs to attach the mirror to the dressing-table of the new bedroom suite which he'd bought at the same Christmas market as the tree, and which would replace my single bed and chest of drawers, and shoulder aside the bookcase with my old William books and George Macdonalds. My bedroom was transformed into a barer version of my parents' room across the landing, and so normality and decorum were restored to Sunnyside. For the first time in our lives (on our wedding night, like a respectable couple) Vic and I shared a bed, and in the morning, after my father had left for work, my mother brought us mugs of sweet tea and that settled the matter. Vic was one of the family. This, of course, allowed for the possibility that he was wretched, disaffected, myth-ridden, what have you. The important thing was that he should join in the general conspiracy to make life seem plausible. My mother wasn't the star of the Women's Institute drama group for nothing, she had a frightening capacity for damage limitation, for pretending that nothing bad had happened, which she must have acquired in her childhood and adolescence, surviving all those murderous vicarage rows. (Once upon a later time, when she and my father were staying in my house, I quarrelled with him into the small hours and, vowing drunkenly that I wouldn't spend the night *under the same roof*, I went out and lay down on the dewy grass – it was

249

high summer – only to find my mother standing over me next morning with a mug of hot, sweet tea.) The show must go on and so it did.

I slept soundly for a change, Vic cupped against my back or vice versa. And I dreamed, one dream in particular, again and again, of a white space – a cinema screen, a canvas, a sheet of paper. From one corner a black line starts indelibly to meander, snaking its leisurely way around and across, doodling aimlessly until little by little and without any system it fills almost the whole empty space and there's only one pinprick of light left, and I wake up gasping for breath, looking for the dawn oblong of the window. My blocked sinuses were the obvious explanation, they reacted badly to all that lying still and so did my insomniac self, which resented rest. Didn't Dr McColl say I had more time than other people? Well now, suddenly, I hadn't. Sleep was dangerous, it spelled regression. Vic and I, having conspired so successfully to become legally independent, seemed strangely more childlike. Cuddling under the covers in our freezing bedroom (all the bedrooms were freezing) had a memory nesting inside of it, long lost: my little brother Clive and I climbing into our parents' empty bed at The Arowry, burrowing under their puffy blue nylon quilt to make a tent and drowsing there in the warm.

It was Clive, now, who showed the most obvious signs of disturbance. He had been sent to a new school in Whitchurch, a private one, for crash courses in numeracy and literacy to compensate for Hanmer school's muck-shovellers' curriculum, and he hated it. Every afternoon he'd burst back into the house like a mad boy, first flinging his football kit along the hall, then his satchel, then himself, in an ecstasy of rage. When Vic and I got back from the Register Office that December day, only Clive let on that there was anything out of the ordinary happening: he danced around us having his own joke, pretending Vic was from outer space or a Frankenstein's monster, pointing at him in mock-terror: 'It walks! It talks!' And so Vic became one of us.

XVII

Crosshouses

The district nurse who visited Grandma – no longer Nurse Burgess with her blunt needles and Hanmer history, but a younger, less substantial woman – shook her head and said that they should try to persuade the baby to turn over, a good midwife would know how to do it with massage. But they didn't bother with that at the antenatal clinic in Shrewsbury. 'He' was, it turned out, a breech baby, the wrong way about, set to arrive in the world bottom first, which meant his head wouldn't get squashed, but I might well have trouble delivering the broadest bit at the start. They measured my pelvis, however, and decided that I could perfectly well manage it, although I'd have to go to the special maternity unit at Crosshouses Hospital where they dealt with Caesareans and difficult deliveries.

Crosshouses was an ex-workhouse twenty-five miles away in the middle of nowhere on the road between Shrewsbury and Bridgenorth, a Victorian pile inherited by the National Health Service. It had a reputation to go with its name. People talked in whispers about the 'complications' that sent you there and over it hung an air of grudging public charity. The Crosshouses consultant, who saw me at the clinic and gave his opinion that I'd been built for child-bearing, made it clear that he thought me a peasant. I never saw him again, though, for he was shortly to be hauled up before the Council of the British Medical

Association and written up in the *Shropshire Star* for charging for National Health beds. He acted on his contempt for the NHS more boldly than most, but his attitude wasn't unusual: you were getting something for nothing, in the good old days you'd have had short shrift and all of this obstetrical expertise would have been reserved for your betters, whose pelvic bones were naturally more daintily designed.

In other words, you should pay and if you couldn't pay in cash you'd pay in dignity. Unmarried mothers had the worst of it, but being married didn't improve your status much with the professionals, for their resentment of patients in general was compounded by the atavistic idea that pregnant women in particular were just walking wombs, only Baby mattered. The clinic was a humiliation which I endured in an impotent sulk, plotting the red dawn, when they'd swing from the lampposts, or – given darkest Shropshire – a handy oak. Meanwhile, the only person on whom I took revenge was myself, since I refused to take the extra calcium Dr Clayton prescribed for my bones and teeth, and didn't rub cream into my stomach, and so acquired a lot of fillings and a set of stretch marks. Smocks I also scorned, I wore Vic's shirts and jeans instead, and they fitted to the end thanks to my mother's menus.

Every day she'd bring us a mid-morning snack of buttered cream crackers and milky Camp coffee in the dining-room where we sat doing our day-long homework, sharing the table with my father's ledgers, huddled over an electric fire. The fireplace didn't work because the chimney was blocked with close-packed twigs: the ground floor of a two-storey bird's nest that went past the fireplace in our bedroom above and stuck out of the chimney pot on the roof. Sunnyside wildlife wasn't confined to the garden and the paddock. There was a spring that came up in the cellar and occasionally flooded, as it did that first year, when it must have brought frogspawn with it before it receded, because one day the cellar floor was swarming with tiny albino frogs who couldn't get out, who'd been eating each other down there in the dark. In May came may bugs, big gold-and-green armoured beetles who threw themselves against our lighted windows late at night like a shower of stones. My mother shuddered with horror at each new plague, but didn't really mind. She greeted the cat when he knocked at the back door using a mouse or a vole for a door knocker with little, pleased screams.

She was much happier than she'd been at The Arowry. Once she'd got used to my disgrace, she liked having Vic and me around the house, so long as we were out of the way. The same applied to everyone at Sunnyside. Grandma spent a lot of the time rearranging her treasures in her room, or watched children's television in the sitting-room. My father would often be working on a crippled truck down the back garden and Clive, when he wasn't at school, would be pulverising the things in the billiard room with his friend Jeff. My mother could walk into town to see Mrs Smith or do some light shopping whenever she chose (the groceries – still called 'the rations' – were delivered weekly by Gail's Uncle Jack from the shop in Hanmer, because we couldn't afford to settle his account, which was months, perhaps years, behind). But she didn't yearn to get out as she once had. She had the kitchen to herself and it was the room she wanted, for her own purposes. There she half listened to the radio, read the paper, learned her lines, pottered and, as she said, was never at a loose end.

Now that the stables were a kind of depot my father's drivers – 'the men' – called at the back door for cups of tea on a tray, and Uncle Albert would drop in from his coal round and sit on the *Daily Mail*s. She even cooked on weekdays sometimes and, although she almost never ate the results, she was perversely proud of them. One meat pie was inspired by eggcups that came free with the cornflakes. At last she could prop up the pastry on top. However, disappointingly the pie came out of the oven sunken as usual. It wasn't until we'd eaten our glutinous portions (and Vic was on his second helping) that she poked around in the dish and burst out laughing. Eureka! Those eggcups were plastic, silly her! They'd dissolved into the gravy! Hadn't we noticed, she asked incredulously, didn't it taste funny? This was one of her best roles, the travesty housewife, the dreamer in drag, and she revelled in it.

It was well known that I couldn't act, so I wasn't expected to understudy cooking and cleaning. Vic and I worked at our books and started sending out the haulage bills (*Please*) in return for pocket money. The notion that he'd find a suitable job receded when he failed the Civil Service examination for entry to the Executive Class because he couldn't do maths, although he did far too well in English and French. At his interview they told him to forget it and go to university. We were back in the same boat, then. The headmistress had told my father that while a teacher training college, a truly Christian one (she was devout), just might accept a moral cripple like me, universities would not, but I didn't believe her. Nor, amazingly, did the senior ladies on her staff.

Miss Macdonald the music teacher, who'd despaired of me years before, stopped my mother and me one day in the middle of the Bull Ring to tell us at the top of her voice that seventeen was the ideal age to have a healthy baby and get on with your life. The geography mistress, Miss Heslop, sent encouraging messages along the same lines. And Miss Roberts timetabled weekly Latin tutorials at her house, and advised me to put in for Scholarship level as well, to impress the selectors. These women, who were all around the same age as the century, all unmarried, were not only unshocked, but somehow pleased with me, it was their younger colleagues of my parents' generation who were censorious. And the Davieses, the youngest, must – I realised much later – have been horribly mortified. Did people think them somehow responsible for our fall? This didn't occur to us at the time, for it was so far from the truth. They were certainly embarrassed and a bit distant, although Mrs Davies set essays and marked work for us both.

As it turned out, we learned a lot more in those five months than we would have at school. Until the summer (the baby, the exams) we were in hiding, safe from distractions, self-exiled from the mesmerising teenage game of looking and being looked at, wearing our unisex uniform for the duration. And in any case, school – at least the county kind that Whitchurch schools aspired to – was stoutly anti-intellectual. Clever was always too clever by half. So we had a honeymoon with books once we'd left, especially Vic, who'd been much more popular at school, a much better clown and time-waster than me. He swapped his own Latin textbook for *Bradley's Arnold* on Latin prose composition, the one Miss Roberts swore by, and came along to revise over tea and cake to keep me company. Latin was the subject that meant most to me, for the same reason as it had when I started at the high school, because it was lucid, learnable, dead to the world. Whatever else had changed, that stayed the same.

Bradley's Arnold trusted to Caesar and Cicero, so most of the examples came from war and the law. On every page, cool constructions made order out of mess, cruelty and corruption: to translate 'Caesar having taken the enemy massacred them' you'd say, not *'Captis hostibus eos Caesar trucidavit'*, but *'Caesar captos hostes trucidavit'*. The main murderous verb, of course, stayed the same. There was a grim wit at work in *Bradley's Arnold*. In Exercise LXVII, 'those hanging back were punished *non verbis solum sed etiam verberibus*', not only with words but also a flogging, a bit of imperial wordplay that sounds like a sly threat to the public-school boys the book was originally designed for.

Miss Roberts herself had a steely quality. Her bearing was upright, and her hair was white and swept back stylishly from her bony, powdered forehead. Unlike the other spinster teachers, who tucked their hankies into their enormous bloomers and lost their tempers, she went in for irony and dressed formally in tailored suits. Orderly in herself, she always had trouble with discipline and conducted lessons with her jaw set, speaking very quietly through clenched teeth against a noisy hum of indifferent gossip. She regarded most of her pupils with patient contempt and they judged her stuck-up, for she had an unmistakable air of inhabiting in her head other times and other worlds that were a lot more spacious than post-war England, let alone Whitchurch.

One winter she appeared in an aggressively smart costume she'd obviously bought somewhere else, made of deep-purple tweed. After lunch in the staff room – and after tea at home – she would hungrily smoke a cigarette, inhaling deeply and flaring her nostrils. When she taught us modern European history in the fifth form she used a textbook illustrated with period cartoons and caricatures, and concentrated on the French Revolution; and for her, Latin meant stoic, Republican virtues, classical civilisation, progress, enlightenment. She was an agnostic, adored reason and savoured satire. Her tidiness was essentially of the mind and she wasn't irritated by my messy hair or slovenly handwriting, but praised my prose and showed me how to tighten my arguments.

She took the latest blot on my copybook coolly for granted, only insisted more discreetly than ever on mind over matter. I had always felt flattered by her approval and now I clung to her good opinion. She was still reserved – although she did unbend to the extent of passing on to me her copies of the *New Statesman*, which I read religiously and which introduced me to a style of socialism very different from Uncle Bill's proletarian party line. The *Statesman* had caricatures, too; in the back half there were mocking group portraits of intellectuals at play, in which Bridgid Brophy stood out because she was often the only woman. Miss Roberts seldom said what she thought directly, and when she learned that Vic and I were poring over visionary epiphanies out of Blake and Shelley, and that he was fascinated by Gerard Manley Hopkins, she drily loaned us Aldous Huxley's *Doors of Perception* (including *Heaven and Hell*) and *The Perennial Philosophy*. Her interest in us impressed my parents and helped make the prospect of university look real, for she lent authority to our amorphous conviction that you could live on your wits. But most of all, and most urgently, the grades she gave me for Latin prose helped me survive day by day, because they weren't just reassuring mock results, they meant that I had a brain, that I wasn't engrossed in breeding as Dr Clayton had foretold.

The time crept by all the same, the baby stretched and lunged but didn't turn over, and Crosshouses loomed. One day Grandma, visited and reanimated by her old anger, made a speech in which she denounced Vic, my father, Grandpa and all males everywhere including Clive, who'd grow up to be a hairy ape like the rest, throwbacks to a man (except for her Billy). Then she cried over me, remembering the horrors of childbirth. I refused to think about what would happen in any detail. Words like 'delivery' and 'confinement' (threats, promises) hung around in my imagination, but stayed just words. In truth I was more fearful of the hospital than of the event itself and I had evolved a secret plan (secret even from Vic) to have the baby at home – simply not to tell anyone that I was in labour until the last minute, when they'd have to call 999 and improvise kettles and clean sheets, which seemed, judging from the movies, the only props you needed. Peasants – real peasants – gave birth between one shift in the vineyards or the paddy fields and the next, didn't they?

The date they'd worked out at the clinic was 29 May and punctually at dusk on the twenty-eighth, when I was pacing restlessly in the garden tugging at weeds, the first twinge came and soon there was no question. Contractions. True to my resolve, I said nothing all evening, we went to bed as usual and although I couldn't sleep, that wasn't odd – my sleeplessness had returned with the discomforts of pregnancy, and Vic and I would read to each other into the small hours. That night it was his turn. The book we were in the middle of was John Wain's novel *Hurry on Down*, which would be fixed for ever in our memories by the grotesque coincidence of its title and the event.

It was a variant on the angry-young-man theme – a young man evading his middle-class destiny, a portrait of the artist as gag writer, recounting the string of comic misadventures that led him to this low-life calling. The jokes were laboured (ho, ho), but I laughed, let out a groan at the same time and gave the game away. Perhaps I'd lost my nerve. In any case, matters were taken out of my hands, the ambulance was called and Vic came with me for the long, bumpy and increasingly painful ride along back roads to Crosshouses. When we got there, around 3.30, I stepped down into a puddle of my own making, in a state of panic. The Sister on duty, who seemed instantly to know that I was late on purpose, briskly slapped me in the face two or three times, sent Vic off back to Whitchurch with the ambulance and hauled me into the Delivery Room.

There, time caught up with me. While the slap-happy Sister woke the doctor, I lay where she'd put me and watched the clock on the wall between my knees. Things were happening too fast. 'Don't push!' she yelled (she wanted the doctor to be there) but I couldn't stop pushing, and although it felt as if I was being torn apart (I was) and the second hand loitered round the dial as slowly as it does for someone on speed, the adrenalin of my fright and my seventeen-year-old's abdominal muscles soon brought an end. The ruffled, sleepy Indian locum who arrived, pinning up her thick plait of hair, was too late, the Sister was already crooking my nerveless arm around a baby girl (girl!) wrapped in a blanket, her face streaked with blood (I remember thinking, whose? mine?) and whisking her away again. Then it was all over except for the stitches, which hurt like hell, so they gave me some gas and air, and left me alone until the real morning came. I watched the clock, fascinated. It was still only 4.15, the liminal pre-dawn hour, and I'd never felt so awake, as though I'd died and been born again knowing how to tell the time. Ages later an orderly pushed a mop into the room and, seeing me there, brought me a cup of hot, sweet tea under telepathic orders from my mother, and I was immediately, violently sick (never mind, she said, mopping it up) and fell asleep.

I came to consciousness on the Maternity Ward, where the Crosshouses day was beginning. The regime was rigid: it wasn't only that temperatures, blood pressure, bedpans and medication were done on the dot, there were endless other rules. Hairwashing was strictly forbidden, even if you were well enough to walk to the bathroom; bathing was rationed; and make-up was frowned upon. Anything that might make you feel less wrecked and dirty was disallowed on principle, because Baby came first and by Crosshouses logic washing your hair was vanity, therefore traitorous to Maternity, morally unhygienic and dangerous. As a result, everyone had stiff, sweaty hair sticking out in tufts, some of it grey, for one of the offences several of these mothers had committed against order and decency was to go on having babies into their forties. By contrast the nurses, Sisters and Matron were as good as vestals, unmarried or at least childless, their baby worship was pure. They served the cause of motherhood selflessly, unlike the feckless women in their charge, who'd probably been thinking of sex, or failed to plan, and who didn't deserve babies.

So mothers were dirt and fathers hardly came into it at all, for visiting hours were brief and the hospital was nearly impossible to reach by bus. There were no public phones. The ward was the world. The babies were segregated in a nursery a couple of corridors away, where mothers weren't allowed, and where they were bottle-fed in the night and cried continuously, waking each other up. In the daytime they were handed out at four-hour intervals for breast-feeding, which had suddenly become the rule and created many more minor offences to do with having too much milk or not enough, or the wrong sort of nipples. When Matron made her rounds, I said I didn't want to breast-feed, but luckily she wasn't listening, she'd spotted down the ward an enormity, a woman with red nails. Marching smartly to the bedside she picked up the woman's hand and flung it back at her with disgust: 'We don't feed our babies on nail varnish!' she announced, looking around her in triumph, and sailed through the swing doors.

Although I was pretty sure that bottle-feeding had been

officially best for baby until recently, I didn't question the breast-feeding rule again, which was just as well, because my daughter brought out all the possessive zeal of the nursing staff. When I saw her next I didn't recognise her: she wasn't wearing her cowl of blood, she had on instead a mop of blonde curls like Shirley Temple's. Not only had they bathed her and shampooed her hair, they'd wound it round their fingers and fluffed it out. Every day she had a different hairdo, depending who was on duty. My favourite was a stand-up Teddy Boy quiff with a DA effect at the back, but after that first time I had no trouble recognising her whatever the style, since none of the other babies had any hair at all to speak of.

She was the ward's model infant: she weighed a (then) exactly average seven pounds seven ounces, she'd arrived precisely on schedule, her long hair – her freakish crowning glory – was the outward sign of this state of grace. I didn't share in the nurses' idolatry. I was impressed by the simple fact of her separate existence, which struck me all the more because I'd imagined her in the womb as a boy, although, as I now realised, I hadn't imagined a material baby at all. But then nobody else had either – my pregnancy had caused such a fuss none of us had been able to see past it – so now Vic dashed out to buy nappies, pins, vests, nighties, bootees and a sun bonnet, and my parents, suddenly finding themselves grandparents, were shopping around for a pram that could double as a carrycot for the baby to sleep in when I brought her home.

But when? Rumour and speculation were the only source of information, since any direct question was dismissed out of hand. People said that they usually kept you in five days or a week, but they'd only ever tell you you were leaving the day before, when the Sister would phone your husband or a number where they'd take a message so that he could come to pick you up, and bring your outdoor clothes and shoes (which you weren't allowed to keep with you). Confinement was the right word, but it wasn't solitary. The curtains round the beds were only drawn for intimate examinations or bedpans – except for one bed where the curtains were always drawn, because the large, sulky girl in there was an unmarried mother. Her privacy was a badge of shame. When I made the mistake of saying to a Sister that I needed to get out to take my A-levels, I was told that I should *count myself lucky* (with a dark glance at the curtained corner) and that Doctor (whom we never saw) would discharge me at the proper time.

I had a sinking feeling they'd keep me in to punish me. There were empty beds and they always kept you longer then, said a woman who'd been in before, because they wanted to look busy. These women had very little reverence for the medical mysteries and told gory tales of incompetence. One woman who'd had a Caesarean had to go back for a second operation because they'd left some swabs behind. The young woman in the next bed to mine had come to Crosshouses because her last pre-natal examination had shown something strange, but it was only in the delivery room, after she'd given birth to a son, that they'd realised what. 'One of them said, "There's something else in there,"' she told me, 'and another said, "It's twins!"' They were her first babies and she wouldn't be sorry to stay a day or two extra to get used to the idea, because she and her husband lived in an isolated smallholding and she'd no one to help. Other older women felt the same, much as they hated the hospital they treasured the opportunity just to lie in bed, especially those with large young families. But I was desperate to leave. I'd been there a week, my stitches were healing, I'd been allowed a hot salt bath, it couldn't be long. Then suddenly my temperature shot up. I had an infection.

After a couple of feverish days, when I was more and more frustrated by the impossibility of revising – we don't feed our babies on books – sleepless and unable to read at night because my light would keep other patients awake, a Night Sister I'd never seen before and never saw again came like a good fairy to my bedside and said I shouldn't fret, she was married with children, it *was* all possible. But not according to daylight rules (they kept her dark). I had to leave. Screwing up my courage and trying to sound calm I said to the Day Sister that if they wouldn't discharge me then I'd sign myself out. She went off to confer with Matron and came back in fighting form. I couldn't, she said, I was under age. Yes I could, I said, I was married. Then I needed my husband's permission, she said. That's not true, I replied. In any case, she said, I wasn't well enough to leave, I had an infection. And where did I get it? I said nastily, in this foul hospital. I'll be better off if I leave. 'If you leave,' she shouted, losing her temper, 'you'll die!' But if she was in a rage, I was in a bigger one. 'I'd rather!' I shouted back, and she spun on her heel and retreated.

The wise women laughed and shook their heads: you shouldn't get on the wrong side of them like that, you can't win. I was shocked and elated. I'd never had a row as savage as that with anyone outide my family, in public. When Vic and my father came to visit, I told them what had happened. My father said he was sure they knew best, and Vic was dreadfully divided because he couldn't believe anyone would tell me I was in such danger if I wasn't, and he wouldn't promise to smuggle in my clothes. I didn't care. I had a nightie that looked enough like a dress, my slippers would serve and I'd resolved that if they wouldn't let me sign the papers the next day I'd climb out of the bathroom window, cross the fields and hitch to Shrewsbury. My daughter would be fine with the hairdressers

until we could claim her. I'd already washed my own hair in the sink when I had my salt bath and was waiting for it to dry when a nurse (looking the other way) announced that they were discharging me with a prescription for antibiotics and that Matron had already called my father. I was free to go.

As I was leaving, they cooed over my daughter and said to Vic what a pity it was that her pretty hair would all fall out, baby hair always did. (It didn't.) Sunnyside looked wonderful, while I'd been away the leggy, overgrown rhododendrons had all flowered – scarlet, purple, pink, white. 'Nature never did betray / The heart that loved her . . .' Nonsense, of course, but wonderful nonsense. Now I'd be in time to quote it. Certainly it was a lot easier to have a baby than to be delivered of the mythological baggage that went with it. Crosshouses was grim, but the fact that they were so much better at moral hygiene than the other kind had taught me a lot. From now on I was making my way against most people's assumptions, I'd have to count my friends and fight back. True, for the moment I felt shaky and the antibiotics upset the baby's digestion, but my infection was soon cured and so was her windy pain. Grandma greeted me as though I'd come back from the Other Side and in a sense I had.

XVIII

Eighteen

When I handed the baby to my mother she passed her straight back, saying she was afraid she'd drop her. She was only forty-two, could have had another child herself – she looked a lot younger than some of those mothers at Crosshouses – and she was reliving the reasons she hadn't, and the dread of children's vulnerability I remembered from when Clive and I were small. Everyone was a bit shaken as the generations were reshuffled, although she showed it most. She recovered herself to choose a name, however. Sharon was a pretty name, she said in the same faraway voice she used to muse over mother-of-pearl, wasn't it in the Bible, the Rose of Sharon? And it did sound romantic, a name that had blown in from America along with rock and country music: in 1960 hundreds of girls were called Sharon, although until that moment we'd almost never heard the name. Vic's father looked down on her in her pram and said, 'She's a Sage, anyway.' Vic's mum, blushing for him, knitted cardigans, boots, a quilt. My father doubted that we were competent, although we managed the bathing, nappy-changing and getting up in the night. He'd probably have liked more children, but valued my mother's girlishness at a higher price. Grandma welcomed the baby as another member of the doomed race of blonde, blue-eyed females (doomed to sleep with the enemy, doomed to reproduce). Uncle Bill, who turned up at Sunnyside with a suitcase full of leather bootlaces, the last remnants of stock from Hereford Stores, sat down on the *Daily Mail*s, asked why didn't we wipe our behinds with them and told me that motherhood didn't suit me. From then on he transferred his ideological attentions to Clive (who'd become an uncle himself and found it hysterical), but for purely political ends, since he didn't fancy boys.

For Bill I was a thing of the past, I'd missed the bus of history and reverted to mindless generation. Like most of the comrades, he had very conventional views on conventional sex. But I didn't believe him. I wasn't a realist, Vic and I lived in a different dimension of fantasy-freedom he couldn't see.

When I turned up at the high school for the first exam I felt light-headed, although my fever had subsided. It was very strange to be back there in a summer frock and high heels,

only six months on but a world away, and when Miss Dennis, the headmistress, appeared at the gate, asking with pseudo-solicitude if I was quite well, shouldn't I be at home, I walked around her as if she were a mere personification of prudery. Her school was the local 'open' centre, the lines she drew had lost their power, you could just step over them. And as if to compound the transgression, Miss Heslop came into the exam room halfway through with a cup of tea rattling and slopping into its saucer, and I drank it down – although it was the last thing I needed, I was already leaking milk. Miss Dennis, despite herself, was much more useful; she fuelled my conviction that I must *mean* something – although I don't think I realised quite how annoying my reappearance, undeterred and unrepentant, was. After that first day she ignored me and I played the outsider without her help, caught up in a kind of euphoria, scribbling for my life, high on the sense of being terminally out of tune with the school song – 'Just the schoooo-ool for me.'

So the only exam I'd missed was the French oral and dictation, which had happened while I was in hospital – and which I didn't regret too much since my spoken French was hopeless. It didn't occur to me that I might have written to the Board and explained why I couldn't turn up.

Years later, when I marked A-levels, I'd find myself sitting on committees that tried to quantify the disasters that affected candidates' performance. One had found her grandfather hanging from a tree in the churchyard on her way to sit her Eng. lit. paper. How many marks was that worth . . . ? But perhaps having a baby would have seemed no excuse and alerted the Board, who mercifully knew nothing about me, to the fact that I was a freak. Dr Clayton certainly thought so. When I said I wanted to stop breast-feeding, he looked disapproving but prescribed a course of diuretics and then – prodding my breasts dubiously – another course, trying to reduce them to flab and puzzled by his failure. One side effect was that I lost weight dramatically everywhere else and got my figure back faster than I'd hoped, and new, slender legs, but the district nurse told me I should stop taking the pills whatever the doctor said and I did, although I knew Byron had lost weight this way.

Next I went to ask Dr Clayton about contraception and braced myself for an embarrassing discussion of rival methods, but I needn't have bothered, because all he said was, 'Now that you're married your husband will take care of that.' What he was saying (since he knew that Vic was only a year older than me and hardly on present showing an expert) was that he wouldn't aid and abet me in acquiring any control over my own fertility. In any case, he must have thought, I was now in all probability going to revert to white-trash type and have more babies, and in a way decorum demanded that I should; I was some sort of nymphomaniac, and mustn't be allowed to have my cake and eat it.

Or was *he* embarrassed? Surely not. The best we can do for Dr Clayton in this narrative is to assume that he was a mere mouthpiece for Whitchurch, with its snobbery, moral paralysis and prurient daydreams. I didn't pursue the question. Although I was still fairly ignorant about kinds of contraception, I had inspected with dismay the diaphragm my mother kept at the bottom of her wardrobe and decided I wouldn't have been able to bring myself to trust the available ones in any case, nor would Vic trust condoms. So instead we gave up sex. Or rather, we gave up sexual intercourse. If collective Whitchurch had known it would have been scandalised, it being an article of faith that a wife shouldn't refuse her husband his 'rights' (and my offence was worse, because he'd been decent enough to make an honest woman of me). One way and another, we seemed bound to act against the grain, but this time our sin stayed our secret.

We thought – we hardly spoke about it, hardly needed to – that we'd find a way out of this impasse, but as time went by it was our secret sexlessness that cemented our intimacy. We were brother and sister. We'd regressed to amoeboid caresses – we talked baby talk, and called each other by queasy, furtive nicknames (Creep for him, Crumble for me) that reflected our guilty innocence, and we kept up an endless dialogue of one about other people and ideas and images. Behind it all was a visceral dread that easily defeated common sense. Every month I was convinced, despite our abstinence, that I was by some bad miracle pregnant, and I raged and despaired. Pre-menstrual tension wasn't yet something people took seriously, although many knew it from experience, but even if we'd been able to label my lunacy, I doubt if we'd have tamed it.

Vic bore with me and didn't jeer, for he saw the force of my unreason. The boundaries between us had been breached for good, we gave a new meaning to the notion that man and wife were one flesh. You could track back this kind of alchemy in books: '. . . intimately to mix and melt and to be melted together with his beloved, so that one should be made out of two'. This is Shelley translating Plato, who was putting words into the mouth of Aristophanes, who's the only defender of heterosexual sex in the *Symposium*, although he makes it sound perverse.

So we sublimated our wants and that cut us off further from our friends. I'd got Gail back – in truth she had never deserted me, I'd been in hiding – but of course it wasn't the same, our paths had diverged and I had something new to conceal. She'd been more *strange*, more different and more dominating than

271

Vic, but now he'd supplanted her. He and I acquired each other's friends as a double act: in some ways we seemed older than our contemporaries and more sure of what we wanted; in others we stayed younger, for we'd take our adolescent passion with us wherever we went next. University, we meant, but although our A-level results were good enough we still had to get places and money. In 1960 you applied to as many colleges and universities as you liked, there was no centralised system. All of them, however, required a confidential reference from your school and I could tell from the speech day in September what would be in mine.

Once I'd have jumped at the opportunity not to attend – if you'd left you could do it *in absentia*, they'd simply read out your name – but this time I was determined to go and collect my prize from the previous year. The headmistress seemed prepared: the speaker was her predecessor, Miss Lester, a plump, popular woman who'd gone on to better things, and her chosen text was Charles Kingsley's famous line, 'Be good, sweet maid, and let who will be clever.' Listening to this sermon, I basked in my pariah status, but I wasn't prepared for what happened next. As I crossed the awful town hall stage behind the banked hydrangeas to receive my book token, the weary applause quickened and my fellow pupils cheered. It was my first and last moment of popularity in six years at Whitchurch Girls' High School and it was as the gym mistress had feared from year one; I was setting a bad example. I shook and blushed as usual, but for different reasons, and was very glad I'd slimmed so Byronically that people could see that I was a sinner in spirit, near-weightless and soon to be out of Whitchurch.

It proved, still, a bumpy ride. Oxbridge women's colleges returned my forms, saying that they were unable to consider an application from me, since they only took mature married women (mature meant over twenty-three). Otherwise, I was accepted with alacrity and without an interview wherever we applied. Miss Dennis's story of my fall – which, one of those admissions tutors remembered a lot later, began 'Lorna is attractive and intelligent, but . . .' and warned that my shyness concealed a corrupt character – went down well in English departments. It was Vic who was sometimes summoned to explain himself (academically, that is) and so met William Empson at Sheffield, where we both wanted very much to go and sit at his feet. But it was not to be: the Shropshire Education Authority refused me a grant. They had no problems with Vic, they'd given money to young men who'd come back married from National Service until it was abolished; however, they were still stopping the scholarships of woman who slept with men, married or no – although in another year or two grants would become mandatory and they'd lose their power of 'discretion', as they must have known, but I didn't.

I couldn't have waited anyway, the suffocating nightmare possessed me, I had no time to lose. If I didn't do it now, the prospect would recede and fade, books would become a hobby and I'd turn into a housewife (which I foresaw not so much as a lifetime of domestic drudgery as one of impotent make-believe). There were state scholarships without strings, but thanks to French I was 15 per cent short. You could qualify by another route, however – some universities had entrance exams of their own devising, with scholarships worth quaint sums like fifty guineas a year, which the state would top up. The first of these, in January 1961, was (a good omen) Durham, and we applied and travelled by train across the Pennines, further north than we'd ever been, into early-afternoon darkness. We stayed in separate colleges and sat our papers in the shadow of the cathedral whose slow bells nagged like toothache.

All the buildings were angular, hard-edged, ill-lit and draughty, with red-hot radiators. It was where you went if you couldn't get into Oxford or Cambridge, but the university premises seemed confusingly cramped and scattered, as if they had been squeezed into the interstices of some other institution, the Church by the looks of things. This was the first time I'd been in a university, but a vicarage ghost lurked in the dark corners and whispered in my ear — 'Immortal, invisible . . . dilapidations . . .'

My interview dashed my hopes of finding a place there. Professor Clifford Leech sat back behind his desk, welcomed me expansively and handed me over to Nicholas Brooke, a sliver of a man on the edge of the pool of Anglepoised light. He was as thin as a rail, tense, his tone rasping, impatient, ironic. When we talked about Shakespeare (he was riffling through my exam script, looking for something he couldn't find) and I struggled to resay what I'd written, he raised a quizzical eyebrow and returned my ideas to their real authors — L. C. Knights's *How Many Children had Lady Macbeth?* Yes. And that rhapsodic stuff about the late plays and levitating into immortality, wasn't that *Wilson* Knight? I nodded, hot in the face. Answering in person for what I'd written was agonising. On paper I'd been confident, I'd been someone else — a lot of someone elses as it turned out. A fraud.

He asked about contemporary novels and I mentioned the respectable ones I'd read, including C. P. Snow's *The Masters.* Yes? I thought it unconvincing, I didn't think dons would engage in such petty, low-minded intrigue. My interviewers both laughed. They obviously thought me sadly naive. I called my mother from a freezing phone box, reversing the charges. When she answered with seven-month-old Sharon under her arm (she'd become blasé about baby-minding) I told her there was *no chance.*

But I was wrong. The inquisition in that stone study was an ordeal designed to establish that I was scholarship material – and that it was worth changing Durham's conventual college rules on my account. When I met Miss Scott at St Aidan's, she turned out to belong to the same generation as Miss Roberts and shared her no-nonsense view of my offence. In future St Aidan's wouldn't be sending women students down for anything other than intellectual shortcomings. She had set a dangerous precedent, but she took it in her stride, only warning me against the mind-rotting side effects of the washing-up that she'd heard living with a man involved. She was witty and kind, and coolly pocketed the fifty guineas I was awarded each year for unspecified college costs and uneaten lunches of lukewarm macaroni cheese. It didn't matter: my state studentship was assessed on my father's means and so I got a full maintenance grant, as did Vic, who was assessed on his mother's meagre wages. We were well off and able to pay some of our way at Sunnyside, where Sharon would stay during Durham term-times.

She had found her place, too. She and my mother communed in the kitchen: Sharon in her high chair, playing with a horrible wet mixture of toys and rusks on her tray, my mother talking to her about what the cat was up to, or the birds out of the window, or the pretty colours in the fire, or the postman's rattle at the door, or Clive's teatime explosion into the hall – from the boys' grammar school now, but just as violent. She learned to talk back very early and for a while it looked as though she found her life so satisfactory, sitting there giving orders and making polite conversation, her hair in precocious pigtails, that she'd never trouble to learn to walk. She preferred her grandparents to her fly-by-night, insubstantial parents; they were much more like parents were supposed to be, like the parents in picture books – and she was much more their baby than I'd been.

When Sharon was asleep and my parents tucked up in bed, Vic and I would go out to play at the rugby club with the town's boozers and bohemians. In the months before we went up to Durham we rejoined Whitchurch life, on the louche fringes. That winter he'd played rugby for the Old Boys' team, most of whom were – like their opponents – at least ten years older and eighteen stone, and his courage won him a certain prestige, along with the scars and bruises. Once he was so concussed that he didn't recognise me after the match, although from his fond grin I could tell that he was quite taken with me even as a perfect stranger. The best thing about the Old Boys, though, was their club, a shabby prefab on the edge of town, with tightly closed curtains advertising Guinness, which came to life after the pubs closed at 10.30. There I learned to drink and smoke. Vic had the advantage of me, and to start with I'd have to dash to the Ladies and throw up after a couple of gin and bitter lemons, but I found by experiment that gin on its own stayed down. We both became quite good at darts, too, which was handy in Durham – the other Durham we lived in, that wasn't the university, where you got lectures after hours on dialectical materialism from part-time window-cleaners.

But we were only part-time outsiders ourselves, moonlighters in bohemia. At Durham we conspired together to work, driven by the desire to get away from Whitchurch for good, and anyway more and more obsessed with words, so that it was a labour of love. When we remet Nicholas Brooke, I couldn't understand why I hadn't recognised him in the first place – the brilliance, the theatricality, the edge of bitterness (he felt trapped in Durham), the cradled cigarette, the flapping black gown . . . this was my first mentor as I'd never known him, in his prime.

We'd be at home at university after all, even though we were
well known from the beginning as freaks and had appeared in
the local paper with the headline THE SAGES TAKE UP LITERA-
TURE (gazing wide-eyed into an imaginary future), along with
a former Congregationalist minister in his forties from Hartle-
pool. I sent the clipping to my mother, who kept it with my
letters, which read like disapproving dispatches from a foreign
land ('Durham is a very Conservative, traditional sort of place,
with privileges for men') in a shoebox, along with the picture
from the front of the *Mail* that appeared when we graduated
in 1964.

We're news once again because we're the first married couple
of ordinary student age to graduate in the same subject at the
same time, both with Firsts. This time we're pictured with
Sharon, though, and that's the real point – she's four by now,
and looks very large and very distrustful. This picture stands

instead of a wedding photograph in our story. Sharon is the one looking beyond the ending, nobody seems to know yet that it's the 1960s, except perhaps for her. She's the real future, she tells the world that we broke the rules and got away with it, for better and for worse, we're part of the shape of things to come.

Afterword

When the graduation-day picture appeared in the paper, the girl from the next bed in Crosshouses wrote to me saying that she remembered how much I'd wanted to take my exams and was pleased it had turned out well. She sent me a photograph of her family – she herself had five children now – another set of boy twins and a daughter, and here they were, behind them a tiny house and acres of scrubby Shropshire fields in the background.

Deaths: Grandma died in 1963 and joined Grandpa in Hanmer churchyard. Shortly afterwards the headstone fell over, doubtless because the gravediggers and masons had disturbed it, although I like to think she was at it, hammer and tongs, with Grandpa down below.

Vic's father died in 1967 and the local Jehovah's Witnesses must have heaved a sigh of relief, for he had taken to inviting them in when they called and asking them to listen on their knees for hours to Channel 13.

Vic's mother died in 1970, after a lonely breakdown which took the form of borrowing her husband's madness and putting on his airs. The doctors said she was prematurely senile, but it was more a case of the mystery of marriage. She recovered and became her sane, patient self again in time to die of cancer.

My mother died in 1989 of a stroke (her second) and is

279

buried at Hanmer. It was her death that set me thinking about writing this book.

More loose ends: Gail trained as a teacher and married Terry, whom she met at college and who also looked rather like Paul Anka, in Hanmer church. They have no children.

I never got to know Miss Roberts well, although I wish I'd tried harder. She gave me her academic gown when she retired from the high school in the 1960s and was pleased when I started reviewing for the *New Statesman* in the 1970s, not long before she died.

My father, who was and remains bereft without my mother, lives with my brother Clive and his family.

Clive left school at sixteen, has a PhD in engineering and acts nowadays as a consultant when he isn't helping his wife run their pub.

Sunnyside is no more, or at least you wouldn't recognise it. It proved a good investment: in 1964 my parents sold half the paddock to a developer who built two semis and a bungalow on the land; and in 1988 they sold the rest of the paddock and the orchard to another developer who built three Tudor mansions with double garages, using bricks from the stables, which were demolished – my father had retired from business – along with the billiard room, thus turning Sunnyside into a normal-shaped house with a garden. After my mother died, in the 1990s my father sold that too.

Sharon came to live with Vic and me when we left Durham, although she still spent school holidays with my parents. Now she is married and has a daughter called Olivia, but she broke the family pattern by doing both in her thirties, so the generations are back in order. I've broken the pattern too, I'm not bringing up my granddaughter.

Vic and I survived the 1960s, but the contraceptive pill and legalised abortion came too late to resurrect our sex life together and we separated in 1974, although we've remained friends and colleagues ever since. Neither of us has had another child.

I married again in 1979 and thereby hangs a tale. In the bathroom of the council house where Vic's parents lived when we met there was a sturdy stool with a woven seat of green-and-cream cord which Vic's father had made from a kit in occupational therapy between jolts of ECT in mental hospital. When I went to meet my new in-laws in a stockbroker hamlet in the home counties in 1979, I took refuge in a remote bathroom and found there a stool with a woven green-and-cream cord seat. Nothing else in this house resembled anything I'd been used to, but this was *exactly the same*. Later I asked whether the bathroom stool had a history: well, yes, his father had had a bad breakdown in the 1960s and had made it when he was recovering, in occupational therapy, from a kit.

I'm not sure what the moral of the bathroom-stool story is. Perhaps this: it's a good idea to settle for a few loose ends, because even if everything in your life is connected to everything else, that way madness lies.

4th
Estate
Matchbook
Classics

In the mid-twentieth century, the matchbox industry was booming. Matchboxes became the host of tiny canvases which displayed a range of ideas: foxes skipping through Polish forests, celebrations of Russia's space race successes, orchards coming into blossom. Such micro-masterpieces serve as the inspiration for the new 4th Estate Matchbook Classics series. The ten books – novels, memoirs and one very unusual biography – are some of the best loved and most admired that 4th Estate has published, each of them as unique as the matchbox that inspired its cover.

Bad Blood
Lorna Sage

The Things They Carried
Tim O'Brien

The Blue Flower
Penelope Fitzgerald

The Shipping News
Annie Proulx

The Corrections
Jonathan Franzen

Stuart: A Life Backwards
Alexander Masters

The Diving-Bell
and the Butterfly
Jean-Dominique Bauby

Half of a Yellow Sun
Chimamanda
Ngozi Adichie

Empire of the Sun
J.G. Ballard

A Place of Greater Safety
Hilary Mantel